ROAM.

ROAM

THE ART OF TRAVEL

+DEAN STARNES

HarperCollins*Publishers*
New Zealand

For Mum, Dad and Debbie,
who make returning home
the best part of leaving

National Library of New Zealand Cataloguing-in-Publication Data

Starnes, Dean.
Roam : the art of travel / Dean Starnes.
ISBN 978-1-86950-711-4
1. Starnes, Dean—Travel. 2. Independent travel. I. Title.
910.92—dc 22

First published 2008
HarperCollins*Publishers (New Zealand) Limited*
P.O. Box 1, Auckland

ISBN 978 1 86950 711 4

Cover design by Natalie Winter
Cover photos by Dean Starnes
Inside cover photos by Shutterstock
Internal photos by Dean Starnes unless otherwise credited
Typeset by Dean Starnes

Printed by Everbest Printing, China, on 128gsm Matt Art

Contents

Looking through a window at the Ishak Pasa Sarayi, Turkey, the palace fortress built by a Kurdish chieftain in the 17th century.

The long road ahead

'Travel is fatal to prejudice, bigotry and narrow-mindedness; and many of our people need it sorely on these accounts. Broad, wholesome, charitable views of men and things cannot be acquired by vegetating in our little corner of the earth all one's lifetime.'

– MARK TWAIN

Advice is like an STD – nobody wants it, but everyone is happy to pass it on. Some of the advice contained within this book was hard won, other bits were told to me by more experienced travellers or gleaned from friends. And even though I've tried to weed out all the obvious in favour of the practical and pertinent, advice is not always meant to be followed. Sometimes it's better to turn left when everyone else went right. Sometimes it's more fun to follow your heart than to follow a guide book. That's fine by me; travelling is, after all, about the journey, not the destination.

There is also a number of travel stories contained within these pages and this book has turned out more autobiographical than I had first intended. I've always felt that many people who write autobiographies must be fairly arrogant. My only excuse for such vanity is that if I had to wait until reminiscence was justified by achievement, I might have to wait for ever. I would like to point out that the stories are not meant to be representative of countries or of their people or their history. They are moments taken out of time and written here out of context. They span two decades of backpacking and in my defence – should I need one – within that time things have changed; China has become easier to travel in, Pakistan more difficult, Russia has relaxed her borders whilst the United States have tightened theirs. Rwanda recovers from war while Nepal battles with Maoist insurgents.

But whilst places change, other things stay the same. Travellers are still bitten by bed-bugs, con artists still rip tourists off, taxi drivers still overcharge foreigners and airlines still won't let you sneak on that bronze Buddha from Thailand as hand luggage. The world, for all its ups and downs, remains an exhilarating place; one moment fascinating and intoxicating, the next uncomfortable and alarming. It's quite a ride.

Scratching those itchy feet

When my parents were young – probably about the time fire was discovered – there were no guide books, no cheap airfares and no pre-arranging your accommodation over the Internet. Now, for the first time in history, the independent traveller doesn't need to be a polar explorer to visit the Antarctic or a multi-millionaire to fund their own African safari. We were all born lucky; for now is the perfect time to travel. When I say now,

BATTLE TESTED

I mean just before the peak season but not during school holidays, Ramadan, Chinese New Year, the wet season, the dry season, local elections, political upheaval or any major sporting event you don't hold tickets for.

Should everyone travel?

Of course they should. Unfortunately, most don't. Lengthy stays abroad shouldn't just be for WWII criminals hiding out in Uruguay to escape UN retribution. Nor is it just for those keen to escape their country's heavy tax on alcohol. And while it may be true that just across the border is a whole new six-pack of beer, there are other reasons to sling your pack.

For starters, it's a great way to meet others – other cultures, other religions and those with other ways of viewing the world. While I doubt you will necessarily 'find yourself', it can be fun to find a few foreigners. After experiencing the planet's diversity, its trying bureaucracy, its crushing poverty and its squalor and wealth, it comes as a comforting realisation that you may have more in common with strangers than you ever thought possible.

If all that sounds a bit too namby-pamby for you, travel is a great way to run away from a problem. Many people believe that running away never solves anything – clearly they haven't been travelling. I prefer the motto 'when the going gets tough, the tough get backpacking'. Travel is also a great way to diet. After three months of the shits you'll make Twiggy look like a whale. It's a great way to learn a foreign language – even if it is all the swear words – and it's a great way to avoid getting a real job. Travelling to exotic places can help you with your tan and allow you to invent exciting stories about your past without fear of contradiction. While travelling you get to try new things, meet new people and take on new challenges. It's a lot of fun.

Catching the bug

A warning: once you've been travelling, no matter how pleased you were to get on the plane and fly back home, travel can become addictive. Somehow the gossip around the water cooler just isn't as scandalous as the time you took a Thai lady-boy home by mistake.

My favourite border – the immigration post high in the Andes that separates Chile from Bolivia.

BORDERING ON THE INSANE

Many of the difficulties in travelling overland through Central Asia boil down to the difficulties in arranging visas. Some require specific entry and departure dates, others require an invitation from a local operator and all require patience. I blame my friend Steph for the trouble we had with our Kyrgyz visa. She believed me when I said that we could effectively extend our visa by altering the dates. This was a stupid idea and she should have known better.

The alterations were hard to detect but the border guards examined our visas closely with a magnifying glass. While we tried to convince the guards that we weren't American spies warranting KGB intervention, our bus passed through the checkpoints into Kazakhstan. Fearing that we would never see our backpacks again I started after them across no-man's land without a passport. This was a mistake. Steph found herself stranded in one country facing a jail term, our luggage found itself stranded in another country, presumably to be sold at the next bazaar, and I was caught in the 200 m gap in the middle, without a passport or entry papers for either country. It took a while and a small bribe to sort that mess out.

Cloth drying on an Uzbek porch.

All dressed up
with everywhere to go!

Fancy yourself in a Kalahari loin cloth or penis sheath from Irian Jaya? Not your thing? Understandable. What about a Japanese *kimono*, a Scottish kilt or a nice pair of *lederhosen* from Germany? Are you brave enough to get a traditional Samoan tattoo or insert a lip plate in the style of the Mursi women of Ethiopia? Perhaps not. More appealing then, a Mexican sombrero to keep the sun off. Oh, what to wear, what to wear!

The first dilemma most travellers face is deciding what to wear and what to take off. The travelling community is divided on the issue. There are those who maintain it's best to 'go native' and embrace the clothing style fashionable with the locals. This is all very well if you are travelling in Italy but more difficult to get away with if you are the only white guy with a penis gourd on your wanger.

Others – like those found wearing a camera around their neck, 'walk shorts' barely big enough to cover their beer belly and sandals over their socks – insist on dressing as a cliché. In its extreme form some couples take to wearing identical clothing. The most humane thing under these circumstances is to have them both put down and keep their coffins closed during the funeral.

So what should a traveller wear? It's obvious, trust me, you'll know instinctively what to take once you have boarded the plane. My advice: follow your heart and, in the spirit of the Federated States of Micronesia, which tried to outlaw baseball caps, set your own rules. After all, whatever you take, you are the one who will have to wear it day in and day out for the length of your trip.

Things I have learnt about packing

- When choosing a backpack, go small; you're not as strong as you tell your girlfriend.
- If you are mocked for having wheels on your backpack, crush the mocker's toes. If you run the bag over their little toe, three or four times, the mocking stops (and their toe falls off).
- You need fewer undies than you think.
- Don't keep toilet paper at the bottom of your pack. If you find yourself uttering the words 'Uh oh', it's already too late.
- Sometimes you'll need more undies than you think.

- If you are overcome by a desire to pack a safari suit, you might want to think about increasing your medication.
- The best thing to take is money – ideally a whole backpack full. The American dollar is the most widely accepted, and if you pack plastic, make it Visa.
- It is perfectly acceptable to wear your clothes inside out and thus cunningly get more mileage from them.
- Wearing the same pair of undies for two, even three, days in a row (per side) is also perfectly acceptable. Why wouldn't it be?
- Never admit to wearing your undies for two or even three days in a row, especially on an online dating profile.
- Swimming in any item of clothing is tantamount to washing it.
- Tie-dyed T-shirts never look good; not even in Goa. Just accept this and move on.
- Always take your favourite clothes – you'll have to wear them day in, day out for months. You may as well like them. Of course they'll probably be ruined or stolen or both.
- While taking a friend will mean that you will always have someone to blame shit on, remember that taking your partner will seriously diminish any chance of holiday romance.
- If your backpack is new, take it outside, throw it in a puddle and back the car over it a couple of times to give yourself some cred.
- Take drugs. I'm talking the legal kind; they can be life-saving and you can always sell them to your under-prepared fellow travellers. When faced with shitting their pants they'll pay anything for a broad-spectrum antibiotic.
- Forget the laundry powder, you cheap bastard. For a few dollars someone will take care of it and you'll help the local economy.
- Don't follow anyone's advice if they recommend a 'universal plug'. What makes you think there will be any running water?
- Money belts are worn under your clothes and are meant to be inconspicuous. It is not inconspicuous to thrust your hands down your (or someone else's) pants every five seconds to fondle the contents.

No matter how beautiful the colours or how fine the silk, it remains a sad fact that no Westerner can wear a sari like an Indian woman. If you find yourself in a sari, call your emergency insurance number; you've just gone native.

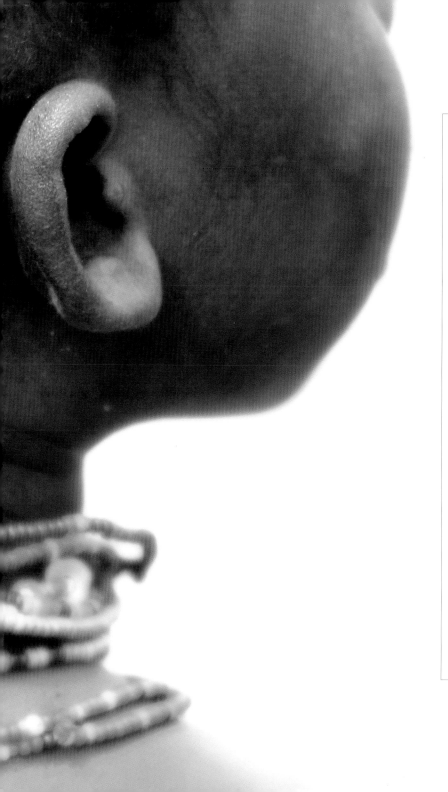

BEAD THERE, DONE THAT

The world over, people dress in order to convey a message, even if that message is simply 'I don't care about clothes or what I wear'.

This boy belongs to the El-Molo tribe, one of East Africa's smallest and most threatened tribes whose population has dipped below 4000. They live by Lake Turkana, a remote and arid area in Northern Kenya. Their staple is fish and their unbalanced diet leaves them susceptible to rickets.

The giveaway to his tribal roots are the beads and red ochre body paint he wears. More than this, African beads are also an inventory of identity.

Necklaces of green and blue beads are reserved for families of witch doctors. Simple white beads are worn by widows; thin multicoloured necklaces are worn by those who are unmarried. A thick, ropy beaded necklace indicates a young woman who is betrothed.

Married women decorate their ears with leaves and those with children often have a lip fixture (used as an aid when washing a child, by dribbling water held in the mouth).

Weird? Not really. Are we so different with our use of engagement and wedding rings to signify our marital status?

PACKING CHECKLIST

There are two principal methods of packing. The proponents of the first school of thought have a 'trial' pack about six months before their actual departure. This approach involves putting items (no matter how questionably useful) on their bed in a series of neat little piles. Here they stay, effectively forcing the 'packer' to sleep on the floor or on a pile of dirty laundry in the corner of the room. The second widely employed tactic is to wait until the cab taking you to the airport has arrived. When it starts to honk its horn, the 'packer' springs to life and starts stuffing the first things they see (pot plants, small children, etc.) into their bag. In either case it is worth remembering that you can usually buy whatever you have forgotten on the road for a fraction of the cost it is back home – besides, the airline will probably lose it all anyway.

Everyone has their own heart-felt opinion about what goes and what stays. I've found that once you have decided on what you're going to take, halve the clothes and double the money. Here is what I would take if I was backpacking in a climatically temperate Third World country, say Australia, for two months.

Bags

- [ ] Backpack – side opening and lockable with the mandatory non-American flag sewn onto it. To seem mysterious, choose a really obscure country.
- [ ] Day pack – lockable and sometimes sold as a 'zip-on' to the main pack. Under no circumstances attempt this. I once saw a tiny Irish girl tip backwards under the combined weight. She looked like an upended turtle with her skirt over her head. As far as I know she is still there.
- [ ] Money belt.
- [ ] Wallet.

Documents

- [ ] Passport – some countries need them to be valid for a minimum of six months after the trip's completion. Carry a photocopy as well.
- [ ] Two ATM cards – Visa is the most widely accepted. Take a spare card (eftpos is fine) in case one is stolen.
- [ ] Cash – US dollars are the most widely accepted.
- [ ] Yellow vaccination certificate detailing all your shots.
- [ ] Passport photos – useful when applying for entry visas.
- [ ] Airline tickets/confirmation of hotel reservations.
- [ ] Travel insurance.
- [ ] Student card – ISC (US) and ISIC (UK) cards are more widely accepted than ID supplied by universities. Not a student? You can buy forgeries in South-East Asia.

Shoes

- [ ] Shoes or boots – whichever are sturdy, semi-waterproof and you can walk in for bloody ages.
- [ ] Sandals or thongs.

Clothes

- [ ] 4 x Socks.
- [ ] 4 x Underwear.
- [ ] 1 x Thermal underwear – it may not be hip but nothing keeps you warm like these babies.
- [ ] 1 x Trousers/skirt.
- [ ] 1 x Belt – so if you get sick and lose weight you can still keep your pants up.
- [ ] 2 x Shorts – if it is hot enough I live in them, but then again that could be the New Zealand influence. In the past, businessmen in New Zealand wore 'dress shorts' with their suit and tie. Now that's a statement.
- [ ] 1 x Swimsuit – only required if you can't swim in your shorts.

BATTLE TE

- [ ] 3 x Shirts/blouses – I like T-shirts, but that's just me. Usually I take two T-shirts, and one either short-sleeved or long-sleeved shirt. Whatever you choose, make them baggy and any colour except white. Always take your favourite 'getting lucky' shirt if you are looking for some action.
- [ ] 1 x Tank top
- [ ] 1 x Sarong – courtesy of Asia and the Pacific, these things are great. Wrap one around you on the way to the shower, use them to sit on at the beach or as a stand-in towel when your regular towel becomes too stinky to bear.
- [ ] 1 x Travel towel – get one that is thin, easily wringable, compact and dries quickly.
- [ ] 1 x Hat – choose one that still looks okay when crushed and, if you are a college student, cool when worn backwards.
- [ ] 1 x Sweater – the one I take is flash enough to go out in – but my idea of going out is so low key, some might call it 'cheap'.
- [ ] 1 x Rain jacket – lightweight and wind-resistant.
- [ ] Something to 'go out' in.

Toiletries

- [ ] Toothbrush and toothpaste – available everywhere in small tubes. Top up as you go.
- [ ] Shampoo and, if you must, conditioner. You don't need as much as you think you do. A 75 ml bottle is enough.
- [ ] Soap in its own soap box.
- [ ] Deodorant – now available in 'travel pack' sizes.
- [ ] Toilet tissue – you don't need the bulk of a whole roll; just a couple of tissue packs is enough to start with, then 'stock up' from well-appointed toilets as you go.
- [ ] Tampons – apparently they can be very difficult to get in some countries.
- [ ] Comb/brush.

- [ ] Shaving stuff – razor and a tube of shaving cream. The cans of foam are bulky and can explode at altitude, which usually involves a serious clean-up operation when you reach your destination.
- [ ] Lip-balm/ChapStick – some people, and I'm tempted to name names here, won't share. Bastards.
- [ ] Sunscreen – fill a 'trial size' bottle.
- [ ] Insect repellent – strength depending on where you are going, but typically the more DEET the better. Of course DEET will eat through plastic and in large enough quantities is probably lethal.
- [ ] Condoms – probably won't get used.
- [ ] First-aid kit – see the checklist in Chapter 3.

Books

- [ ] Guide book – sure it's bulky and expensive but it's also full of valuable information.
- [ ] Novel – you'll be amazed at how much reading you get through while waiting for buses and trains. Make sure it has 'trade-on' value. No one will swap with you if your book features a Fabio-like hero and a windswept sky.
- [ ] Diary and pen.

Miscellaneous

- [ ] iPod and charger.
- [ ] Camera and lens.
- [ ] Swiss Army knife.
- [ ] Sleeping sheet – leave the sleeping bag at home.
- [ ] Cutlery, camping set and maybe a stainless-steel mug.
- [ ] Flashlight – the smaller the better.
- [ ] Watch – the cheaper the better, equipped with a reliable alarm.
- [ ] Padlocks – combination, so you can't lose the keys.
- [ ] Sunglasses.

DANCING ON GOLDEN LILIES

With the decline of Mao's ubiquitous blue suit, Chinese are once again free to wear jeans like the rest of the world.

China, however, is no stranger to anomalous fashion statements. One of the most grotesque (at least by today's standards) was the infamous art of foot binding. The practice emerged in the courts of the southern Tang dynasty who thought these diminutive feet attractive and dignified, fragile and elegant. It gradually became the prevailing style and 'golden lilies' became a synonym for bound feet.

Outlawed in 1911 the practice involved a long strip of bandage being wrapped extremely tightly around a young girl's foot. Over the course of two to three years the bandages were wound ever tighter, breaking the four smaller toes and bending them backwards under the sole of the foot. Eventually the arch of the foot was also broken and the foot pulled in line with the leg. The procedure was accompanied by the reek of infected, gangrenous flesh. A real turn-on, I'm sure.

Ideally, if all went to plan, the feet would be left a twisted and deformed 7.5 cm long.

Dressed in a costume provided by the photographer, a shy Chinese boy waits his turn to be photographed outside Beijing's Forbidden City.

Looking the part

One of the best reasons for travelling is that it enables you to buy clothes; clothes that are normally difficult to justify. Safaris, for example, are great because they have a very strict dress code. It's like being in a club.

Firstly it is imperative to wear the right colour – khaki or, at a pinch, army green. Also it is important to wear sturdy walking boots. I'm not sure why. Every safari I have ever been on was spent locked in a jeep; you could be butt-naked in high heels for all the walking you did, but I'm sure there is a reason for it.

Secondly, it is important to have lots of buckles, button-downs and strap-like stuff incorporated into your clothing. For my part, my pants have a complicated tie and strap arrangement for rolling them up into shorts and fastening them – it's like putting up a tent. It's important that all safari clothes have lots of pockets. It's cool to have pockets on your pockets and I recently met an American who had teeny-weeny pockets on the pockets of the pockets. Very cool! He explained they were very useful for carrying his cellphone. When I asked him how many cellphones he was planning on bringing, he told me not to be 'fastidious', which I thought was the same as 'fascist' and replied, 'I'm anti-terrorist too, but still don't believe in dropping bombs on Iraq', which kind of killed that conversation.

The exception to the khaki rule is at night when you get to wear multicoloured polar fleeces – except no one calls them polar fleeces any more. Everything has an extremely long and technical name. I now refer to my woollen jumper as a micro-weave-thermo-dynamic, nuclear-armed GORE-TEX® outer shell. The socks that I stole from Dad are my bipedal, poly-syllabic, multi-functional foot shields.

And then there are all the really neat gadgets that outdoorsy types have a proclivity for. My favourite is the quintessential Swiss Army knife. Mine has about 500 tools nested inside; it's fantastic. It is also bloody useless but that's not the point. The point is that it arouses serious Swiss Army knife envy. No one has a bigger knife. With so

Dressed in iridescent blue huipile, *a young Mayan highlander at the local market in Santa Catarina Palopo (Guatemala) clutches two roosters as her mother negotiates with the buyer. She won't get much. There are leather shoes more tender than these fowl. The trouble with Guatemalan chooks is that they tend to range a tad too freely, acquiring the physiques of poultry marathon runners.*

many things that fold out, it's like opening a never-ending Christmas present with the added thrill that you risk losing a finger when they all snap back into position. I have no idea what most of them do, but if I'm ever lost on a remote South Pacific island I'm certain that the nail file and toothpick will be handy. I once met an English woman who had a nifty little torch with an in-built compass. Fantastic. Of course, due to the positioning of the compass on the torch handle, you couldn't actually shine any light on the thing, but still it was brilliant. I mean who thinks of all this stuff?

iPod therefore I am

We all have our weaknesses. If I could somehow have my iPod surgically grafted to my body I would. It saved my life on the Trans-Siberian. Seven days on the train from Beijing to Moscow and a whole lot of nothing in between – although it's not technically called nothing; technically it's called the *taiga* and refers to a forest the size of India that blankets Siberia. When you are standing on the platform of Moscow's Yaroslavl station you are closer to the USA than you are to the other end of Russia. Most people don't realise this; I didn't. If it wasn't for my iPod (and vodka) I might have died of boredom.

However, many argue that an iPod is an intrusive gadget that does nothing more than cut off the wearer from the audible world around them. By plugging yourself in, you are also switching yourself off. Real travellers seek out new, unfamiliar music and attempt to communicate, despite language barriers; antisocial iPods hinder this. Now, you may well be thinking to yourself, what a load of self-aggrandising, egotistical bullshit (I know I am), and you'd be right.

True, it may be hard to hear the screeching calls to Islamic prayer and the tracts of incessant chanting that will undoubtedly be broadcast at maximum, speaker-rattling volume on your dusty, bumpy trip across the Moroccan Sahara, but does this really matter? And while Hindi pop music may be catchy, there are only so many times you can hear the same gyrating, effervescent track before you 'go postal' and there is blood on the dance floor (so to speak).

IPOD TIPS FOR THE SAVVY TRAVELLER

BATTLE TESTED

- *Some museums and tourist centres have downloadable walking tours for iPod users on the Internet.*
- *It's a great device for storing your foreign-language lessons to help you study as you travel.*
- *You can back up your photos on to them once your camera's memory card is full.*
- *Download podcasts from other travellers to see what they did wrong.*
- *Maps can be stored here if needed and printed out later on demand in Internet cafés.*
- *It's a great way to make friends. Children love to hear what you are listening to – even if it is Michael Bolton.*

©Eddie Torremans   www.globetrotters.be

GOURD FOR NOTHING

The first thing one notices when meeting a Dani tribesman from Irian Jaya (West Papua, Indonesia) is their distinct lack of traditional dress.

It can, for the prudish, be a bit disconcerting when you first meet a man with a dried orchid gourd attached to his wanger. True, some of these gourds are beautifully decorated with shells, seeds and tassels but nonetheless it's difficult to maintain eye contact with a man whose scrotal sack is dangling from an elongated vegetable.

The Dani tribesmen are proud of their penis gourds (and who wouldn't be?) and wearing them is seen as an act of defiance against the Jakarta government which tried to impose a ban in the 1970s. An elder once famously clutched his erect gourd and exclaimed 'Freedom to Papua', when a reporter asked him how he felt about Indonesia.

Today the preferred custom is to affix your gourd at a jaunty 'present arms' angle and keep it in place with a piece of string tied around the waist. Not only do these dried gourds contain the chap's Johnson but may also house tobacco and money. Which, considering the lack of pockets inherent in a piece of string, is only to be expected.

So if you find yourself in Irian Jaya wondering what to get that special man in your life who has everything, get him a nice penis sheath.

UNDER WRAPS

When Steph and I travelled the Silk Road – much of which is Islamic – Steph also had to abide by Islamic sensibilities and stay covered. Unfortunately her most shapeless pants were a pair of pyjama bottoms. Even though she maintains they weren't pyjama bottoms, I'm telling you, they most definitely were. Not many people have travelled through Iran in their pyjamas but Steph has.

She questioned me several times if people could see the shape of her legs through the thin material and I always told her they couldn't, although if the sun was right you could – like a tent lit from within. I did this because I wanted to see how tolerant people were of this shoddy dress standard and if the reports so often retold in the Western media were accurate. It was a very interesting experiment and now I can comment with authority on the matter.

When people see the shape of a woman, say for example a person dressed in slightly see-through pyjama bottoms, the men usually ogle for some time, declare their undying love and, to prove it, follow it up with a quick marriage proposal.

The women were mostly unfazed by Steph's clothing although occasionally one would click her tongue at us to signal her disapproval. Iranian culture prides itself on its hospitality so a tongue click is quite a statement.

In many Muslim countries, Pakistan for instance, women seem oddly absent. But look carefully and you'll soon see black tent-like objects gliding between stalls in the local market. Believe it or not, there is a woman inside each of these gliding tents. Under no circumstances attempt to invite yourself into one of these tents. Their capacity is strictly one person.

UNDER WRAPPED

During the Japanese Festival of Yamagasa in Fukuoka, thousands of men voluntarily give themselves a wedgie and carry gigantic floats through the streets. If this sounds like you (or perhaps you have a deep-rooted desire to see thousands of tight Japanese buns) there is a catch – the festival is held at 4 a.m. when it is completely dark – so you will need to take a torch or night-vision goggles with you.

At the other end of the Japanese wedgie spectrum is the sport of sumo wrestling. Guaranteed to set the treatment of any anorexia-nervosa sufferer back 10 years, the sight of a man whose buttocks consist of multi-layered rolls of soft and dimpled flesh, swaddled in a nappy (mawashi) is not for the faint hearted. No one is sure who was the first to decide to leave his undies pulled up his crack, but sumo is an ancient martial art (gendai budo) spanning many centuries. Even today, sumo contains many ritualistic elements; one relatively obscure (but in my mind important) rule: should a wrestler lose his mawashi completely, he is justifiably disqualified.

Keeping your shit together

Lurking ominously near the front of nearly every guide book and foreshadowing, as it were, your early demise, is the chapter on health. Under no circumstance read this chapter. I know it's tempting – after all, forewarned is forearmed – but trust me, you'll only be left with the impression that the world is a seething, fizzing petri dish of disease. It is – but do you really want to know that before you travel?

Simply know that rabies, cholera, sleeping sickness, leishmaniasis, yellow fever, the Plague (yes, it is still kicking around), typhoid, Ebola, hepatitis A, B and C, meningitis, polio, chicken flu, dysentery, giardia, bilharzia, AIDS, Japanese encephalitis, dengue fever and my personal favourite, malaria, are only a plane ride away.

Let's not be pessimistic. The chance of actually contracting any of these is slight, although, it must be said, significantly higher than if you were to stay at home wrapped in cling film. There's more good news: smallpox was eradicated in 1979, so that is one to strike off any hypochondriac's list. Most diseases aren't fatal, and the ones that are, often kill so quickly (Ebola, rabies and chicken flu for example) that you won't suffer for long. And, for all those budding virologists out there, the world must be a very exciting place, a veritable boiling cauldron of disease and pestilence. Yes, there is much to be thankful for.

Shit happens

Let's face it – you haven't really travelled until you've had 'the shits'. By far the most common form of ailment while on the road is diarrhoea which is also a great source of amusement and interest to other travellers. Every traveller I have ever met can fondly recall the first time they spent an evening squatting over an unsavoury pit latrine making sounds like a bus backfiring. Backpackers, who have a preponderance for fart jokes at the best of times, spend an inordinate amount of time talking about their bowel movements. If you ever find yourself in an awkward silence at some hostel, nothing will jump-start the conversation like a casual enquiry about the consistency and regularity of your listeners' stools.

Acoustics in toilets are usually outstanding due to the hard tiled surfaces; every groan, every plea to a merciful god, is amplified and broadcast, pitch perfect, not only to any newly acquired loved one, but the entire hostel. It is possible to receive a standing ovation after an impressive performance, such is the solidarity between backpackers. Indeed, at times you may feel like inviting other travellers into the loo just to show off, but this is not a good idea; a lengthy description will suffice.

STAY AND DIE WITH US

Every sunrise, tens of thousands of Hindi devotees descend the Varanasi ghats (steps) that line the river Ganges to bathe and pray. Known as the Ganga Ma (or Great Mother), the river is one of the most sacred sites in India. To die here and have your ashes emptied into the heavily polluted river is to be guaranteed a release from the cycle of reincarnation and deliver you directly to heavenly Nirvana. From my hotel, which advertised 'come stay and die with us' I could hear the bones cracking and skulls exploding in the cremation fires.

Even if you are far from death, bathing in the Ganges carries its own risks. Recent tests indicate faecal coliform levels range from 21,000 to 80,000 colonies per 100 ml. The safe level for drinking water is zero, for bathing water, less than 150 colonies per 100 ml.

MONTEZUMA'S REVENGE

I had been up all night, vomiting and shitting (almost) in the toilet. By the time my alarm went off at 5.30 a.m. I thought the worst had passed (at speed) through me and I was looking forward to visiting the Brobdingnagian Mexican Mayan ruins of Palenque, a four-hour drive from San Cristobal where my friend, Lenseça, and I were staying.

While we toured the darkened alleys of San Cristobal picking up the other members of our tour I am ashamed to admit that there was a demonic gurgling sound coming from my butt. An extremely self-centred and irate German proceeded to complain at length that he did not wish to sit next to me, until told by a young Englishman to, and I quote, 'Fuck up'.

Our tour began smoothly, albeit punctuated with several spew-poo stops (for me) and several waterfall stops for swimming (for everyone else) on our way to Palenque. The ruins, I later heard, were fantastic. I wouldn't know, as I spent my time dragging myself around in the sweltering heat looking for toilets. Lenseça was great and asked every 2.65 seconds if I was feeling better. After I was completely dehydrated we set off for home.

During the drive home a loud squeak developed in our left front tyre which sounded to me like a small monkey from the jungle. I tried to explain to the driver that if we could get hold of a plate of peanuts, we should be able to lure the monkey out. I may have lacked credibility. Instead the driver found a mechanic who, after much deliberation, got out both his tools (a big and small hammer) and began to remove wheels and bang around at the chassis.

In the meantime, Lenseça found a goat with huge nuts. I myself did not see this goat as I was busy dying, but from all accounts they were truly impressive. I only wish she had taken a photo.

There was absolutely nothing to do while we waited for the mechanic. I would normally have thrown pebbles at the back of the irate German's head, but we had already ditched him at an earlier bus stop. Needless to say, the mechanic couldn't locate the small monkey and we continued on our way at the breakneck speed of 20 km per hour, arriving tired, sick and hungry, long after all restaurants had closed. On days like this it hardly seems worth chewing through the restraints.

Doctors recommend that if suffering from diarrhoea you should avoid fatty foods, spicy hot foods, acidic foods and fruit. This leaves rice, but there is only so much rice any one person can stomach before they start hurting people.

Instead, eat what you want and wait for the bug to run its course – things usually improve after a day or two (or get horribly worse).

What a shit-hole

Not all toilets are created equal. The word 'toilet' doesn't really capture the myriad styles and shapes that can be found in the bathrooms around the world. Locating the handle (lever, piece of string dangling from the ceiling or foot pedal) to flush can be a time-consuming exercise and then of course there is the great 'Western sitting style versus the Eastern squatter' debate.

On the whole I'm a big fan of squatting rather than sitting because no part of your body touches any part of the toilet and, if you saw the state of these things, you'd realise that this is a good thing. The only disadvantage I can see with the squatters, is that when you are drunk, it is all too easy to stand in them. This is more difficult, although not impossible, in a Western loo.

THIS IS CRAP. View the toilet that brought tears to my eyes when forced to use it in Uzbekistan. See the movie – rats, crap and all – at www.deanstarnes.com.

HOW TO USE A SQUAT TOILET

When you gotta go, you gotta go, and for most of the world when nature calls, it tells them to squat.

Squatting takes a bit of practice. Try this – holding on to something for support, lower yourself down until your bum cheeks are almost touching your heels. Many Westerners will need to go on tiptoes to maintain their balance but Asians stay flat footed. Now, let go with your hands and stay in this position for a couple of minutes. If you fall backwards you'll be sitting in your own shit which, trust me on this, isn't a good look.

- *Empty your pockets first, as your pockets can end up upside down and it's no fun searching through other people's shit to find your hotel key.*

- *The worst part is figuring out which way to face. If it's just a hole in the ground, any direction will work. If the toilet has a hood-like arrangement at one end (as in Japan), that is the front. Otherwise face the door and look for treaded pads which indicate where your feet should go.*

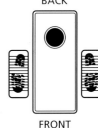

BACK

FRONT

- *Drop your pants to your knees. If you drop them to your ankles you'll end up pissing in them. Doh!*

- *On trains, take a wide stance for added stability.*

- *If you are doing it 'sans paper' then wash your butt with your left hand with the water from the hose or bucket in a front to back direction. Otherwise carry your own paper and put it in the bin next to the toilet. Don't be tempted to flush it, as the narrow pipes aren't designed for paper and they will block.*

- *Don't flush until you are well clear of the toilet. These toilets tend to spray water across the whole floor and it ain't pretty.*

WHAT'S BUGGING YOU?

*Travelling through Mongolia's Gobi Desert and sleeping with nomads
in their gers (felt tents) is an incredible experience. The vast lonely
countryside, the unforgiving glare of the midday sun – it all helps put life's
problems into perspective. So does getting lice in your shorts.*

*I don't know how I got them; one moment I was crab free and the next,
there was a party in my shorts and the lice were inviting friends. I feared
by the next day I would have more wildlife in my pants than the rest of
the Gobi combined. I was practically becoming a national park, worth
protecting. Maybe I had picked them up from an infected bed; maybe I
had gotten too close to a yak – who can say?*

*Sure, pubic lice down your pants may sound fun but it made me very
depressed. I was hundreds of kilometres from a pharmacist, let alone one
who might actually stock lice treatment and so, in desperation, I decided
to shave off all my body hair. I know in some circles hairless bodies are
considered de rigueur, but the sight of my hairless wanger has left me
with unresolved issues.*

*The thing with deserts is that water is somewhat scarce. I'm not an
anthropologist or anything, so don't quote me, but I'm pretty sure it's
considered rude to shave your crotch in a Mongolian family's only barrel
of water.*

*So there I was, pants around my ankles, standing over a pit latrine,
flashlight clenched between teeth and armed with my friend Steph's
pocket knife (she doesn't know this) and a blunt razor with no water. I'm
not going to say any more, other than it got messy.*

*Steph had been incredibly supportive (from a distance of about 10 feet)
and recommended that I bathe the infested area with iodine for good
measure. This would have stained my skin yellow and while I may have
been hairless, at least everything was still the right colour. I could not face
the prospect of having a bald, bright yellow wanger. I'm sure Marco Polo
didn't have to deal with this kind of crap.*

*Unfortunately I was doing one last inspection by shining the torch down
my pants when our jeep driver walked in. It is very difficult to mime, with
any degree of respectability, what I was trying to accomplish. Never had
the language barrier felt more acute than when caught searching for body
lice in my undies under the disgusted stare of a Mongolian herdsman.*

Yaks grazing in front of a Mongolian ger. During the day these yaks, along with the goats, were free to wander off and graze in the surrounding countryside. At nightfall they returned to their respective camps and patiently waited to be milked.

I do have two real bits of advice on toilets. Firstly, always carry toilet paper unless you are into the whole left-hand routine. Secondly, if you do come across a clean toilet, say in a hotel lobby or McDonald's, use it while you have the chance; although technically you should be a patron of that establishment – technically.

There are some frighteningly unhygienic toilets in Third World countries and many don't have access to running water. In rural China, toilets are often no more than simple platforms on stilts above a pile of shit. This is what is commonly referred to as 'atmosphere' or 'local colour' by guide books. If that isn't bad enough, you can expect an audience as you are in full view of the crowd that often gathers around tourists in rural China. The Chinese are inquisitive to say the least; not only did they not look away, they cheered when I managed to shit on top of a pig that was foraging in the sewage beneath. This has left some deep emotional scarring. I don't want to talk about it.

It's in the water!

Water may seem harmless enough and many argue that you should actually drink the stuff, although I suspect they're only joking. Water carries lots of bugs like giardia, which can leave you squatting over a pit latrine for days at a time. But it's not all bad news; alcohol, as luck would have it, is reliably safe (thank you, God).

Nonetheless, because water remains a significant threat to your health, it is essential to find a reliable source of drinking water if you are to avoid getting sick. Bottled water may not be all that it appears; many enterprising

---

HOW TO PURIFY WATER ON THE GO

In poor countries, recycling can no longer absorb the amount of plastic water bottles discarded by foreign tourists fearful of waterborne diseases. Bearing in mind these countries' lack of infrastructure, an environmentally responsible choice would be for travellers to filter or treat the local tap water themselves. Here's how.

- *If you want to filter the water first, repeatedly pour the water through a piece of cloth (silk is ideal but a handkerchief or clean white socks will do) until it is clear. This will not remove the harmful microbes. For that…*
- *Boil the water for at least five minutes at sea level and a minute longer for every 300 metre increase in altitude to pasteurise it. Skim off any residue that may form on the top.*
- *Carry, and use, a specially designed water purifier capable of filtering out amoeba and other pathogens.*
- *Add a few drops of iodine to the water (different brands require different concentrations) and wait at least 15 minutes before drinking. Disguise the bad taste with cordial.*
- *In an emergency, add 2–4 drops of household bleach per litre of water. Stir and wait 30 minutes before drinking. If you cannot faintly smell the chlorine, repeat.*

BATTLE TESTED

HOW TO REMOVE A LEECH

Rainforests are a natural storehouse of disease. This alone makes for a strong argument for slash-and-burn agriculture. Malaysia's Taman Negara (pictured below) is a huge national park of virgin rainforest and one of the few places where tigers, Asian elephants, rhinos, deer and leeches can be seen nightly at the salt licks. I can only vouch for the leeches, which were particularly problematic after the heavy rain (a common phenomenon of most rainforests).

Because they are attracted by vibrations, I recommend walking near the front if walking single file in the jungle and leave those who follow to cop the leeches that drop from above. Pause for more than a micro-second and you'll see them inching towards you from all directions. Mosquito repellent, tobacco, salt, toothpaste and soap are supposed to keep these little bloodsuckers at bay. They don't.

To remove a leech, carefully slide a fingernail under the smallest end, attempting to push the leech sideways until its anterior sucker's seal is broken. The leech will stop feeding while it attempts to reattach itself. To prevent this, flick the small end of its body while you slide your fingernail under the other end. Leeches do not carry disease, but because of the anticoagulant in their saliva the wounds bleed profusely. It is important not to squeeze or yank the leech as this may cause the leech to regurgitate into the wound, causing an infection.

FLICK AT THE ANTERIOR SUCKER

locals have invested in 'bottled-water-cap-sealer' machines which enable them to sell you the tap water you have been so desperately trying to avoid. Don't be discouraged; simply run a few tests for viscosity, pH balance and specific gravity and you'll be fine. Otherwise just check the seal, see if it looks kosher and keep an eye out for any signs of aquatic life, like fish, swimming around in your bottle.

Finally, remember it only takes a drop. No singing in the shower. No ice in your drinks. No salads or other foods that are washed and then served raw.

And if all that sounds bad, consider the tiny urinophilic candiru fish (*Vandellia cirrhosa*) of South America. Forget the piranha, forget Jaws, this is the most feared fish in the Amazon. A candiru fish will follow a stream of urine back to its source – which could be a skinny dipper taking a leak. It then swims up the urine stream into your urethra where it extends its spiny fins to lodge itself firmly in place, thereby drawing blood. The candiru gorges itself on both the blood and body tissue of its host by using the teeth on its top jaw as a rasp. Unfortunately it is almost impossible to remove due to its spines and the resulting haemorrhaging can be fatal. For men, the suggested treatment is penile amputation. Oh God, please no!

There's something about malaria

'She has no rigors or shaking chills, but her husband states she was very hot in bed last night.'

– Charted on a malaria patient's medical record by her doctor.
– www.rinkworks.com

When I caught malaria I thought I was going to die. I even phoned home to tell my parents. They phoned the rest of my family and before long, everyone thought I was going to die. Nothing makes you want to live like everyone else expecting you to die.

I was a little disappointed by how well everyone coped. It would have been nice if someone – anyone – became a little unstuck.

Admittedly a mental breakdown would have been too much, but still, it would have been nice. Unfortunately my family are very well adjusted and they soldiered on.

Malaria is a vicious little parasite that lives in your blood. People obsess about the bird flu, but unless you have a thing for dead ducks, you'll be fine. Malaria, on the other hand, is a real problem. Bill Gates recently gave $250 million to help combat this disease. This was the world's largest single donation to any cause.

I suspect that I contracted malaria in either India or Pakistan, but it didn't rear its ugly head until the end of an Annapurna Circuit trek in Nepal. To further compound my predicament, I had a non-refundable plane ticket to London leaving from Delhi.

Fortified with Panadol I walked with a raging temperature back to Pokhara and boarded my bus for the 10-hour trip down the Siddhartha Highway to the Indian border. I can't remember much of the trip, except bouncing around in a seat near the front clutching my head, and my teeth chattering so hard I thought they would rattle free of my jaw. By the time I got off the bus, my eyes were no more than red fissures in my grey and pallid face. Before catching the train to Varanasi, I had time to find a doctor who gave me a shot of quinine and assured me that things would soon improve.

Things did not improve. My temperature spiralled upwards, my headache became so blinding that I could no longer focus and I had trouble staying conscious. My sight faded until all that remained was like looking through a long, lonely tunnel. This is the point where I left the train, phoned home and told my parents of my impending death. Even in death I managed to give a few instructions, the most important of which was that if they hadn't heard from me within 24 hours they could assume the worst and contact the embassy to claim my body. I wanted to be cremated with a first-class ticket.

There then followed another doctor, further treatment and a long overnight train trip to Delhi.

I woke a day later in a small room, lying on a makeshift cot staring at a slowly revolving fan. My backpack was propped against the far wall and I could make out the excited babble coming from a crowd of people on the other side of the wall. Apparently a kind-hearted station official had seen my plight and helped me to this recovery room. I never met the person who had led me from the train and I never had the chance to thank them and I really wish I had. Because I had slept for almost a day, my plane was due to leave from the airport in a matter of hours so I rushed by taxi to the airport to fly home.

I had forgotten all about the melodramatic conversation with my parents until I reached London. By that time the 24-hour period had long expired and my parents were sick with worry. My sister was about to board a plane from New York to come and find me. If they weren't so relieved to hear that I was okay, they would have killed me.

Travel tip: Malaria is often underrated by travellers, but unless you are planning a hermetically sealed trip to Geneva, take precautions as malaria remains a very real problem in many parts of Asia, Africa and Central America.

HOW TO FIT A BACKPACK TO AVOID BACKACHE

You can reduce the risk of back injury by choosing a pack that is a good fit, ensuring that most of the weight is carried on the hips. Torso length (not overall height) is the crucial length.

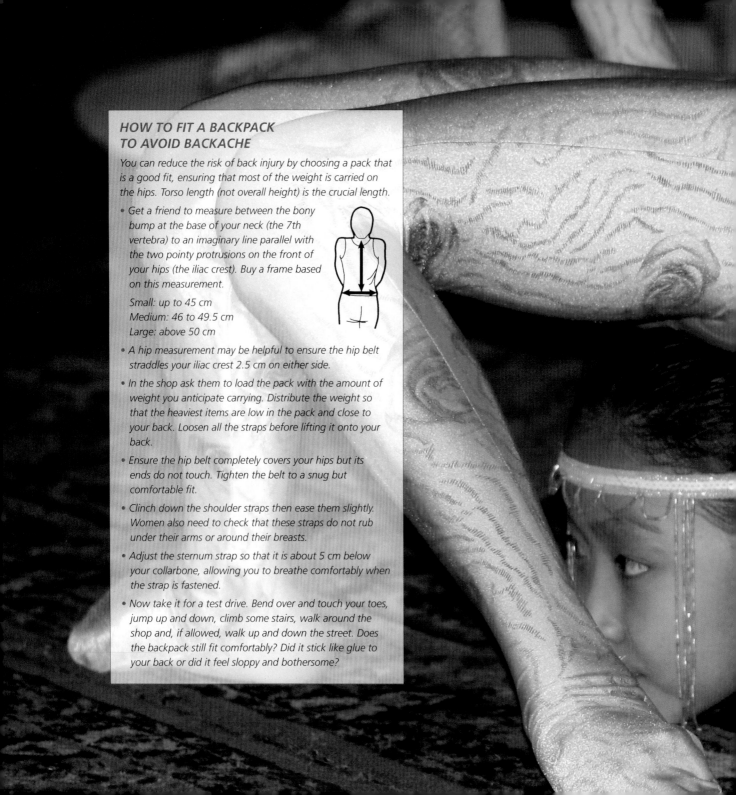

- *Get a friend to measure between the bony bump at the base of your neck (the 7th vertebra) to an imaginary line parallel with the two pointy protrusions on the front of your hips (the iliac crest). Buy a frame based on this measurement.*

  Small: up to 45 cm
  Medium: 46 to 49.5 cm
  Large: above 50 cm

- *A hip measurement may be helpful to ensure the hip belt straddles your iliac crest 2.5 cm on either side.*

- *In the shop ask them to load the pack with the amount of weight you anticipate carrying. Distribute the weight so that the heaviest items are low in the pack and close to your back. Loosen all the straps before lifting it onto your back.*

- *Ensure the hip belt completely covers your hips but its ends do not touch. Tighten the belt to a snug but comfortable fit.*

- *Clinch down the shoulder straps then ease them slightly. Women also need to check that these straps do not rub under their arms or around their breasts.*

- *Adjust the sternum strap so that it is about 5 cm below your collarbone, allowing you to breathe comfortably when the strap is fastened.*

- *Now take it for a test drive. Bend over and touch your toes, jump up and down, climb some stairs, walk around the shop and, if allowed, walk up and down the street. Does the backpack still fit comfortably? Did it stick like glue to your back or did it feel sloppy and bothersome?*

A Mongolian contortionist bends over backwards as part of her eye-watering, limb-popping routine.

FIRST-AID KIT CHECKLIST

'To combat infections many travellers carry a "purpose built" medical kit. These are plastic boxes with a red cross on their lid full of their local chemist's slow-moving products. With names like "Out of Africa" and the "Adventurer's Pack" (it's the one with condoms), they cost a fortune and are full of completely useless stuff like leeches and Band-Aids.'

– No Shitting on the Toilet, PETER MOORE

What makes up a practical medical kit varies from traveller to traveller and to where you are travelling. Will you be in the Australian outback or downtown Austin? In many Third World countries prescription medicines are readily available over the counter at a fraction of the price you'll pay back home, but you will need to know what medicine is right for you. Obviously medicine should be taken under medical supervision but sometimes an illness may strike when you are a long way from a hospital or clinic. In such circumstances it's great to be able to crawl from your sleeping bag, dragging your snotty nose to a medical kit filled with hard-hitting drugs fresh from the research facilities of Switzerland. Listed below are what I take in my emergency stash. At this point bear in mind that I am not a doctor. I once shagged a medical student, so I do have some similarities to many surgeons, but you really should seek a professional opinion about what medicines (if any) you should carry.

Diarrhoea treatments
Diarrhoea is the most common ailment to affect travellers, but usually clears within a day or two if left untreated.

☐ Imodium – think of this as a plug for your arse. It's not helping the problem and you're not cured. It's great for an unavoidable bus trip and little else.

☐ Antibiotic – used to treat bacterial diarrhoea.

☐ Giardia or amoebic dysentery medication (usually Fasigyn or Flagyl will clear these up).

☐ Antispasmodic tablets (e.g. Buscopan) – for treatment of abdominal cramps.

Other medications
☐ Broad-range antibiotic (such as Roxithromycin) – for the treatment of chest, sinus and skin infections.

☐ Cold and flu medication.

☐ Panadol.

☐ Iodine solution – great for cleaning cuts and treating water prior to drinking.

☐ Location-specific treatments and prophylactics such as malaria tablets.

☐ Motion-sickness pills, if you require them.

☐ Antibiotic eye drops – conjunctivitis is surprisingly common.

☐ Fungicide to treat athlete's foot and the like.

Medical equipment
☐ Thermometer.

☐ Syringes and needles – a letter from a doctor stating they are for medical reasons will stop an over-zealous customs officer spending the afternoon ransacking your bag and orifices looking for your stash.

☐ Bandage.

OPPOSITE: The fly-encrusted sea life and the thick, oily odours of fish baking in the sun in this Zanzibar market were all that were needed to kick-start my new diet.

HOW TO COUNT ON YOUR HAND IN CHINESE

Chinese even count on their hands differently. I once waved two fingers at a Shanghai fruit seller and was given seven oranges.

At other times I would hold up a single finger, and if it wasn't straight enough for the vendor's liking, I ended up with nine!

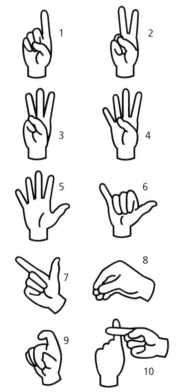

Not only is Chinese difficult to speak, the written language consists of thousands of distinctive 'pictographs'. No wonder this guard, standing beneath Chairman Mao's portrait in Tiananmen Square, China, looks glum.

It's all Greek to me

I can't, in all honesty, offer any practical advice on language acquisition. The truth is, even my grasp of English is tenuous; and despite years of travel, I've never been able to pick up anything beyond the cross-cultural noncommittal grunt. Two years in Japan and it's still Greek to me.

God knows I've tried – sometimes for minutes at a time – to learn a new word, but (and I'm going to be frank) foreign languages are inherently boring. If they weren't so dull I'm sure I could learn several. French, for example, a very important language (although not as important as the French would have you believe), can be divided into masculine and feminine words. This is clearly not right. And, even though they stubbornly refuse to speak English, they have an uncanny ability to understand it, should you insult them.

Maybe I can't learn languages because I'm lazy. This is okay by me; reticence is better than stupidity.

This is not true of others. There clearly are some sharp knives in the linguistic cutlery drawer. When someone yells 'Run for your lives!', I'm always the last to know. Once, helping a guide pull a cobra from a bush in the Amazon he screamed (in Portuguese) 'Run for your lives!' and everyone did. Everyone, that is, except me, who was left holding an eight-foot snake. Snakes, even long ones, can turn really quickly, quicker than the words 'let go, you stupid bastard' can be translated. Not many people know that.

Chinese, with consonant groupings such as zhou, ixia, us, gap, you, gnu, up and gust, will always be beyond me. I've accepted this and moved on. The closest I've ever come to articulating any of these sonorous sounds is farting which, ironically, is culturally insensitive. I accept that language is the bedrock of culture and any phrases

Graffiti and greetings on a section of the old Berlin Wall in Berlin, Germany.

'It is easier for a cannibal to enter the Kingdom of Heaven through the eye of a rich man's needle than it is for any other foreigner to read the terrible German script.'

– MARK TWAIN

that can be gleaned inevitably pay gold. I've seen it happen (to others obviously). However, if, like me, you don't have an affinity for anyone else's tongue, don't be discouraged. Knowing the language of the country is not a prerequisite for travelling through it. Naturally if you do speak the local lingo, things are smoother, you'll probably learn more, find making friends easier and have a richer experience than a moron like me. But morons are people too; we can still learn and have rewarding experiences even if we have no idea what is going on.

I once travelled through Latin America with a friend whose Spanish was worse than mine, which was an impressive feat in itself. After two months she still hadn't figured out the word for 'women's' and could still be found taking a crap in the 'men's'. I didn't ever tell her and guarded the dictionary to see how long it took her to learn these two words – it turned out to be 64 days, 11 hours and 46 minutes.

Despite advice you'll hear to the contrary, understanding the local language – even a superficial understanding – is not necessary. People are friendly and surprisingly patient and resourceful in their endeavours to understand you. It's amazing how well you can make yourself understood without uttering a sound. Nonetheless there are a few things that you can do to help.

Tips for the linguistically impaired

Speak LOUDLY and s-l-o-w-l-y

This is an excellent technique and being so naturally ineffective it is almost instinctual. Within moments of arriving in a foreign airport you'll find yourself speaking abnormally loudly and slowly to immigration officials, taxi drivers and hotel receptionists. Don't be fooled by their blank stares and expressionless faces; of course they understand you! How could they not when you are speaking so loudly and so clearly?

The easiest way to learn a language is to throw caution to the wind; don't worry about the mistakes you are undoubtedly making and give it a go. The locals loved Bronwyn's attempts at Swahili – no matter that they couldn't understand a word she said.

Sign of the times. The written word can be as amusing as the spoken. During Eisenhower's election the Japanese are reported to have slung a banner across a Tokyo street that urged the Japanese citizenry '... to play for Eisenhower's erection'. Excellent.

According to the Indian sign above, freedom fighters can ride the bus for free. Trying to overthrow the government? No need to pay, my friend; we welcome anarchy.

Use terrible English

It is not unusual to find yourself omitting small words; prepositions and conjunctions are usually the first to go. Who needs 'em? Instead, speak a kind of pidgin English of your own construction. Of course, no one will have any idea what you are banging on about – not even native English speakers – but despite what may seem to be a fundamental flaw, this approach has many devotees. Instead persevere; a breakthrough is imminent.

Carry a phrase book

These pocket-sized aids have been carefully designed to provide no real help to the hapless traveller. Presumably essential words are omitted and others are grouped in nonsensical chapters making them virtually impossible to find. You'll often see a traveller spend 10 minutes with his head buried in his phrase book, frantically searching for the words 'can I buy you a drink' long after the bar has closed and the Swedish babes departed.

Speak in song lyrics

This may sound ill-considered but desperate times call for desperate measures. You will be pleasantly surprised at how well you get by with a few well-placed Ricky Martin lyrics and the odd *'que sera, sera'*. Yes, as long as you are happy living *'la vida loca'*, nothing can possibly go wrong.

Mime it

Sign language and mime have proved to be excellent forms of communication although, it must be said, should you lose the use of your hands you would be mute, and should you go blind, you would also be deaf. Despite this risk, it is possible to effectively communicate all manner of things to a receptive audience. Think of it as a giant game of charades on which rides the successful completion of your vacation. No pressure.

In Nicaragua I mimed my whole life story, including my hopes and aspirations, to a Mayan villager. Despite him laughing at inappropriate moments, he seemed to follow what I was saying. In turn he mimed his life story back and from what I could gather he left his village at a young age to join the merchant navy where he worked as a shrimp fisherman until he met a young lady, who, I can only hope, became his wife, and with whom he enjoyed both prolonged and frequent biblical relations. After a terrible attack by an octopus he left the fishing industry and now works as either a mechanic or small radio operator – I'm not sure which.

I confess I rely heavily on this approach and the only time it has ever failed me was in Chile when I had a haircut. I clearly indicated I wanted a little taken *off* but what I got was a little *left*. The part that was left was just a tuft on the top of my head so I looked like a sad rabbit that had been mauled by a dog.

Draw it

This tactic is prevalent throughout Asia where English in uncommon and miming often only adds to the confusion because body language there is so dissimilar to our own. Basically you draw whatever you are trying to communicate and then, just like in Pictionary, you stab at it frantically with your pencil until the other party gets it.

An exciting variation is *Fear Factor* Pictionary which is best played in China. Simply go into a restaurant and eat whatever you can draw. No matter what animal you draw, chances are it will be on the menu. Baby seahorses; a bull's testicle; crickets – yummy! I usually draw a chicken and *usually* get a chicken – but be careful not to draw the feet first as they may focus just on this detail and bring you only chicken feet. Cows are more problematic; sometimes my cows look like cows and at other times they, unfortunately, look like rats.

Only go to places you can say

It can be hard to buy a ticket to a place you can neither say nor spell. To avoid embarrassment, a quick squizz through a map is recommended. The only place I could pronounce in Guatemala was a town called Livingston on the Caribbean coast (I even got to say 'Livingston, I presume' when the boat pulled up – incidentally no one thought this was funny but I pissed myself laughing). Other places like Quetzaltenango and Chichicastenango were clearly trying to discourage tourism (or morons). It didn't get better as I travelled south. The capital of Honduras is the unpronounceable Tegucigalpa. What's wrong with these people? Thankfully the world's longest place name, Taumatawhakatangihangakoauauotamateaturipukakapikimaungahoronukupokaiwhenua-kitanatahu, in New Zealand, has nothing of interest to encourage a visit.

Shack up with someone bilingual

The first time I went to South America I was so helplessly out of my depth that I spent the first three days holed up in my room, too afraid to set foot outside. Thankfully I met a multilingual German girl called Gretcha from whose side, for neither love nor money, would I leave. It took the long-suffering Gretcha three countries to shake me and even then I was able to track her down by hanging out at the long-distance bus station until she showed. Ahhh … those were the days.

THE FIVE MOST USEFUL PHRASES IN THE THREE MOST USEFUL LANGUAGES

While some cunning linguists seem to master languages effortlessly, I stick to the basics. A well-placed 'please' and 'thank you' work wonders but the phrases listed below are essential for your survival. If you are too stupid to learn anything else it is possible to travel using the words below conveniently grouped into five phrases and three languages, English (E), Latin American Spanish (S) and French (F).

E *How much is it?*
S *¿Cuánto cuesta esto?*
F *C'est combien?*

E *One, two, three, four, five, six, seven, eight, nine, ten.*
S *Uno, dos, tres, cuatro, cinco, seis, siete, ocho, nueve, diez.*
F *Un, deux, trois, quatre, cinq, six, sept, huit, neuf, dix.*

E *Do you have any rooms/beds available?*
S *¿Tiene habitaciones/camas libres?*
F *Avez-vous des chambres/lits libres?*

E *Can I have a ticket to _____?*
S *¿Puedo tener un billete para _____?*
F *Est-ce que je peux avoir un billet pour _____?*

E *Nice place. Where can I get a beer?*
S *Que sitio agradable. ¿Dónde se compra una cerveza?*
F *C'est un lieu agréable. Où est-ce que je peux acheter une bière?*

If all else fails, try alcohol

The more you drink, the more fluent you become in another's language. You may begin to slur your own native tongue but I have seen a South Korean, drunk on vodka, start chatting fluently in Mongolian. I tried a few shots myself and I swear the more I drunk, the easier it became. I have no idea what I was saying but apparently I was telling jokes, discussing European foreign trade agreements, the works! Brilliant.

Swear like a local

Every province has its own dialect and colloquialisms, every tongue its own particular stock of swear words and nothing amuses locals more than teaching foreigners to talk dirty. As luck would have it, I have a natural affinity for profanity and can tell people to 'fuck off' in several languages. The locals love it.

Other expressions that pay off handsomely are political statements that reflect local sentiments. In Eastern Turkey the Kurds taught me a solidarity expression with the PKK separatists and every time I trotted it out someone brought me tea. Conversely when I asked if they thought fighting for peace was like screwing for virginity I was given the evils and invited to leave their country. Go figure.

Communication through osmosis

This is really only for the truly pathetic. I have tried it several times and I can reliably report that it never works. I'm only going to try it a few more times and then I'm giving up. I employ this when it is vital I understand something I am being told and have exhausted all other options. What I do is listen really, really hard, hoping that somehow I'll understand what bus I'm supposed to be on or where my luggage now resides.

Don't be afraid to ask

Normally I encourage people to ask questions but there are limits. Here are some questions that have been asked at North American national park offices:

- What time does the two o'clock bus leave?
- Did people build this, or did Indians?
- Do you know of any undiscovered ruins?
- How much of the cave is underground?
- Which beach is closest to the water?
- Where can we find Amish hookers? We want to buy a quilt.
- What's the best time of year to watch deer turn into elk?
- Why did they build the ruins so close to the road?

Teach everyone else English

Admittedly this is a long shot but I'm doing my part. Linguistic imbeciles unite! Instead of us learning a foreign language, let's teach everyone else English. It's a great idea which has already been adopted by citizens of the United Kingdom who are unabashedly monolingual despite having a whole plethora of languages and peoples as neighbours. Way to go, Britain!

RIGHT: This Kenyan hat speaks volumes. After all, a fake rose sticking out of your hair must be some kind of statement. In this case, the floral motif is common to the Turkana people.

Thanks to the Internet, even remote Borneo tribesmen now have access to shots of Pamela Anderson's tits. Yes, pornography has come a long way in the past few years.

Gone are the thrills of receiving battered-looking letters covered in exotic stamps, months after they were posted. Instead, the first thing many travellers do when they arrive in a new town is to seek out an Internet café and update their blogs in mind-numbing detail.

Think twice before giving out your email address. This may sound unduly pessimistic but cruel experience has taught me that only those who want something ask for your email. Unless it is sex (whoa!) they are after one of the following:

- *A job, sponsorship, a green card or your passport when you have finished with it.*

- *A free place to stay on their next trip.*

- *To expand the size of their group mailing list and inflict the story of their life on you in hourly instalments.*

Making yourself clear

In countries like Indonesia it is important to avoid 'yes' or 'no' questions because they always answer 'yes' even if they don't understand the question or know the answer. They feel it would be rude to answer with an emphatic 'no'. In Bali, my friend Terry and I hired motorbikes and headed off into the countryside. When we became lost we would ask, 'Is this the way to Ubud?' and point in the direction we thought was correct. Invariably they would answer 'yes' even when the village was in the opposite direction. We spent days riding around Bali, which might sound like fun but got boring by the third lap.

Another thing to avoid is the double negative. It is important to remember that most people who have studied English can probably speak it better than you, so for your own sake, keep it simple. My friend Bronwyn and I once tried to order banana fritters in Uganda. Because I started the conversation with a negative ('don't you have', instead of 'do you have') it became painfully convoluted:

'Don't you have any banana fritters?'

'No.'

'But they have some.'

'Yes.'

'When you say no, you don't have, does that mean yes, you do have, or yes, you don't have?'

'No, I don't have.'

'So you have some?'

'Yes – of course' (looking at me like I'm a moron).

'But you said, "No, you don't have any," and now you are saying yes.'

'No, I'm saying yes I have and no I don't, it's the same you see.'

'So do you have some?'

'Yes.'

'Can I have two please … with vodka?'

Money talks

As Neil Diamond noted, money may not sing and dance but it talks and, the world over, people speak its language. No matter where you are, if you want to spend some money, you'll have no problem making yourself understood. The San Blas archipelago is strung along 226 km of Panama's Caribbean coast and is known as the Comarca de Kuna Yala, after the Indians who make their homes on the islands and run the area as an autonomous region. The islands have their own laws and local government based on traditional beliefs and social structures.

The Kuna have a shrewd sense of money – shrewder than I have, as it turned out. I like to pride myself on my pretty sharp negotiating skills, but when dealing with the Kuna I got the rough end of the pineapple. Some of those little old Kuna ladies may look harmless but trust me, they are ruthless capitalists who have no mercy. It is such tenacity that has enabled the Kuna to preserve their culture in the face of European contact ever since Columbus sailed past in 1502, completely lost.

The going rate for a photo is a reasonable US$1. If you don't particularly like paying for your photos, they don't particularly want to be photographed. Not everyone likes this about the Kuna but they don't care; it's their island, so it's their rules. I asked a crinkly old lady in my best Spanish (which is the same as my worst Spanish) if I could take her photo. She eyed me up and down, looked at my camera, looked at my scruffy clothes (I could practically see her calculating my worth), added tax and finally came up with an outrageous figure of US$10. I smiled and signalled that I was a poor traveller without a job, a long way from home, struggling to make ends meet. She signalled back that she was impressed that even the poor from my country could fly halfway around the world to vacation and that I must come from a land (an undoubtedly generous land) uncommonly blessed. She was good; what could I say to that? I made to leave (see 'Talk then walk' in the Shopping chapter) when she relented – round one to the street-savvy backpacker.

By the time I had walked back a few metres and composed the picture, she'd had time to drag a few kids and a puppy into the shot. Suddenly a baby appeared on her knee and there were some additional people three hundred feet away, practically on the other side of the island, waving – all clearly commanding a dollar when in fact I was just wanting to photograph the crinkly old lady I had first approached – round two to the old woman.

I took the shot anyway and since I had a motorised drive I thought I would go for the second shot an indiscernible instant after the first. All the people who had squeezed themselves into the picture, even the puppy, screamed 'two photo, two photoooo' and the price was doubled. I handed her the ten dollars she had originally asked for – round three to the crinkly old Kuna lady.

As consolation, she sent me off with her granddaughter and the puppy to look at her turtles. The turtles were kept in a bamboo cage of stakes driven into the ground, forming an enclosure. In the enclosure, swimming around in circles, were about seven turtles of varying sizes. The turtles were kept there until they were eaten. I'm not sure that was legal, but the Kuna are self-governing and no one likes to quibble over international law with a 10-year-old girl and her puppy – it makes you feel like an idiot.

It was while we were sitting on the makeshift jetty that formed one side of the enclosure, with our feet dangling in the water, that the girl pointed at a long dark shark resting on the sand beneath us. I hate sharks, always have, and keeping a shark with your turtles is like keeping a tiger in your pantry. After retrieving my foot I learnt that the shark was a real coup for the family. In the summer, big American cruise ships would sometimes call in, buying *molas* (traditionally patterned textiles) and taking photos. The whole island stood to make a lot of money and they would pay to swim with that shark. I asked if any got eaten.

By way of demonstration, she dived into the enclosure, grabbed the

Some of the Kuna islands, like the one these children live on (Nalunega), are so overcrowded that every inch of the island is covered in palm shacks, leaving no room for anything but narrow paths criss-crossing between the huts.

shark by its tail and started pulling it towards the shore. It was a very complacent shark; it had obviously been pulled ashore many times before and had the kind of lazy, resigned expression sharks sometimes get. The girl tried to lift the shark out of the water so I could stroke it (for US$5) but it was way too big for her and she barely got its back half off the bottom.

Further along the beach, three women worked on *molas* for the tourist market back in Panama City. Kuna women still wear brilliantly coloured *molas* over their short-sleeved blouses and vibrantly patterned wraps. Their legs and forearms are adorned with tightly bound strands of beads and their noses are decorated with golden rings. By zealously protecting their language, traditional dress, legends and decision-making processes the Kuna have carved a unique niche in which they are saving their culture by marketing it to tourists. Game, set and match to the Kuna.

RIGHT: Women make molas *to sell to visiting tourists. For the traveller, a visit to the Kuna results in a series of charges and visitation fees that some find unreasonable, but ultimately benefit the Indians, helping them survive independently in a modern world.*

Testosterone-fuelled teenagers celebrate Vietnam's victory over Thailand in the South-East Asia Games soccer final by riding their motorcycles at speed through the streets of Hanoi.

From A to B

My advice – never take advice from anyone who maintains that *just* getting there is half the fun. It's a pretty sad indictment on their holiday if the most exciting part of their vacation was being frisked by airport security.

That said, things do improve once you're clear of airport customs. Travellers face a dizzying array of strange and improbable contraptions, all willing to whisk you from A to B, stopping only for repairs, petrol and prayers. Nothing smacks more of travelling than getting down and dirty with the locals on their public transport. I'm not just talking planes, trains and automobiles, I'm talking rickshaws, dugouts, *bemos*, donkeys, buses and *túk-túks*.

Come fly with me – air travel

'If forced to travel on an airplane, try and get in the cabin with the Captain, so you can keep an eye on him and nudge him if he falls asleep or point out any mountains looming up ahead.'

– MIKE HARDING

Air travel tends to be very boring or very exciting – mind you it's a fine line between exciting and crashing. There's little to do on a plane besides watch movies, scoff cashews and drink booze, although these days the drinks trolley doesn't rattle past with the same degree of regularity that it used to. To pep things up there's nothing wrong with a few harmless diversions to pass the time. During a long-haul flight most people, sooner or later, allow their mind to dwell on the possibility that their plane might crash. While the aerophobic traveller might be tempted to start scrawling out their last will and testament on the nearest fireproof surface, many choose to make light of the situation through humour. At any given time half the passengers are actually telling each other bomb jokes or making exploding noises when any of the passengers around them press any of their buttons. This usually results in someone *accidentally* changing the movie channel of the person next to them at the climax of the in-flight movie. You know this because that person will then mutter about it under their breath although of course they are in fact ranting at twice their normal volume because of the sound-cancelling properties of their headphones. Since it can be very embarrassing for all concerned to hear someone's little old grandmother mouthing off I find it best to avoid humour on aircraft and particularly in airports. These days airport security just don't get sarcasm, irony and bomb jokes.

In the past few years a string of dodgy, no-frills airlines have started operating from obscure airports, offering cheap seats and little service. These carriers offer little appeal other than the cheap airfare, although that's enough for me. On these flights it's worth taking a cursory glance at any place you might expect to find a logo

– the *In the Event of an Emergency* card, the embossed fold-away table, seatbelt buckle or cutlery – to see if the logos printed there match the insignia on the plane's tail. If not, don't panic unless you find yourself on a second-hand Aeroflot plane in which case you may as well assume the safety position then and there.

The best seats on the plane are the ones in front of the emergency exits where you'll get more leg room. If you know the type and model of the aircraft a quick search on the Internet (www.uk-air.net/seatplan.htm) will soon reveal which aisles these are on. If you are tall or just don't like resting your chin on your knees, consider making an advanced seating request. Advanced seating requests is the process by which travellers inform the airline of the one seat that they will not be given on check-in.

The short haul – local transport

Unlike air travel, local transport offers an unparalleled opportunity to mix with locals, see the countryside and save a lot of money. Forget the pre-arranged tours; do it yourself, on the spot, at a fraction of the cost the travel agent would have charged you. The physical act of travelling itself lies at the heart of the independent travel experience. The first step for any would-be backpacker is to acquaint themselves with the various vehicles they are likely to encounter, if for no other reason than to accurately describe them when relaying how much they overcharged you at the hostel later that night.

Indonesia has more than most in the arena of local transport and is an excellent case study. Firstly there is the ubiquitous Balinese *bemo* – a tiny pickup truck with two rows of seats down the side. Ideally suited for eight people but with imaginative layering of disproportionately sized people inside, careful stacking of passengers on the roof, combined with a handful out the side with a precarious toe-hold on the running board, it is possible to get at least 25 on board. A step-up from these – in the sense that they can travel faster downhill and therefore cause more carnage in the likely event of an accident – is the *oplet*, also known around Java as the *microlet* or *colt*, but to you and me, it's a minibus. Then there's the ever-popular *becak* or bicycle rickshaw or, for the yuppie, the auto rickshaw or *bajaj*, a three-wheeler powered by a noisy, fume-belching two-stroke diesel motor. Hair-raising near-misses are guaranteed and glancing-blow collisions are common. They are the same height off the ground as most truck exhaust pipes and their small wheels and rock-hard suspension make them supremely uncomfortable; even the slightest bump will have you airborne. In quieter towns you may find *dokars* and *andongs* – horse or pony carts with two wheels (*dokars*) or four (*andongs*). These horses are half-starved and you're liable to kill them should you and a friend along with your backpacks attempt to use them.

Of course in most towns there are taxis (in Jakarta one even used its meter) and a ride in one is a thrilling experience. Indonesians believe that their (and your) survival is at the whim of the gods, and to curry the favour of their deity of choice they dangle garish religious paraphernalia from the rear-view mirror and festoon

A rusted truck limps across the Salar de Uyuni. When it rains here the painfully white salt plains are transformed into giant, sky-reflecting mirrors.

THE WORLD'S TOP FIVE ROAD TRIPS

PASS THE SALT
Bolivia's Salar de Uyuni
Stretching like a giant white tablecloth over 12,000 sq km, the Salar is the largest saltpan on earth, containing an estimated 10 billion tonnes of salt. There are no roads; just pick a direction and watch your vehicle rust around you.

AMERICA'S MAIN STREET
Route 66, United States
Although it's now getting superseded by interstate highways, it's still possible to get your kicks on Route 66. All you need is a Yank tank (a Pontiac or Chevrolet will do) capable of the 4000 km run from Chicago to California and an unhealthy appetite for burgers and fries.

RIDE LIKE THE WIND
Italy's Amalfi Coast
Don an Armani and straddle a Vespa. The 50 km ride from Sorrento to Salerno is a vroom with a view. Postcard-perfect towns, dramatic cliffs and turquoise waters demand some serious rubber-necking.

THE HIGH ROAD
The Karakoram Highway (KKH), Pakistan to China
The KKH took 20 years to plan, push, blast and level. The word highway is misleading as the road is nothing but metal and decaying asphalt laid over some of the world's most rugged, mind-bending terrain. The highest point reaches 4800 metres before plummeting down to the Pakistani lost kingdom of Shangri-la.

GENTLEMEN, START YOUR ENGINES
The Paris to Dakar Rally, France to Senegal
If all of the above seem a bit namby-pamby, retrace the skid marks out of Paris to turbulent West Africa. Deep sands, land mines, police checks and volatile borders are guaranteed to get your motor running.

their dashboard with spiritual trinkets that serve to obscure the windscreen and increase the likelihood of crashing. Thus protected, Indonesians feel free to drive as if competing in an international motor rally with you as their co-driver. Resist the temptation to yell advice. If the driver does hear you over the screaming engine he will only take it as encouragement.

Over the years I've been in a few crashes at the hands of reckless drivers – notably two in one day on a bus ride from Bocas Del Toro to Panama City but, like a first kiss, I recall mostly fondly the day my friend (Terry) and I almost died in a *colt* (minibus) travelling from Ngadisari to Probolinggo on Indonesia's Mount Bromo.

The driver, for reasons that defied logic, preferred to roll down the mountain without first starting the engine. I suspect it was a fuel-saving tactic but I had no chance to ascertain his exact reason on this point. After what may have been as long as five or six seconds, gravity had us hurtling down the road, without the use of the van's power-assisted brakes. Unable to start the engine, and with ever-increasing velocity, it was all our driver could do but clutch at the wheel and scream at the top of his lungs. We screamed for him to deploy the handbrake, but instead, again for reasons beyond logic, he attempted to negotiate a 90-degree turn at something approaching the speed of sound. Now we were no longer racing down the mountain but running perpendicular across its slope into a large bowl-like depression. As we climbed the opposite side of the bowl we slowed and came to a standstill, an ideal time to apply the handbrake. He didn't. Instead we started rolling backwards.

I shall never forget the faces of the locals, many of whom had never seen two white men, screaming like school girls, race backwards past them in a minibus before. While it was possible to roll as quickly backwards as it was forwards it was not possible to steer as effectively and the inevitable crash was pretty nasty. The back (where we were sitting) took the full brunt of the concrete wall, ripping off the back axle on a rock in the process. As shaken as our driver was, he still had the gumption to ask for our fares.

The whole nine yards – long distance

The two most common forms of long-distance transport are buses and trains. Varied tactics are called for on each and differ from country to country. Throughout the world you will find yourself stuffed inside an eclectic group of vehicles loosely described as buses along with mounds of baggage in the aisles, chickens and other livestock under the seats and in some areas passengers travelling 'upper class' (i.e. on the roof).

Buses tend to be frustratingly slow, stopping frequently – often for seemingly no reason and for long periods. Local music, like Hindu pop, is usually played at maximum volume and will screech on, day and night, without end. Requests to turn it down are treated with amusement and complete disbelief. Deluxe buses have a slightly more refined set of tortures: they usually screen videos, macho karate epics, also played at full volume for hours on end. The accepted procedure for two travellers is for one to guard the baggage and the other to

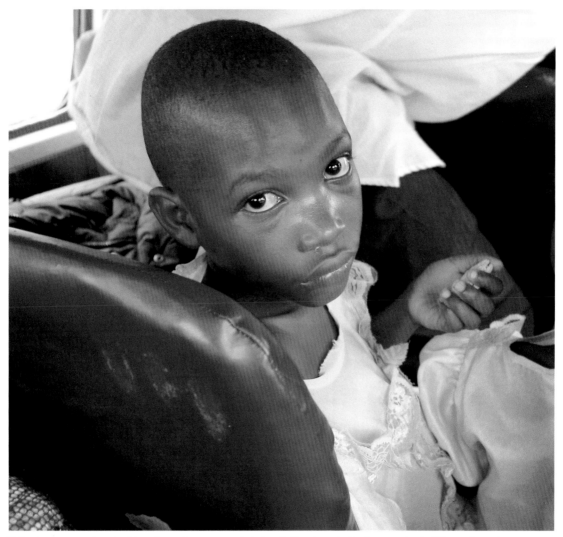

This photo was taken inside a Rwandan matatu (minivan). For the whole three-and-a-half hours it took to motor 35 km – we stopped every 500 yards to enquire about the price of bananas – this girl stared at me. I tried several times to make her smile but she was clearly horrified to find a mzungu (white person) on the bus.

HOW TO STOP A RUNAWAY HORSE

Horses are big, strong and dangerous, except in Mongolia where they are small, strong and dangerous. Horses kill more Australians every year than either crocodiles, snakes or sharks – this isn't necessarily a bad thing. My best advice for novice riders is to ask for a gentle, preferably dead, horse.

Experts advise that if you do find yourself on a runaway horse keep a firm grip with one hand on the saddle and the other on the reins. Resist the temptation to lean forward and keep as upright as you are able. When pulling back on the reins do not use excessive force in case you unbalance the horse and cause it to fall. As the horse slows, get it to circle by pulling the rein to one side. With any luck you'll then be able to bring the horse to a standstill by pulling back on both reins with steady pressure. Dismount.

Mongolian horseman.

storm the bus in the hope of a seat. In India a seat may be reserved by throwing a newspaper or hanky through an open window or asking a passenger to place an item of yours on an empty seat allowing you to claim your place after things simmer down.

A bus driver's skill, particularly in Asia, is judged by his ability to use the correct horn from the impressive array that every vehicle comes with. In China, law requires that drivers announce their presence to cyclists (which number in the tens of millions), and for this they use a tweeter for preliminaries, a bulge or bullhorn if they get annoyed and, if the situation calls for it, an eardrum-shattering air horn. Apart from their ability to use these horns in the correct manner, most drivers are, as a rule, atrocious. They are loath to change gear and prefer to almost come to a complete standstill on a slope rather than change from third to second.

It is not uncommon for buses to start competing for roadside passengers. The usual scenario is for the following bus to get perilously close to the leading bus's rear bumper and to blast furiously on an armoury of horns before, in a hair-raising exhibition of reckless daredevilry, sweeping around the opposition, usually on a blind corner.

Things can sometimes get nasty even before you've actually set foot on your bus or train. China's national sport, the Huddle, is played at train stations with thousands on the 'field' at any given time. The rules are simple: every day all of China's 1.1 billion people go to the train stations to shout at the government official who is employed to refuse to sell, under any circumstances, a ticket.

People don't queue for their turn to shout, but huddle, pushing and shoving (it resembles a riot) towards the front. After four or five hours a lucky backpacker may find themselves at the ticket window where they too can shout their destination at the person who sits there and drinks tea. After a few minutes they're replaced by someone else. This goes on for days until frustrated and hopelessly behind in their travel schedule, everyone turns to the black market and buys their ticket at an inflated price.

CHOOSING A BUS SEAT

- *Remember, you're not in high school so avoid the back seat (and those directly over the axles). Bus physics – which are different than elsewhere on the planet – mean that the effect of every bump, every pothole and every squashed rodent will be magnified to the point that the force will be sufficient to launch you into the lap of unsuspecting passengers several rows removed.*

- *Third World countries' roads are largely a series of interconnected potholes. This, coupled with bus manufacturers' proclivity to upholster bus seats in vinyl, means that you will often find fellow travellers – particularly those prone to buttock perspiration – sliding into your lap. Be prepared.*

- *Figure out which side of the bus the sun will be on for the majority of the trip. These tin cans on wheels can be unbearably hot and cause excessive buttock perspiration. See above.*

- *Ask someone to write down your destination in the local lingo so you can show the bus driver and avoid any misunderstandings. If you are forgetful like me, have someone stencil it across your forehead.*

- *Sit somewhere you can see your luggage get nicked.*

BATTLE TESTED

TOP FIVE TRAIN JOURNEYS

RUSSIA ALL THE WAY – The Trans-Siberian and Moscow Underground

The Trans-Siberian makes all other trips seem like once around the sand-box on Thomas the Tank Engine.
Not to be outdone are the metro stations of Moscow, with their bas-reliefs, stuccos and mosaics of Soviet patriotism.

ROCKY MOUNTAIN HIGH – The Rocky Mountaineer through the Canadian Rockies

From Vancouver there are three routes through five national parks, all over two days, and all thoughtfully stopping at night so not a single mountain vista, glacial lake or rugged escarpment can go un-photographed.

THE BIG RED – The Great Ghan through Australia's rusty-red heart

Named after the Afghan camels that once trekked this route, the Ghan runs from Adelaide to Darwin through the outback of the world's driest continent. Fair dinkum.

MAKE MINE AN EXPRESSO – Riding the Japanese shinkansen

If the others all seem a bit tame and speed is your need, then the Japanese maglev bullet train is just the ticket, holding the 2003 world record of 581 kph. In contrast, regular shinkansen dawdle along at a mere 300 kph.

SHOOTING THE CANYON – The Sierra Madre Express through Mexico's Copper Canyon

There's nothing quick about this express; you'll have plenty of time to goggle at the deep chasms, sheer canyon walls and high deserts as you traverse 36 bridges and wander through 87 tunnels.

Moscow's Komsomolskaya Metro with its chandeliers and grandiose baroque-style ceiling.

TIPS FOR THE
TRANS-SIBERIAN

- There is no point scanning a timetable for the term 'Trans-Siberian' as this name refers to the track, not the train. The Trans-Mongolian and Trans-Manchurian also share much of the line.

- Since hundreds of trains use the track, be sure you don't end up on the excruciatingly slow mail trains. All trains are numbered and the larger their number, the slower they travel. The fastest number 1 Rossiya train takes a week.

- Save your money and buy the tickets yourself as you go. It's easy.

- The hard part is getting a visa to travel independently in Russia. Go to www.waytorussia.net for help.

- Consider going in winter to see the taiga in all its frigid, freezing glory.

- Make friends with the provodnitsa – the carriage attendant who keeps the place clean, the rabble orderly and dispenses the boiling water for your noodles. Bring your own mug.

- On the Chinese and Mongolian routes be prepared to fight for your space. Traders will attempt to turn your compartment into their warehouse by storing their goods on, under and over your seat. Do what the Russians do – push the whole lot into the corridor.

Once around the block

The Trans-Siberian is a rail trip without parallel. For 9289 km the track spans mighty rivers, crosses isolated steppes and rushes headlong through the mighty, virtually uninhabited forests known as the *taiga*.

My own Trans-Siberia odyssey was a roaring success although the start was a bit shaky. I had convinced Steph that pre-purchasing tickets was against the spirit in which the trip had been conceived. Who would have thought that the sole weekly train from Beijing to Ulaanbaatar, the first leg of our trip, would be booked solid?

Because neither of us spoke Chinese, Mongolian or Russian, formulating a 'plan B' was tricky. On the second day, at a Beijing bus station we met a Mongolian girl who understood English and could translate our request to Mongolian which in turn was translated to Chinese via her mother and from there to Russian. It was like playing Chinese whispers. There was a whole string of people involved in trying to figure out what we wanted. It took several attempts to confirm that we didn't have a ticket for the train but still wanted to go to Moscow, one-third of the globe away, and needed a bus ticket to the border where we planned to join the train.

After that, tickets were easy to come by although I can't remember much beyond the first few rounds of vodka. I've never been a cross-dresser but I have a photo of myself dressed in the *provodnitsa's* (carriage attendant) uniform so I can only presume we had some kind of party. I have a vague recollection of losing a chess game against a four-year-old and debating Tolstoy's *Crime and Punishment* with his grandfather in Russian.

Steph, who was even more worse for wear than me, said that a soldier named Alex had taught us the art of drinking vodka Russian style; which is straight, frequent and accompanied by sausages and cucumbers. When I asked her what I had thought of the scenery she said I found it to be very tree-ey.

CLIMB ABOARD THE PEACE TRAIN at www.deanstarnes.com to view the Trans-Siberian slide show. Just like being there but without the hangover.

BATTLE TESTED

TRAIN TIPS

- The only time to pass up an opportunity to ride on the roof is when it's raining.

- A Euro-rail pass is a ticket that allows young Americans to rush from one train station to the next without seeing any of the sights or meeting any of the locals. In an effort to get the most 'value' from their pass many manage to eat, sleep, shit and screw without ever leaving the train. Even though the newer passes are more flexible it's worth calculating how much you will spend if you just buy the tickets as you go.

- The top bunk is safer than the bottom but even then, keep your valuables stuffed down your pants during the night.

- Don't screw up your nose at the food sold by vendors – it's less likely to give you the shits than that served by the railway.

- In Africa, Asia and Northern Ireland, 'first class' merely indicates that the train is in better condition than the others. Since most are creaking dinosaurs, left over from colonial days, this isn't saying much.

- In India, poverty is such that riding without a ticket is commonplace and the aisles will soon fill with families. If you have paid for a sleeper, like Steph pictured below, don't be afraid to either stretch out if need be or share your seat when sitting upright. Non-ticket holders are happy to relinquish your seat when asked. Don't sweat it.

Watching your steppe

The Gobi Desert is a vast, scrubby area of Southern Mongolia, thinly populated with rabid dogs and semi-nomadic families. Because water supplies are scarce and dust storms frequent, it is essential to ensure that your transport is reliable from the get go. Most travellers congregate in the guesthouses of Ulaanbaatar, Mongolia's capital, where it's easy to form groups and share the costs associated with hiring a jeep and driver. Steph and I met an Italian couple who were also keen to visit Yolyn Am – the dramatic, ice-filled valley in the heart of the Gobi Desert.

We didn't anticipate that our driver, Kharajoul, might have a death wish. I now believe that a key consideration when arranging local transport is the mental stability of the driver. I feel that guide books should include a cunning psych test that enables canny travellers to evaluate the likelihood of inadvertently embarking on a suicide mission. Kharajoul believed that the prudent approach to crossing the Gobi Deseert was a mad dash through it with a two-fisted grip on the steering wheel. This technique made no concession for anything: wandering camels and rough terrain were all treated with disdain. Sometimes our jeep would become airborne, *Dukes of Hazzard* style, off sand banks. Mid-air, Kharajoul liked to turn and wink at us. I believe at one point he may even have attempted to high-five the Italians. These were the only times that Kharajoul acknowledged our presence within his jeep.

Generally, I'm a great supporter of the *Dukes of Hazzard* driving style, and some of the best times I have ever spent in a car have been the airborne moments just before impact. Unfortunately, despite the sturdy construction of the Russian-made jeep, the passenger front seat was torn off its brackets after a particularly rough landing. Kharajoul seemed unconcerned when this seat took on its own psychopathic personality and started ricocheting around the jeep's interior. As is the tradition in these parts, the car seat was upholstered in a Persian carpet, which in itself is rather worrying, but now that this particular seat was free to move about the jeep's interior it took on a deadly significance. It's really difficult to enjoy the desert ambience at 100 km an hour while fighting off the advances of an Islamic seat on a personal *jihad*. I suggested that Steph hold the seat in position with her knees from the back seat. This technique proved to work rather well although her knees did get rubbed raw and began to bleed. I suspect it was at this point that she first began to suspect that I was not as much fun to travel with as I had told her at the New Year's party a couple of months before.

Upon our safe return to Ulaanbaatar we decided that a second trip, this time across the rolling steppes of Western Mongolia, was warranted – although this time we hired a slower, and therefore presumably safer, Russian-made Furgon minivan. As an added precaution we also hired an interpreter, Ziggy, should it prove necessary to communicate with our driver beyond the occasional high-five. It was an excellent trip and we went to places I can't even say, let alone spell. In preparation we took vodka and an extra roll of toilet paper. In hindsight some kind of map, a compass or even a GPS thingy would have been better as we were hopelessly lost by the third day.

I can assure you that Mongolia is one of the best places on earth to get lost in. Because there is little private land, people, including tourists, are free to drive where they like, camp where they want and generally treat the entire place as a giant national park. We drove from one nomadic camp to the other looking for a town. It was a lot of fun until our brakes gave out.

Initially this was okay because with the careful employment of first gear and cunning use of the road's camber we could almost slow down. Unfortunately the gear box, which was showing increasing signs of wear, broke as we crested a large and steep hill. I am still amazed how quickly we gathered speed and despite hitting several boulders on the way down our velocity was close to breaking the sound barrier. We tried to throw ourselves out of the door but it was all we could do to stop braining ourselves against the minivan's roof. My life, several yaks and some rocks flashed before my eyes.

I'm no mechanic but I think the technical term for the state of our van at the bottom of the hill was 'rooted'. As we pitched our tent I explained to Steph that it couldn't get worse.

The storm came later that night and the wind was so strong that it blew our tent flat against our faces as we lay in it. The only thing keeping it on the ground was our body weight. In the night I almost heard wolves; they were the 'special' kind of wolf that only Steph could hear.

Attempting to rescue our van in Mongolia.

Third car – new driver.

Things were going splendidly until we tried fording a swollen river. We almost made it, but not quite. We were in a very remote area, and hadn't seen another car for days so we decided to strip to our undies and try pushing the minivan to the bank, but it was trapped in the rocks and swirling water.

At this point, Ziggy our translator burst into tears and declared this to be the worst holiday she had ever been on although I'm sure this was not true. I pointed out some other low points in her translating career but this did little to cheer her up.

Steph and Ziggy went for help; the driver and I went for the vodka. We were extremely cold from the freezing water and the driver mimed that vodka was our best shot of avoiding hypothermia and that we should drink some now for medicinal purposes.

We must have been very cold because we drank the whole bottle without so much as a wedge of lemon or swizzle stick. By the time Steph got back with help I was having a good old time.

We were rescued by a nomadic family who invited us into their *ger* (traditional felt tent) to spend the night. This was great except we saw the real Mongolian way of life; it isn't flash. We discussed their livestock and spent the rest of the day viewing what we were assured to be very attractive yaks (like cows but with bad hair).

My idea of 'roughing it' is sleeping with the window open but that night we slept, along with everyone else, on the floor in a row amongst the baby sheep and goats that are also brought in to keep warm. If you have to sleep with livestock I can say that baby goats are less aromatic and shit less than lambs.

Safely back in Ulaanbaatar, Steph told me that I was a bit moody on the day we lost our brakes; to which I explained how I always get a bit edgy after near-death experiences.

 BUT WAIT THERE'S MORE
Visit www.deanstarnes.com to view the Mongolian slide show.

The world's most dangerous road

It's a mere 65 km long, but since its construction in the 1930s by Paraguayan prisoners of war, Bolivia's North Yungas Road has claimed thousands of lives. This muddy track free-falls from the Bolivian capital of La Paz to Coroico and is legendary for its extreme danger, hairpin turns, abrupt drop-offs, single-lane width, thick fog and total lack of guard-rails. On 24 July 1983, a bus toppled into a canyon, killing more than 100 passengers in what is said to be Bolivia's worst road accident. In 1995 the Inter-American Development Bank christened it the 'world's most dangerous road' and some estimate that on average one person a day is killed there. Of course on most days no one actually dies, everyone gets down (or up) shaken but not stirred until a whole bus goes over the side killing everyone, bringing up the monthly average. Ironically it's also a popular tourist attraction – 65 km of continuous downhill cycling from a snow-flecked Andean ridgetop to the steamy Amazonian jungles 3600 metres below.

All things considered, biking is actually the safer option than taking your chances on a local bus and it is important to keep telling yourself this when you first see the magnitude of the cliffs and the width of the road – a mere three metres. From the road edge the Coroico River is no more than a thin silver sliver threaded between impossibly sheer canyon walls. It's enough to give vertigo to a condor and many tourists sooner return to La Paz on the minibus than start the cycle.

The plan was that our minivan driver, Rolando, would follow behind us so that we could ride with him if we wanted to chicken out. He also carried spare parts for the bikes and would transport them back to La Paz at the conclusion of the ride to Coroico. We rode around in circles for a while, repeatedly testing our brakes and adjusting our helmets. The mountain bikes had 24 gears although I used only the highest one. To calm our nerves Rolando related the latest disaster story. The day before an Israeli girl had plummeted

Cycling on Bolivia's North Yungas Road.

to her death when she lost control of her bike and rode over the side. At the time I suspected it was just a story told to increase the adrenalin rush but I have since heard that a small memorial has now been built at the site where she died and it's a popular place for cyclists to break their descent.

Once Rolando had us sufficiently spooked we were off at tear-inducing speeds down the narrow, fog-shrouded dirt road. I had planned to sit back and whizz down the mountain watching the scenery flash by. I was partially right – the scenery did flash by, but way faster than I felt comfortable with. Instead of relaxing, I had to concentrate extremely hard on the road ahead and my hands ached from clenching the brakes. At times I imagined crowded lorries in the mists ahead, slamming on my brakes for no reason, and at other times I would round a hairpin corner to be confronted by an overcrowded bus and no room to manoeuvre. Occasionally other tourists – ones who presumably hadn't heard about the Israeli girl – would flash past; some even yelled out that I was driving like their nana. I yelled back that their nana sure had balls.

Pulled by gravity, pedalling wasn't required, the scenery was mind-bending and if you stopped at the crosses and stone cairns which mark the places where travellers have died it was sometimes possible to spot the rusting chassis of wrecks amid the jungles below.

In Coroico I met a backpacker who had come down the road by bus. He was in a state as the bus he had travelled in had knocked another bus over the edge of a cliff as they had attempted to inch past one another. The only survivor that he could see was a baby on a ledge, presumably thrown through a window as the bus toppled over. The worst part he said was that no one was able to reach the child and they were forced to leave it behind, although the authorities in Coroico assured him that a rescue team would be dispatched to search for survivors. The next day the papers reported that the baby had survived along with many others; only 12 had died. I flew back to La Paz in a light aircraft.

WHO'RE YOU CALLING A CHICKEN BUS?

My most memorable bus rides are those on the retired North American school buses that are put to use on the metal roads of Guatemala and Honduras. These are affectionately known as chicken buses because of the locals' predilection for travelling with their fowl and the fact that you'll be squashed into one like a battery hen in a shoe box.

Loading a chicken bus involves stacking people in layers on seats designed for children. Only when the bus is filled to the absolute brim does it depart. It's then that the fun really begins as the bus will tour the town picking up passengers and generally defying Piaget's law of Conservation of Volume.

On one trip I became intimate with several large pairs of Mayan breasts and the general groin regions of those standing. I think Lenesça may even have gotten pregnant.

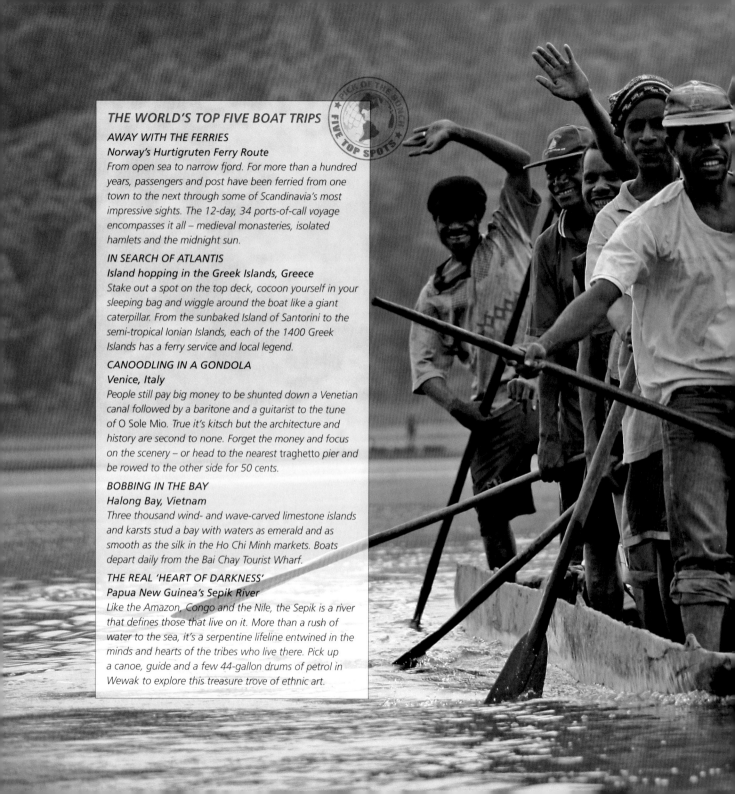

THE WORLD'S TOP FIVE BOAT TRIPS

AWAY WITH THE FERRIES
Norway's Hurtigruten Ferry Route

From open sea to narrow fjord. For more than a hundred years, passengers and post have been ferried from one town to the next through some of Scandinavia's most impressive sights. The 12-day, 34 ports-of-call voyage encompasses it all – medieval monasteries, isolated hamlets and the midnight sun.

IN SEARCH OF ATLANTIS
Island hopping in the Greek Islands, Greece

Stake out a spot on the top deck, cocoon yourself in your sleeping bag and wiggle around the boat like a giant caterpillar. From the sunbaked Island of Santorini to the semi-tropical Ionian Islands, each of the 1400 Greek Islands has a ferry service and local legend.

CANOODLING IN A GONDOLA
Venice, Italy

People still pay big money to be shunted down a Venetian canal followed by a baritone and a guitarist to the tune of O Sole Mio. True it's kitsch but the architecture and history are second to none. Forget the money and focus on the scenery – or head to the nearest traghetto pier and be rowed to the other side for 50 cents.

BOBBING IN THE BAY
Halong Bay, Vietnam

Three thousand wind- and wave-carved limestone islands and karsts stud a bay with waters as emerald and as smooth as the silk in the Ho Chi Minh markets. Boats depart daily from the Bai Chay Tourist Wharf.

THE REAL 'HEART OF DARKNESS'
Papua New Guinea's Sepik River

Like the Amazon, Congo and the Nile, the Sepik is a river that defines those that live on it. More than a rush of water to the sea, it's a serpentine lifeline entwined in the minds and hearts of the tribes who live there. Pick up a canoe, guide and a few 44-gallon drums of petrol in Wewak to explore this treasure trove of ethnic art.

PICK OF THE BUNCH · FIVE TOP SPOTS

That sinking feeling

I've been in many boats throughout the Third World and all their captains have had something in common – a reckless disregard for the sanctity of human life. Life jackets are either non-existent or were last reliably used on the ark. The Plimsoll line is often regarded as decorative and the food will always be served in whatever area is currently being engulfed by diesel fumes.

Capsized canoes aside, no boat I have ever travelled in has actually, despite initial appearances, sunk. That is until I started out for Kerema from a remote village in Papua New Guinea's Gulf Province during a visit to update the *Lonely Planet* guide book. It took a determined effort on the captain's part to sink his vessel. First he had to load it to the brim with 44-gallon drums of diesel followed by half the Kerema Girls' Under-15 Australian Football League team. Despite having only millimetres of freeboard we powered into a tropical version of *The Perfect Storm*.

We didn't last long – about an hour and a half. It only really dawned on me that we were probably going to sink when the bucket I was using to bail out with was plucked from my hands by one of the many incoming waves. I'm not a great believer in signs but I took this to mean we were up Shit Creek without a life jacket.

The last I saw of the captain was him diving overboard when the motor gave up. I stuck around a bit longer to see how the whole thing played out. I shouldn't have bothered as the next wave broad-sided, swamped and sunk us. We went under quickly and I suddenly found myself the sole person clinging to the remains of the boat which bobbed a couple of feet below the surface.

As it turned out the Kerema Under-15 Girls' AFL team are excellent swimmers and it was every man (and school girl) for themselves. Fortunately an incoming tide and strong wind made the 500 m swim to shore rather easy and no one drowned. Even our luggage was eventually washed up but I could have cried – okay, I did cry – as my cameras, iPod and laptop had all been destroyed.

OPPOSITE: Papua New Guinea's Sepik River balancing act.

The floating island homes of the Uros people of Lake Titicaca (Peru). In addition to the islands themselves, the Uros build boats, houses and knick-knacks from tightly bundled reeds. Because the reeds are constantly rotting from beneath, the islands need to be constantly rebuilt with fresh supplies from the top. Walking across their soft and springy surface requires care.

Crash pad

Deciding where to stay while travelling is a challenge that must be faced daily. Accommodation quality varies greatly from one country to the next. While some places are obscenely clean, others change their sheets as often as the Chinese get to vote.

It's important to have a realistic expectation of the level of comfort to be found in the country you are visiting; at home I hit the roof if I can't find my complimentary mint but on the road I'm happy with anything that doesn't smell of damp squid.

As you would expect, budget considerations are the greatest single determining factor when choosing where to stay. To help figure out where you're likely to feel most at home I've listed the idiosyncrasies of the various types of accommodation below.

A home away from home

Camping

Tenting is the cheapest and least comfortable of all the accommodation options presented here. Tents are very small – they may be described as 'two person' but the people the manufacturers are referring to are dwarfs. Most tents are little more than large frocks secured to the ground by a number of ropes that serve the dual purpose of acting as extremely dangerous trip-lines.

If you are not sure whether tenting is the option for you, I recommend sleeping in a bus shelter on a stormy night to see how you like it. Tents are even worse than bus

---

PICK OF THE BUNCH — FIVE TOP SPOTS

THE WORLD'S MOST UNUSUAL HOSTELS

MY HOME, MY CASTLE
St Briavel's Castle, England
Built in 1292 as a royal castle and hunting lodge for King John I it has since been a judicial centre, a prison, a school and a private house. Today it's a youth hostel complete with a moat, gate-towers, armies of backpackers and medieval banquets – but only in August.

A ROOM WITHOUT A VIEW
Peri Pension, Goreme, Turkey
Like something out of The Flintstones, cave rooms here – built into strange rock formations called fairy chimneys – come with and without bathrooms. They're priced accordingly.

A NIGHT ON DEATH ROW
Ottawa Jail Hostel, Canada
For 110 years the Ottawa Jail Hostel was a maximum security facility with 'a long history of mistreating its inmates'. Guests here stay in converted cells and if the ghost stories on their website are anything to go by, there are more than a few former inmates still hanging around.

FALL ASLEEP IN CLASS
Kennedy School, Portland, USA
If the staff here catch you drawing on the chalkboards in this once historic elementary school, you'll be sent straight to the Detention Room – only this time for whisky and cigars.

FLOATING ON A HIGH
Beagle Houseboat, Amsterdam, Netherlands
Four beds, three minutes from the city centre, two levels, one captain and only a few rules. It's the kind of houseboat where the reggae music is free and smoking is allowed.

shelters as they continue to leak long after the storm has passed. Most campers spend their nights huddled together trying to avoid touching the sides of their tent lest it triggers a waterfall at the point of contact. Most people can stand about two nights of tenting before they pack up and check into a hotel.

Youth hostels

Youth hostels have come a long way over the past few years, although not far enough. The general idea is to stuff as many people into a room as the health authorities will allow. Many dorms are unisex and the attitudes of the Europeans can be fairly bohemian – the Scandinavians and Germans love to wander around in little more than their bras and knickers. This of course is enough to get the Australians more excited than a teenager with their first cell phone and the main reason why YHAs are so popular.

Backpackers

At first glance there is little difference between a backpackers and a bona-fide youth hostel. Both offer cheap accommodation, little security and cramped dormitories. The major difference is backpackers are not affiliated with any larger organisation and their dodgy business practices aren't hampered by regulations or constrained by bothersome code of conduct requirements. Safety considerations are non-existent. In fact, many places are made of highly flammable materials and it is the sincerest wish of the proprietor that the whole place (apart from the insurance policy) goes up in smoke.

As a general rule, backpackers are run by people with the moral backbone of a jellyfish. No corner remains uncut, no promise fulfilled and more often than not, no toilet cleaned. To redeem themselves in the eyes of their guests they tend to develop odd, but not altogether unappealing, idiosyncrasies. Sometimes it is worth staying in a backpackers for the comedy alone. My favourite Malaysian guesthouse was one in Kuala Lumpur, run by a little old man who had a knack for mixing his metaphors. The resulting idioms were often better than the originals and most of the guests

STAYING WITH GOD

Before the tenth Sikh guru died in 1708 he (as is the custom in Sikhism) named his successor. But unlike the gurus before him, he chose a book – the Guru Granth Sahib – as his inheritor and it is housed in the Hari Mandir (the Golden Temple), the holiest shrine in the Sikh religion.

Sikhs believe in one god and one supreme eternal reality whose truth is imminent in all things. They practise tolerance, understanding and respect of others. Their hospitality extends to offering shelter to anyone who comes to their gurdwaras (temples) and many backpackers choose to sleep at the Golden Temple itself. The pilgrims' quarters for foreigners are simple dormitories furnished with clean beds and, just like all the other pilgrims, you are expected to remove your shoes and wear a head scarf inside the temple complex.

In addition to free lodgings, the temple provides free meals to any pilgrim who asks and 30,000 meals of chapati and dhal are served daily. The food is pretty good (although the menu never varies) and the communal kitchen is spotlessly clean. What makes the whole thing even more remarkable is that the whole place is staffed by volunteers and funded by donations (most backpackers donate something). Even the logistics of doing the dishes – thousands of items for every meal – calls for a level of cooperation seldom seen elsewhere.

A man completes his ritual bathing in the tank that surrounds the Golden Temple in Amritsar, India.

Bellerophon riding his winged horse, Pegasus, battled the monster Chimaera at Olimpos on the Mediterranean coast in Turkey. Unable to kill the beast he entombed it alive beneath the ground where its fiery breath now attracts tourists.

TREE HOUSES

Everybody loves tree houses; well maybe not those prone to vertigo, but everyone else. Queen Elizabeth II learned of her father's death (and her subsequent ascension to the British throne) while staying at Treetops, a tree house in Africa.

The tree houses in Olimpos (Turkey) have long been a fixture on the backpacker circuit. Sure they are prone to theft, sexual assaults and only have six toilets for the 200 guests, but staying here is a lot of fun. Besides, a night's accommodation costs only $12 and breakfast is thrown in.

Olimpos's big draw is that according to legend the fire that springs from the rocks of the Chimaera is the ignited breath of an imprisoned monster trapped here by Bellerophon on his winged horse Pegasus thousands of years ago. Ever since then, until the first Thursday of September last year, the fires have been burning and at one time served as natural lighthouses for ancient sailors. Last September it fizzled out because I squirted it with my water bottle.

This sparked the most dangerous incident on my journey through the Middle East. Many people became unreasonably upset with me when the flames went out. For a bunch of supposedly laid-back backpackers they sure got irritated over what was essentially a mistake. Thankfully Fadlullâh, our guide, wasn't such a person. He quickly whipped out a lighter and restarted it. 'It happens all the time when it rains – don't worry about it.' I believe I owe my life to that man.

were only staying on to see what he would say next. A few of my favourites:

- Built like a shit hitting the fan.
- Flogging a dead gift horse in the mouth.
- Going through a midwife crisis.
- I could be sitting on a minefield here.
- It's downhill sailing all the way.

Homestays

A homestay is a great way to rub shoulders with the locals. It enables the traveller to have a more 'authentic' experience and see the 'real' thing. Unfortunately family dynamics are the same the world over and living with someone else's children only reinforces my argument that you should need a licence to breed.

Bronwyn and I once stayed with a Kenyan family to whom we had been entrusted to deliver some money. Things were going splendidly until the Masaii attacked in a cattle-raiding enterprise in the middle of the night. Our hosts told us to remain calm while rushing from door to window bolting everything in sight. I told Bronwyn not to worry as I was right behind her; although in truth I was right behind the wardrobe that was right behind her. In the morning we were shown the spot where spears had struck the side of the house (actually those gouges had been caused by a different raid four years earlier – but that's not the way I tell it when showing people the photos).

Bed and breakfasts

In many countries it is possible to stay in someone's home and share breakfast with them the next morning – much like a one-night stand without the sex.

BATTLE TESTED

Tents along the Inca Trail in Peru. Because the hills were so steep and flat land so scarce, tents were pitched along the path itself.

ROUGHING IT

There are a few unwritten rules about camping that everyone should know and, just so there can be no mistake, I'm going to spell out a few here.

- Kids attract kids like shit attracts flies. If you go camping with kids don't be surprised to find other kids in your tent. This is normal. Sometimes these kids stay for days. Don't expect their parents to come looking for them either; with you as their free baby-sitter, they're having the time of their lives.

- Whenever you light a fire the smoke will blow straight into your eyes no matter where you sit. Always.

- You will be assigned a camp site by the camp warden. It is your job to patrol it and stop others from infringing on it.

- If you overhear someone arguing or discussing personal matters in the tent next door it is impolite to yell out advice – even if it's really good advice.

- When going to the toilet in the middle of the night, be careful not to shine your torch on the tent walls of others – they might be having sex.

- Every night check your sleeping bag for unwanted guests like scorpions, snakes or the randy teenager from next door.

- Store things safely away before leaving your tent. It's depressing to find that the local raccoons have made off with your toothpaste, half-eaten chocolate bar and all your knickers.

In an Acapulco hotel: 'The manager has personally passed all the water served here.'

In a Paris hotel elevator: 'Please leave your values at the front desk.'

In a hotel in Athens: 'Visitors are expected to complain at the office between the hours of 9 and 11 a.m. daily.'

On the door of a Moscow hotel room: 'If this is your first visit to the USSR, you are welcome to it.'

In a Belgrade hotel elevator: 'To move the cabin, push button for wishing floor. If the cabin should enter more persons, each one should press a number of wishing floor. Driving is then going alphabetically by national order.'

– FROM THE BOOK *ANGUISHED ENGLISH* BY RICHARD LEDERER (1989)

There are two significant drawbacks with B&Bs that warrant mention here. Firstly, you'll be expected to view all 20 photo albums chronicling the family history and each photo will be explained to you in either a language you don't understand or an accent you can't fathom. Secondly, B&Bs are usually built in obscure suburbs so far from the city centre that they are often in a different time zone.

Business hotels
I try to avoid staying in business hotels because businessmen make me depressed. If they are travelling salesmen they'll be so lonely they'll want to jump from your balcony or, if it's a one-off trip on the company's expense account, they want to drag you to the strip clubs for their last 'big hoorah'. Either way, you can bet there's going to be porn on the pay-to-view channel.

Cruises
The worst thing about spending your holiday far out at sea on an up-turned skyscraper is that if anything unexpected should happen, you are stuck far out at sea on an up-turned skyscraper. We've all seen *Titanic*, we all know what happens. Maybe not. I wonder if the folks who sign up for cruises realise the view is the same on both sides of the boat – surely one patch of water looks much the same as the next? I don't see what all the fuss is about – there really isn't much to a boat cruise that a waterbed, sun lamp and a poster of the sea taped across your bedroom window can't replicate.

Resorts
This is where I would stay if I could afford it. Resorts are often built in poor countries so that tourists can pay the same exorbitant prices they enjoy back home. Take Cancún for example. Mexico is quite cheap with a vibrant culture so it has taken considerable effort to disguise this from tourists. While there is little chance of getting off the beaten track, there is also little chance you'll be expected to fix the plumbing if you want the toilet to flush.

Built to last

Sometimes it seems that all of the world's best architecture was built by a couple of hundred slaves with a few hammers and a couple of logs to roll their stones on. I'm no expert, but I don't think it was the same group of slaves responsible for all of the world's ruins – I suspect there may have been two or three groups involved. I've heard it said that the construction of these ancient buildings baffles modern engineers who, despite having modern machinery at their disposal, cannot replicate them. That might be true – I wouldn't know – but I can tell you what I think. I don't think they are really trying. I suspect the real problem is that we just don't have enough slaves any more. When we say 'Peter the Great built this' or 'Julius Caesar built that' I suspect that neither Peter nor Julius lifted so much as a pinkie down at the construction site.

Looking across the temple-strewn plain at Bagan, Myanmar.

Judging by the number of people who visit historic sights, you would assume that most people find history fascinating since most ruins, even those only a few sandstorms away from disappearing altogether, are crawling with visitors. Because there is so much to see and so little time in which to see it, it's worth knowing how to recognise a historic spot when you come across one.

- Was it built by slaves?
- Is it built at least 20 km away from where all the hotels are and only serviced by outrageously expensive taxis?
- Are the streets surrounding it filled with shops selling bottled water, film, postcards, T-shirts and plastic replicas of the site at 'special one-time-only prices' because you are their first customer of the day?
- Do boys trail behind you offering to shine your shoes even though you are wearing sandals?
- Do you get your sandals shined just to have a chance to sit down before your partner carts you around a group of buildings that look much the same as the lot she carted you around the day before?

LEFT: A windmill from Schermerhorn, Netherlands.

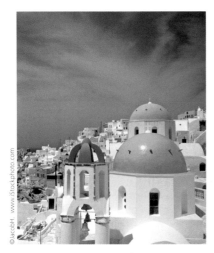

The vivid blue domes of Greek Orthodox churches on the island of Santorini.

- Is there a laser light and sound show on every Wednesday that 'really captures' the atmosphere of what it was like 2000 years ago?
- Do you arrive to find that although there are a number of ticket booths, only one is manned? When you finally reach the front of the queue two weeks later, does the cashier insist on being paid in US dollars and not the local currency?
- Is the exchange rate she kindly offers to convert your currency back to US dollars nothing short of criminal?
- Do you recognise the place from a James Bond, Indiana Jones, or Lara Croft film?

If you have answered 'yes' to at least two of these questions, congratulations, you have found yourself a genuine historical site.

Variations on a theme

Of course not all interesting architecture is old. Some of it is just weird. Just as every country has its own cuisine, language and culture, building styles are equally as eclectic. Often it is the homes of the everyday people that are the most interesting.

Sometimes it is possible to stay in these buildings and an opportunity to do so shouldn't be missed. From the igloos of the Inuit to Dutch windmills, it seems that no two cultures build their homes in the same way. Even churches are many and varied. I'm not talking about the differences between mosques and synagogues, but the differences within the same belief. From the onion-shaped, multicoloured domes of the Russian Orthodox churches to the aquamarine domes of the Greek Orthodox ones, the moment a border is crossed it seems that everyone is keen to do things a little differently from their neighbours. This of course doesn't apply to Las Vegas; they think nothing of building an Egyptian-style pyramid next to a medieval castle.

Moai, *carved by ancient Polynesians, gaze silently out to sea on Easter Island, Chile.*

THE 'NEW' SEVEN ARCHITECTURAL WONDERS OF THE WORLD

With so many impressive buildings scattered around the globe, it proved impossible to choose just five highlights, so I chose seven. Here then are my nominations for the 'New Seven Wonders of the World'. Let's try not to destroy this lot.

TAJ MAHAL *'The Taj Mahal is like a solitary tear suspended on the cheek of time.' – Rabindranath*

SYDNEY OPERA HOUSE *'In the hot sun of the day it will be a beautiful white shimmering thing.' – Jørn Utzon*

THE MOAI OF EASTER ISLAND *'That primitive head, so ambitiously vast, yet so rude in its art is as easily read for the woes of the past as a clinical chart.' – Robert Frost*

BIG BEN *'All through this hour, Lord be my guide. And by thy power, no foot shall slide.' – The words to its chime*

THE PYRAMIDS *'From the heights of these pyramids, forty centuries look down on us.' – Napoleon Bonaparte*

THE GOLDEN GATE BRIDGE *'The Golden Gate Bridge's daily striptease from enveloping stoles of mist to full frontal glory is still the most provocative show in town.' – Mary Moore Mason*

SAGRADA FAMÍLIA CHURCH *'The Temple de la Sagrada Família is an hymn in praise of God intoned by the Humankind, and each one of its stones is a strophe.' – Puig Boada*

Early morning workers clear leaves at Copán Ruinas, Honduras. These ruins, along with Palenque (Mexico) and Tikal (Guatemala), are considered to be the finest architecture the Mayans ever built.

THE WORLD'S TOP FIVE RUINS

WITH THEIR HEAD IN THE CLOUDS
Machu Picchu, Peru

Like llamas on a trail, tourists trot along the Inca Trail – the most famous hike in South America – to Machu Picchu, the 'Lost City of the Incas'. Most people take four days to trek from a place called Km 88 to the often crowded and cloud-shrouded city precariously balanced amid the jagged peaks of the Andes. Others just take the train.

NOW THE HOME OF JAGUARS
Tikal, Guatemala

For a thousand years it was considered the middle of nowhere – a vast tangle of impenetrable forest, home to jaguars, tapirs and a dizzying array of birds. A thousand years before that it was one of the greatest cities on earth, a sprawling conurbation of stone temples, terraced gardens and bustling market places. Tikal, the largest city the Mayans ever built, is the perfect place to 'sit-on-your-butt-and-bump-down' a few pyramids.

Lenesça runs out of steam, halfway up a Mayan pyramid, Tikal.

Continued on page 89

Continued from page 87

PICK OF THE BUNCH ★ FIVE TOP SPOTS

THE WORLD'S TOP FIVE RUINS

IN A TANGLE OF ROOTS
The Temples of Angkor, Cambodia
Straight from the set of Tomb Raider, the root-encrusted ruins of Angkor Wat is a stunning tour de force of classic Khmer architecture – that is, once you have battled through the gangs of youths selling postcards, books and bottled water.

CARVED IN STONE
Petra, Jordan
Petra was once famously described as 'a rose-red city half as old as time'. But even these eloquent words fail to capture the sense of awe the carved rock facade of The Khazneh inspires when it is first glimpsed between the narrow canyon walls of The Siq.

AS WRITTEN IN THE BIBLE
Ephesus, Turkey
Ephesus gets my vote as the best of the Roman ruins; arguably more impressive than Rome itself. The partially reconstructed Library of Celsus is the official highlight, although clambering over the lesser ruins and the lavish brothel is more fun. Start early, as the Mediterranean sun is fierce.

Tree roots snake down walls and thread their way between celestial maidens at the Ta Prohm temple near Angkor Wat in Cambodia.

©Matteodel. www.istockphoto.com

Like it or not, you better get to used to it – rice is a staple for a large part of the world and the most consumed cereal grain on earth. Here a Balinese woman works in a rice paddy.

The world on a plate

Food can be an adventure all in itself. Many first-time travellers are unprepared for anything more disagreeable than the airline food on the way over but be warned, food is the social glue of society – indeed in some countries it even tastes like glue, and you'll be expected to partake.

As an esteemed guest you may even be treated to the local delicacy which can be a dubious honour. Considering that the locals are doing all they can to merely scrape by, it's a grave insult to turn up your nose at their freshly grilled dog. Sure, chowing down on Lassie may not seem much of an honour, but refusing to eat their pet pooch can make things uncomfortable. As a general rule, keep an open mind, pray that it tastes like chicken and try to sample everything you are served. Although, that said, it's prudent to avoid anything that has appeared on a postage stamp or the WWF calendar.

All countries have their national oddities: the Scots have their haggis, the Americans have their preservatives, but it is the Asians who have taken the motto 'waste not, want not' to heart and to their stomachs. You don't have to venture far into a Vietnamese market before you'll be confronted by all manner of local fauna fried, boiled and served with a tasty dipping sauce. Nor is it just the flesh being offered. In Asia no part is wasted – chicken cartilage (*nankotsu*, Japan), fish eyes (it's acceptable to spit out the cornea in the Philippines), monkey toes (deep fried in Indonesia) and blood from a freshly slaughtered cobra, drained into a glass and served still warm while its body is left to wither in front of you in Thailand. (It's appropriately called *ran* and run you may well do.)

Beyond the backpacker restaurants of Phnom Penh, Cambodia offers a wealth of dishes that back home the health authorities would ban. From top to bottom: coiled snakes, maggots and fried frogs.

IN IRAN, UNDER THE BRIDGES OF ESFAHAN, men gather to eat dates, drink pots of tea and smoke *ghalyuns*. Visit www.deanstarnes.com to see a quicktime movie of Steph's and my first courageous foray into the belly of Iranian culture.

HOW TO SMOKE A WATER-PIPE

Throughout the Arab world the use of water-pipes (known regionally as the hookah, ghalyun, chillam, hubbly bubbly or shisha) together with sweetened and flavoured tobacco is very widespread. Middle Eastern cafés and teahouses, like pubs in the UK, are popular gathering places for men, and many social hours soon go up in apple-scented smoke.

In the West, water-pipes are mainly used by university students and South Africans on their O.E. to get stoned. However, drugs (besides tobacco) and alcohol are strictly forbidden under Islamic law.

1. The waiter places burning coals on top of the flavoured and sweetened tobacco in the head of the pipe and covers them with perforated tinfoil.

2. Inhale via the hose. Air is pulled through the coal and tobacco which produces the smoke. This smoke travels down the body and bubbles up through the water into the jar. When a smoker next inhales he sucks in this smoke and simultaneously draws more smoke down the body.

• Excess smoke can be released with the valve.

• Some hookah are multi-stemmed allowing several people to smoke at once. If not, then place the hose on the table to signify that it is free, or pass it directly to the next smoker.

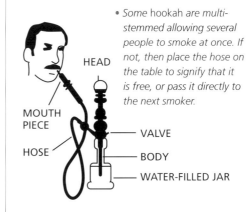

HEAD

MOUTH PIECE

HOSE

VALVE

BODY

WATER-FILLED JAR

Alphabet soup

Here's a quick, not very useful but alphabetically sequential guide to 'travelling your tongue'.

A The locals of the Caribbean island nation of **Aruba** serve up a mean iguana which tastes a lot like chicken (but then again, what doesn't?). Not only will it satisfy any rumbling tums but being an aphrodisiac it will also 'strengthen your back'. Nudge, nudge, wink, wink.

B Two words: **Belgium** and **Beer.** If God didn't want us to drink beer he wouldn't have made Trappist monks and clay bowls of garlic mussels. Be it *Duvel*, *Hooegaarden* or the cherry-flavoured *Kriek*, the words on everyone's lips are *schol!* and *santé!* (Cheers! in Flemish and French.)

C **Ceviche**, can it get any healthier? Raw seafood marinated in lime juice and coconut, served fresh on beaches the length and breadth of Central and South America. Served not so fresh, probably with **cholera,** in the interior.

D Say cheese, **Dutch cheese**. Gouda, blue, edam … So many types and so little time; someone pass a cracker. Better still, pass two.

E Good **English** food is often considered a contradiction in terms but there is more on offer than mushy peas and mashed potatoes. There are jellied **eels**, for example. Yum. Things have improved … the Indians arrived and now everyone eats curries.

F **French** cuisine even sounds delicious, just rolling off your tongue directly to your waistline. 'Come here, you naughty little croissant.' Of course there are **French fries** but I'm holding Belgium and McDonald's responsible for that contribution to the world kitchen.

G Breakfast? How about a soup called *khachi* made from tripe and cow hoof? If you can stomach that you may be in for a real treat: beetroot paste mixed with garlic and walnuts (*pkhali*). Delicious I'm sure but I'll pass; thanks anyway, **Georgia.**

H Ask any God-fearing Saudi Arabian how they like their camel and the answer is always the same – **Halal slaughtered** (as an offering to God while the butcher faced Mecca) served on a bed of steaming rice.

I From *biryanis* to vegetable *thalis*, **Indian** with its exhaustive selection of curries is a vegetarian's dream cuisine. Interestingly enough there is no such word as 'curry' in India itself; the English coined the phrase to generally describe spicy Indian food. At any rate wash it down with a sweet or salty *lassi* (drinking yoghurt) and, for more bang for your buck, the *special lassi* comes with hashish.

Around the world you'll find many taverns, pubs, restaurants and cafés have their own small claim to history. Built in 1837, the Trafalgar Tavern in Greenwich (London) has been frequented by famous writers and politicians, including Dickens and Thackeray, who came here to enjoy a whitebait supper. It was boasted that whitebait could be caught, cooked and served within the hour. Whitebait is still a house speciality but, looking at the murky waters of the Thames outside, it's hopefully caught elsewhere.

J Arguably the most famous of all **Jewish** foods – the humble bagel, and there are none better than those you'll find in any New York deli. Ironically, they go great with bacon, but it's hardly *kosher*. Luckily they are also great with lox (salmon) and cream cheese.

K If you ever find yourself in North **Korea** you might want to try *bibim naengmyeon* (cold noodles), *bi bim bap* (stir fry) or *kimchi* (spicy cabbage pickle). Who am I trying to kid? Just go with whatever the official tour and your compulsory escort will allow.

L **Lebanon** is the biblical land of milk and honey and the Lebanese make the most of their resources. Pop into any one of Beirut's bakeries for a sugar high on tooth-achingly sweet *baklava* (filo pastries drenched in honey).

M **Malaysians** say the durian fruit is delicious. But as one traveller phrased it, 'They smell like shit, taste like shit and look like shit – unless you have the durian ice cream which smells like shit, tastes like shit but looks like ice cream.' Its odour is so offensive that it's banned on buses in Singapore.

N Oodles of **noodles** – what would Asia be without them? Start the day with *foe*, breakfast noodles from Laos. Lunch on the Vietnamese staple, *pho*, and for dinner, Japanese *ramen*. Just don't forget to slurp – loudly.

O May I recommend something from **Oman**? *Macboos* perhaps, a delicious meal of meat, rice, limes, spices and onion. Or vegetarians may opt for **okra**, one of the most disgusting vegetables on God's green earth. Okra are pods of mucus, something akin to what you might sneeze out when suffering from a nasty chest cold.

P Not so long ago the main course in a **Papua New Guinean** banquet may have been you, but breathe easy, the last recorded instance of ritualised cannibalism was in 1959.

Q After a hard day haggling in the markets of **Qatar** try a refreshing glass of **qahwe** – it goes great with *wara enab* (stuffed vine leaves) and other Bedouin delicacies.

R Know that in **Rwanda** mutton doesn't come from a sheep; it's goat. No cause for alarm because the two are virtually indistinguishable; both delicious, especially when barbecued over charcoal.

S The **Scots** are responsible for haggis (stuffed stomach – I'm not referring to the bloated feeling you get after a good meal, I mean you'll be eating stuffed stomach). Thank the Lord for **Scotch** (whisky).

Sacks of spices for sale at the bazaar in Diyarbakir (Turkey).

Now open for business. A couple in Tallinn enjoy a late-night coffee in one of the many cafés that have sprung up since Estonia separated from the Soviet Union in 1991.

DO NOT COVET THY NEIGHBOUR'S KNIFE

If faced with an armada of cutlery, check that you have the right restaurant. The general rule is that the more stuff on the table, the more zeros there will be on the bill. The other general rule is to start from the outside and work your way in – like tooth decay.

1. **Napkin.** *When you are first seated, spread this across your lap.*
2. **Soup spoon.**
3. **Fish knife and fork.**
4. **Dinner knife and fork.**
5. **Salad fork.** *Watch this one as the salad can come at any time.*
6. **Service plate.** *Not actually used for eating off.*
7. **Dessert spoon and fork.** *May appear when dessert is served.*
8. **Bread plate and butter knife.** *Sometimes the salad plate appears here, watch the others for clues.*
9. **Water glass.**
10. **White wine glass.**
11. **Red wine glass.**

ONE TEQUILA, TWO TEQUILA, THREE TEQUILA … FLOOR

Mexico's tequila or mezcal isn't for the faint-hearted but with a little practice you too can be downing shots in the local cantina. Be warned, it packs a powerful wallop not apparent until you attempt to stand.

1. *Lick the back of your hand and sprinkle salt on it. The salt will stick to the wet patch and won't end up on the floor.*

2. *When ready, lick the salt, then quickly …*

3. *Down the shot in one gulp (targo).*

4. *Suck on a piece of lime.*

5. *If you find a worm (gusano) in the bottom of your glass, eat that too. There is usually only one per bottle so it's reserved for the (un)lucky last.*

For an exciting variation you may want to lick the neck of your lover (or, if this isn't your first shot, total stranger) and sprinkle the salt there.

I have also heard of people just sipping the stuff; many Mexicans claim it's wasted on the tossers.

Did I mention in the 2005 tequila-drinking championships the winner drank 50 shots of straight mezcal then died? The $100 prize money went to the hospitalised runner-up.

 T Aromatic **Thai** food; an irresistible combination of sweet, sour and salty. Lemon-grass, green papaya, fresh coconut milk, kaffir limes and spiced prawns. With such mouth-watering gastronomic delights it's hard to fathom why all Thais aren't the size of small whales.

 U The **United States** have given us fast food and Coca-Cola. Coming to a previously remote corner near you, a McDonald's, Burger King, KFC and a Wendy's franchise. Cheers, Uncle Sam.

 V Communion at **Vatican City**, the home of Catholicism. Symbolically partake of the Body of Christ (wafer) and drink the Blood of Christ (wine). Amen.

 W Be careful when ordering bread in **Wales**. Laver bread is in fact boiled seaweed mixed with oatmeal. Instead ask for *bara brith* (fruited tea loaf).

 X In the Guatemalan city of **Xela** (Quetzaltenango) be sure to try the indigenous speciality, *pepián* (chicken in a sesame sauce). It makes for a nice change from the ubiquitous tortilla (corn dough bread).

 Y Some like it hot – if you're one of them, have you considered a *salta*, an eye-watering stew of lamb, beans and peppers from **Yemen**? Be warned though: being Islamic there will be no beer to wash it down with, just a nice glass of cardamom-scented tea.

 Z 'Z' is for **zebra** and you can eat one (legally) at Nairobi's Carnivore restaurant where they are grilled on gigantic skewers over an open fire. As long as the flag on your table is flying they'll keep feeding you. While you're there try the ostrich, eland and crocodile.

 WANT TO EAT SOMETHING DISGUSTING but don't know where to start? Download the recipe for Chocolate Cricket Chip Cookies at www.deanstarnes.com.

Playing with your food

Whet your appetite for travel.

Winery and brewery tours

Where there's alcohol, there are tours. And where there are alcoholic tours there's generally a lot of fun. Learn the local lingo for 'cheers' and start toasting everyone in sight. Be it quaffing a glass of *vino* in Tuscany (Italy) or attempting to drink the Guinness brewery dry in Dublin (Ireland), it is important to remember that the world over it's unseemly to be drunk by 10 a.m. Yes, even if it is your birthday and the staff at the Heineken brewery in Amsterdam (Netherlands) said it's free.

Cooking classes

By learning to cook the local cuisine you gain an insight into the culture and at the same time have some control over what goes into the pot. This way you are able to cleverly censure the inclusion of pets. In Thailand, the classes kick off with a shopping trip to the local markets for ingredients. This also allows you to determine how much you were over-charged the day before.

Food factories

Charlie isn't the only one wanting to get into the chocolate factory. The Cadbury chocolate factory in Tasmania (Australia) allows you to eat as much as you can stomach. This is not always so appetising – steer clear of the abattoirs.

Festivals

Festivals are a great way for the locals to flog off excess crops and otherwise inedible food at ridiculous prices. The Wild Food Festival in

---

HOW TO USE CHOPSTICKS

'The honourable and upright man keeps well away from both the slaughterhouse and the kitchen. And he allows no knives on his table.'

— CONFUCIUS

It doesn't take long to master chopsticks – roughly three missed meals. There are two effective techniques and half a dozen ham-fisted approaches that soon make the 'sticks' manageable. Both 'correct' methods call for the lower chopstick to rest in the 'V' of the thumb and index finger and for the chopsticks' tips to remain even. Remember, it's only the top chopstick that moves.

Method 1: Hold the upper chopstick between your thumb, middle and index fingers, as if it were a pencil.

Method 2: Hold the upper chopstick with only the thumb and index finger.

Etiquette

- *Use the provided rests or lay the chopsticks across the top of your rice bowl when not using them.*

- *Never stand your chopsticks in a bowl of rice like a dagger as this resembles ancestral incense offerings.*

- *In most instances, do not spear your food.*

- *Don't wave your chopsticks about as you talk.*

- *In many Asian countries, it's okay to slurp your food.*

- *If there are communal bowls of food but no spoons, use the non-eating end of your chopsticks to dish up your own (or another's) food.*

HOW TO PICK A STREET FOOD STALL

Sure, the hygiene standards are low, but so too are their prices. Here's a few tips to minimise the time spent hunched over a toilet.

- *Make sure it's hot. Preferably fresh from a pot of bubbling oil or water straight to your plate. Heat kills bacteria.*

- *Look at the condition of the chef; better still, look at his dog – they'll both eat the leftovers and if they look green, chances are you soon will be. A fat chef is a good chef.*

- *Choose a busy place where the food is turned over quickly. Not only will it be healthier, but the locals are going there for a reason. Inversely if the diners are scraping their meals off under the table to the local dogs – steer clear.*

- *Avoid all unboiled water, including that on salads and in ice cubes.*

- *It is easy for budget travellers to lose weight. If you are feeling overly tired and lethargic try eating more protein. Eggs are usually readily available and affordable.*

- *If the curries are too hot to handle, yoghurt, curd or fruit will dilute the sting more effectively than water.*

- *If you cannot find clean drinking water, soft drinks are always a safe option.*

BATTLE TESTED

Hokitika (New Zealand) sells out of huhu grubs every year. Those who try these white, globular insects are split into two camps – those who think they taste a little like peanut butter, and those who think they are disgusting.

Street eats

Many people wonder if they should eat from the local street stalls or stick to the more up-market restaurants. I've given this careful thought over the last few minutes and now realise that generally, despite appearances, it's safer to stick to the street vendors than dine alone in a flash restaurant. True, the restaurant might appear to be more hygienic but there is no real difference between the fly-encrusted food on the street and the fly-encrusted food in the kitchen apart from the price.

In many poor countries the locals can't afford to dine in the restaurants and so the food there is left sitting around growing

Our daily bread – women selling wheels of bread in Nukus, Uzbekistan.

salmonella, waiting for a well-heeled tourist. Few things in life are as deadly as a reheated meal in Nepal. If you do eat in a restaurant make sure you leave by the front door – that way you're unlikely to stumble across the dogs out the back 'doing the dishes'.

The only time I ever became ill in Nicaragua was after eating restaurant food. By and large I found it best to get it while it's hot, straight out of the frying pans on the street.

Do-it-yourselfers

For some, hell bent on travelling inexpensively, it becomes a matter of principle to eat cheaply and self-cater. But is it worth the effort? Maybe. Depends where you travel. It might be fun to sip a latte on a Parisian sidewalk but the café owners charge extra for the privilege. In countries like this you may well find yourself nicking the free tomato-sauce sachets from McDonald's to make soup with.

BATTLE TESTED

DYING FOR A MEAL – HOW TO DEAL WITH BEGGARS

If you travel, sooner or later you are going to be faced with beggars and the crushing poverty that exists in many parts of the world.

People sometimes imply that travellers are a callous lot; happy to walk past those in need, feeling no compunction to stop. The truth is, the alternative, staying at home, with your head in the sand, isn't helping the poor either.

In fact those that do travel in Third World countries do help – the money they spend, especially if they travel independently, goes directly into the local economy. The terrible poverty they witness is more likely to foster a desire to help compared with those who stay at home and turn a blind eye to the hardships faced by others.

Of course no one can help everyone and some use this as an excuse to help no one. If you are travelling and do want to help, here are some tips.

• *Volunteer your time. Working in an orphanage or school can be both rewarding and constructive.*

• *If a begging child approaches you, never give him or her money, give them food instead. Children are sometimes kept from school in order to get money for adults. Giving children money only fosters an attitude of dependency.*

• *When giving alms to beggars, do so when you leave, to avoid being mobbed.*

• *It is okay to say 'No' and sometimes you will need to do so firmly to stop being harassed.*

• *If you have to make a choice between giving money to a child, a mother, or an elderly or handicapped person, always give to the elderly. They are the most in need.*

• *Often it is more effective to give a larger lump sum to a trusted charity than dole out smaller amounts on a whimsical impulse. These charities are in a better position to help and (hopefully) can provide more constructive aid.*

• *Read critiques of charities on the Internet to ensure your values match their objectives. Sites like www.charitynavigator.org rank the effectiveness of many aid organisations.*

Squiggles of orange-coloured jalebis for sale at the Patna (India) animal fair.

However, in other countries food can be so ridiculously cheap that it seems miserly to begrudge the locals a crack at your tourist dollar by cooking your own meals. There are times though when price is not the determining factor. Often cheap is synonymous with fried and there comes a point, even for men, when all you really want are some fresh veggies. If you answer yes to any of these questions, that time has arrived for you.

- Are you more likely to see something green coming out of, rather than going into, your body?
- Do you believe that chocolate and sugar should be given greater recognition than vegetables – and possibly given their own tier on the food pyramid?
- Everything you have eaten for the last week has been either battered, crumbed, deep-fried or wrapped in pastry and sprinkled with MSG.
- Is tomato sauce the greatest vegetable component of your diet?
- Can you no longer tell the difference between strawberry-flavoured food and strawberries?

Mincing your words

One of the delights of eating out is perusing menus for English words that have been chopped, tossed, diced and spliced. Indian chefs are particularly gifted in this. Kick start your day with rice burbles – it most certainly will – or corn flaks, corn flexs, or corn flax. Eggs offer some interesting combinations. They come half scribled, screambled, bolid, deep fried, shallow frid, pouched, pooched and scram bled on plane tost.

The brave might care to try their luck with pain-cakes, leeches and cream, carate salad, pork cutarse, or a dreaded veal cutlet which begs the question, how bad is it going to be? No matter, wash the lot down with a nice glass of pineapple blood, orange squish or cow juice (milk?) and ginger bumping milk (your guess is as good as mine).

Rice can be park-fried, plane-fried, part-fried or oiled and served with cowpea; take your pick. Combine that with some chicken cripes, chicken arms (hard to come by I would imagine), bum chicken or children soup and you should be in for an interesting taste sensation. Sometimes it's preferable to stick to processed foods like caned vegetarian, dried meat floss or naked pawns. Otherwise it might be best to order the fish. How about some fried crap, rain blow trout, roast squit or tuna in grease?

The Chinese are more fastidious with their spelling but brutally honest in their descriptions. In China you may be tempted to try the dumpling stuffed with the ovary and digestive glands of a crab, the sweat and sour bone in fragrant spinach or the double boiled forest frog. My favourite is the pork with fresh garbage; presumably far nicer than the pork served with stale garbage on offer down the road. At other times I had no idea what was meant. The benumbed hot flies with belly silk and nuddles proved particularly perplexing.

And finally, if you don't believe me, see for yourself, Japan has *teppan yaki* – before your cooked right eyes.

Beijing night market, China.

FEAR FACTOR *AT BEIJING'S NIGHT MARKET*

A good breakfast is no substitute for a large dinner.

– CHINESE PROVERB

Pizza in Italy isn't the same as pizza in America. Chinese in China isn't like … well it isn't like any other place on earth. Eating at Beijing's night market is like competing in Fear Factor without the prize money. Steph and I spent a night daring each other to eat scorpions that were threaded onto a stick, still wriggling. Thankfully they died in the grilling process and were quite crunchy, especially their legs – a lot like crickets. Also for sale were baby birds, starfish, seahorses, silk worm cocoons and, of course, dog. The highlight was the beer, 30 cents for a large bottle; I was well drunk after $1.50. Not drunk enough to eat the dead rat though.

Steph eats a scorpion.

Culture for sale. The world over, culture groups perform for tourists. Some say that this financial support helps keep minority cultures alive and that some of these groups go on to become great ambassadors for their people, giving old ways new significance and new worth and a better chance of survival. Others argue that the culture is dumbed down to become palatable for foreign tastes and effectively turns minorities into human zoos that do little more than cater to voyeuristic tourists. Here conchero dancers perform in Mexico city's Zócalo.

Culture vulture

Culture is what makes strangers strange. Culture, through language, beliefs, traditions, superstitions and customs, helps define and distinguish one group of people from another and forms the bedrock of many unacceptable jokes. To travel well, it's important to have a deep tolerance of other cultures, or at least be able to hide your incredulity at the insane practices of others behind a mask of indifference.

The most important thing to remember is that when all's said and done, it's their country – if you don't like it you can always go home. If someone asks you how you are enjoying their country, the correct answer is 'I'm loving it'. No one enjoys hearing their motherland criticised by a foreigner enjoying its hospitality. It doesn't even matter if they agree with your observations or not. The point is, they don't want to hear it from you. It's like someone talking about your wife. You might not think she's a great cook but that doesn't mean you want to hear about it from every Tom, Dick and Harry.

If you've read this far through the book, you'd be forgiven for thinking I might have trouble following my own advice – and I do. Even still, trust me when I say, the middle of the immigration hall isn't the time nor the place to comment on the physical flaws of the state leader whose 20-foot portrait adorns the airport.

If the worst comes to the worst – and I know I'm going to regret admitting this – if I simply must say something that I don't want the locals to hear, I try to say it really, really fast in my broadest accent. This of course only works if the locals speak a different language than you do. It doesn't work, say, for an Australian telling his best sheep-shagging joke in New Zealand.

TIPS ON HOW TO BLEND IN

Tired of standing out from the crowd? Is your individuality driving you nuts? Are you always the one to get pickpocketed? Do you stop traffic?

Often there is little you can do to stop yourself standing out. You can hardly change the colour of your skin or the language you speak, but sometimes it's best to try to blend in as best you can and thus be more easily accepted.

- *Leave all your judgements at home.*
- *Respect local dress codes. Attempting to dress exactly like the locals is often impractical and counter-productive (a white man dressed as an Aborigine is only inviting attention), but you should dress modestly in conservative countries and respect religious sensibilities.*
- *When entering a village where your appearance is likely to cause a commotion amongst the children, don't walk around too much. It's better to stand in one place and observe quietly.*
- *Don't talk too loudly. Westerners often speak loudly compared with people of other cultures and it makes them cringe.*
- *Learn a few basic phrases (including how to introduce yourself) in the local lingo.*
- *Familiarise yourself with the local currency so you are not fumbling around like an obvious tourist.*
- *Walk purposefully. Try to at least look like you know what you are doing.*

BATTLE TESTED

BATHING NAKED WITH RUSSIANS

I'm not the kind of guy who habitually gets beaten by large, naked men. That was until I had been to Russia.

Moscow's Sandunovskiye Baths seemed harmless enough; vaguely Victorian, as if I had wandered into a charmingly old-world gentlemen's club. The only thing to suggest I hadn't was that all the men were nude.

I was quite brave to get publicly naked because I had previously shaved off all my body hair as a result of the crabs incident in Mongolia (see 'What's bugging you?', page 30). People can quickly form the wrong impression about you if they see you have a hairless wanger. Great care was required.

The word 'hot' doesn't begin to describe the temperature they had managed to crank their banya *(Russian sauna) up to. The roof of my mouth started to sweat, my lungs began to burn and the cedar benches singed my buttocks. I stuck it out for maybe as long as three seconds before crawling towards the door, only to find it barred by a large bear of a man who grunted 'Minimum five minutes'. There must have been some kind of cross-cultural misunderstanding at this point because despite my vigorous head shaking, a large ladle of water was poured onto the furnace, resulting in a blast of face-melting heat.*

Russians like to belt each other with venik *(birch sticks) while they bathe. I just assumed that the birch branches were included in the admission price. This is not the case. The branches are sold separately on the street outside and, depending on the freshness of the leaves, may require soaking in carefully heated water to bring them to their optimal, back-slapping best. It's fair to say that should you unwittingly steal someone else's pre-soaked birch branch, the locals get a bit funny about it. The only thing worse (or better, depending on your personal proclivities) about beating yourself with a Christmas tree is having someone else do it. The moment I felt that first light brush of another's branch on my buttock I was like a terrorised deer – transfixed in headlights and unable to move. I later learnt that these soft touches are a way to fan the heat evenly over the body. Despite my earlier transgressions the locals were essentially being polite and showing me how better to appreciate the* banya. *They then proceeded to thrash me.*

Russians believe that there are many health benefits to being beaten, notably an improved circulatory system and an invigorated heart. I don't know if anyone has ever said you haven't really lived until you've been flogged by a naked Russian, but I'm saying it now. Once you get over the alienating culture shock it's quite relaxing. Sure it hurts like hell but the rush of blood to your skin, the tingling body-wide sensation and the extreme heat makes every muscle in your body instantly melt to jelly.

It's customary to have more than one crack at the banya *and bathers alternate between steaming in the sauna and plunging into an ice-cold, heart-stopping plunge pool (*basseyn*). I dived in with a bar of soap. As it turns out you can't take soap into the plunge pool. Nor is the soap complimentary – you should bring your own. Again, things got a little tense there for a while.*

For many Russians the weekly banya *visit has become an integral part of their lives: a time to catch up with friends, share stories and escape the gruelling winters. There are even unisex* banyas *that have the added benefit of allowing couples to beat the hell out of each other. Banyas can be found throughout the former USSR and once the etiquette surrounding them is understood, and your anxiety levels regarding public nudity have subsided, a steam-up at a* banya *can be the highlight of a trip to Russia.*

A warrior issues a challenge during a powhiri *(welcoming ceremony) as part of a merger between two design agencies in New Zealand. Sometimes cultures collide – in 2005 a Dutch tourist gave offence by nervously smirking during the welcome and was head-butted so hard that his nose was broken.*

MEET AND GREET – HOW TO RECEIVE A MAORI HONGI

There are more ways to greet a person than merely shaking their hand. Even then you must consider whose hand needs to be shaken first, if it's appropriate to shake the hand of any women present or if, by excluding them, you will give offence. If a bow is called for, how deep do you go? How long should you stay down?

In New Zealand, a traditional Maori welcome – which you may encounter on a marae *(meeting place) – involves the pressing together of noses, symbolic for exchanging the* ha *(the breath of life). To perform a* hongi, *begin by shaking hands and then lean forward to gently press your noses together while exhaling. In some tribes, men prefer not to hongi with women. The* hongi *will only be performed after the protocols of the* powhiri *(welcome) are finished.*

Birds are good luck in Hong Kong.
This man took his parrot to the races.

TOP FIVE
CULTURES TO VISIT

PICK OF THE BUNCH
FIVE TOP SPOTS

CHINA – Follow the dragon
The Middle Kingdom may have undergone some brazen transformations of late, but the Cultural Revolution is well over and the 1.2 billion Han Chinese (the world's largest ethnic group) are enjoying a cultural renaissance.

INDIA – The beat goes on
Bollywood, tandoori chicken, cricket and a whole host of gods – nothing else on earth comes close to the cultural behemoth that is India. Around every corner is a temple, a festival, a marriage or, at the very least, a holy cow. Brace yourself.

BRAZIL – Turning up the heat
True, not all Brazilians are beach-going, samba-dancing, football-fanatic, rum-drinking revellers but it's easy to see why you might think so.

**THE UNITED KINGDOM
– Now that the sun has set**
Fancy a cuppa? The English are still terribly, terribly British and there is more than enough history to keep the culture vultures flocking, or rather queuing, for more.

BHUTAN – A kingdom on the edge
Caught between two worlds, this tiny Himalayan country battles to maintain its medieval ways as it takes its first shaky steps into the 21st century. Traditional culture, Buddhist doctrine and an enlightened king have kept the country's culture so intact that they are yet to install a set of traffic lights.

Culture shock

'In trains, boats, planes or tourist areas one frequently comes across foreign guests. Do not follow, encircle and stare at them when you meet. Refrain from pointing at their clothing in front of their faces or making frivolous remarks; do not vie with foreign guests, compete for a seat or make requests at will.'

– AN EXTRACT FROM A CHINESE TRAVEL GUIDE FOR CHINESE

Travellers often find that certain etiquette, taken for granted back home, is ignored or simply doesn't exist in the wider world. For some, this can be a very disturbing realisation and left untreated can manifest itself as culture shock. The more set in their ways a traveller is, the more profound the adjustment will be required to assimilate new ideas. I once met an elderly Irish man emotionally scarred by the discovery that the men in the village next door drank their whiskey with ice – a sacrilege he told me, which he would not tolerate. The news that in some bars people diluted their single malt with water was enough to turn his face red and get him frothing at the mouth. I find the Irish accent difficult to understand at the best of times, let alone when they are enraged and spitting, so I missed some of the finer points of his argument, although the point 'only the sons of Protestant whores would dilute whiskey with water' was one he felt particularly keen to make. When I added that I myself had drunk whiskey that way in Dublin he tried to beat me with his cane.

The cultural divide can be a bigger obstacle to your trip than just the quiet enjoyment of alcohol. Even more than the language barrier, the culture gap, if left unchecked, can result in a serious bout of homesickness. Homesickness is the realisation that the rest of the world sucks more than the place you were desperate to get out of six weeks earlier. Very soon you find yourself comparing everything with back home and crying into your backpack like a school girl on her first homestay. Therefore it's vital to recognise the early symptoms of culture shock. One sure sign that you have strayed too far from the nest is if you find yourself frequently uttering the words 'back home …' This is an early sign of cultural indifference which, if left unchecked, can manifest itself as intolerance to local customs. These traditions, once endearing, now become a justification for an armed invasion to root out heathen practices and install a good old-fashioned democracy like the one you have 'back home'.

It can be difficult to predict which aspect of a foreign culture will get your blood boiling. For some it's the language barrier, for others it's sleeping in unfamiliar rooms, eating strange food or the rude way that everyone else is acting. And although it isn't politically correct, I'm listing the cultural flaws of others below.

Staring squads

'The program is Aliens *and you are the star, and cinema-sized audiences will gather to watch.'*

– *CHINA* LONELY PLANET GUIDEBOOK

Being openly stared at isn't confined to China. In many Asian countries, a traveller with Western features, once off the beaten track, has the power to stop traffic. However, in rural China the size of the crowds are extraordinarily large and the viewers so unabashedly bold that they'll soon have you ducking for cover. You needn't bother; the crowd, curious to see what you will do next, will only follow. If there is anything about you that is thought to be 'abnormal', the number in the assembly increases tenfold. Eyes of any colour other than brown require detailed inspection. I was once asked if I could actually see out of my blue eyes and then, on learning that I could, if the world looked strange. Likewise, any hair colour other than black will need to be thoughtfully examined by all present, and blond-haired children will be regarded with open awe.

Staring back or getting abusive only attracts bigger crowds and nothing amuses a Chinese peasant more than an irate foreigner standing in the middle of town ranting and raving. They love it.

Some don't like to be photographed, so one tactic is to click off a few shots, in the hope that it will send a few diving for cover. Another is to hire a bicycle, in order to zoom around town without giving the locals time to amass.

Even in a country like Japan, where you might expect a higher degree of sophistication, a traveller will feel themselves being scrutinised from afar. Hairy arms and legs hold a freaky fascination for the Japanese and on the days I wore shorts, my young Japanese students would test my leg hair authenticity by plucking at a few.

Chinese spittle drizzle
'Spitting, the national sport of China, is practised by everyone regardless of how well dressed or sophisticated they may appear. All venues are possible – on board buses and trains, restaurants, streets and even carpeted hotel lobbies.'

– CHINA LONELY PLANET GUIDEBOOK

Most Chinese suffer from chronic bronchitis which clogs their lung passages with mucus and the only effective way to clean out the nasal cavities is send the whole globular mess flying. Although laws against spitting have existed for years, it is only recently, with the 2008 Olympics, that they are being enforced. Fines equivalent to a

MUZUNGU!

'Muzungu' means 'white person' in many African Bantu languages and it's a polite euphemism for 'foreigner', although many travellers take offence at being referred to by their skin colour. While I don't find the word offensive, it does get irritating after you've heard it for the hundredth time in the course of 30 minutes.

Nor is it just Africans. Indonesian kids will harass a traveller by endlessly screaming 'Hello mister' at the maximum volume their little lungs will allow.

Rural Chinese, young and old alike, enjoy standing next to tourists and repeatedly screaming in their ear 'Laowai!' – a term which literally means 'old outside' but is also the Chinese idiom for 'foreigner'.

Bronwyn (in the orange T-shirt) sits on her backpack amid curious onlookers in Rwanda.

Panama is the country that bridges North and South America and as such enjoys a great cultural diversity. Compare these two girls from Panama City to the Kuna ladies on page 51, the indigenous tribe from the San Blas Islands.

day's wages for many labourers have gone a long way to reducing the habit, but outside of Guangzhou, Shanghai and Beijing, the phlegm still flies thick and fast. Only the foolhardy would stand between two buses and be exposed to the resulting crossfire. A cartoon I saw compared it to rain – a slight drizzle in the morning with cultural fallout expected by late afternoon.

Spitting wouldn't be so bad were it not for the long, noisy process of sucking the mucus from the nasal cavity into the back of the throat before it is expelled with the force and accuracy of a bullet. On the plus side, travellers who spend enough time in China eventually appreciate that a well-aimed glob of mucus can be a thing of joy.

Nose picking on the other hand can be more alienating. Most Westerners prefer to pick their noses in private or behind the wheel of their car where they believe the glass windows have magical properties shielding them from public scrutiny. This is not the case in China and on one 40-hour train ride I had the misfortune of sitting opposite a man who had taken nose picking to an art form. Using both hands to apply leverage, he could fish out a bogie so deep that a mining licence was required. For 500 km at a time he would diligently work on his nostrils, examining, rolling into a ball and eventually flicking pieces of snot at his fellow passengers, all of whom would encourage, comment and occasionally applaud.

The Turkish hustle

Turkish men and solo women travellers perform the Turkish hustle up and down Turkey's Mediterranean coastline. It is a firmly held belief that a woman travelling solo is after one thing – well actually two things: sex and a nice carpet. Encouraged by ribald reports from Hollywood on the sexual appetites of young starlets, Turkish men are baffled when their numerous advances are rebuffed. Unfortunately, no matter how many times they are rejected, their enthusiasm for foreign women remains unflagging and the whole thing takes on the tired tedium of a comic routine too often performed. Since their advances aren't subtle, there is no mistaking

A Turkish pedlar repairing a shoe.

TOP FIVE TRIBAL EXPERIENCES

PAPUA NEW GUINEA HIGHLANDS

Huli wigmen, Asaro mud-men and Simbu skeleton sing-sing performers make PNG an anthropological treasure trove. Home to over 800 tribes, most of whom have their own distinctive language, art forms and body decoration.

OMO VALLEY, ETHIOPIA

Southern Ethiopia boasts some of the world's most fascinating people. The Mursi lip stretchers, the body-painting Karo and the Bumi who scarify their torsos, can all be found in this dusty African corner.

LAGO DE ATITLÁN, GUATEMALA

It is here, amid the verdant hills that surround Guatemala's most beautiful lake, that indigenous Mayan still cling to their traditional beliefs, wear their traditional huipiles and tend their terraced corn fields.

KALAHARI BUSHMEN, NAMIBIA

A visit to the San is a lesson in desert survival. Skills, honed over the last 40,000 year, by //Nhoq'ma hunters, will have you recognising the pointy end of a spear in no time.

GOLDEN TRIANGLE, ASIA

In the opium-growing gardens of Laos, Cambodia and Thailand, you'll find an eclectic mix of super-friendly hill tribes who still dress in elaborate costumes and whose artistic expression includes the practice of neck stretching.

Papua New Guinean women at the Mt Hagen sing-sing.

the men are after more than a mere snog behind the kebab shop. Many women, tired of being objectified, resort to wearing fake wedding rings or travelling with male companions to thwart such advances. The Turkish hustle soon deteriorates into the Turkish hassle and the only thing sadder than the way the men view Western women as wanton hussies is the equal perception among women that all Turkish men are sexual predators.

Saving face

Regardless of who is right or wrong, a Taiwanese person is unlikely to admit an error if it involves a loss of face. In Taiwan (as well as many other Asian countries), people often don't say what they think, but rather what they think you want to hear. Thus, the staff at the China Airlines office may tell you that your flight will be here 'very soon' even if they know it will be delayed for two days.

Screaming and yelling doesn't help. To avoid such unseemly confrontations Taiwanese typically resort to smiling. A smile doesn't always mean happiness; some Taiwanese smile when they are embarrassed or worried, but this is often misinterpreted as smug and uncooperative by many travellers. This explains the situation where the foreign tourist is ranting and raving at the staff in the airport check-in, while the person behind the desk stands grinning from ear to ear.

Let's not shake on it

Interaction between any two individuals relies not only on what is said, but how it is said. The body can communicate entirely the wrong message and the independent traveller needs to take care if they are to avoid giving the wrong signals or incorrectly interpreting the gestures of others. The 'thumbs-up' sign for example is considered obscene to many Pakistanis unless you are discussing male anatomy.

Between Pakistani men, a handshake is essential to conversation and may well last the length of the discussion. Don't be offended if someone offers you his wrist; he just considers his other hand unclean. For example, he may have just finished eating and his fingers could be covered in curry. Do not be tempted to grab the left hand, as this hand is reserved for ablution activities and I can guarantee you that whatever that yellowy-brown stuff is under his fingernails – it's not curry. Okay it might be curry; people do wash their hands after all.

While every country has its idiosyncrasies when it comes to body language, let's look at a few more from Pakistan. Never point the sole of your shoe or foot at a Muslim, step over any part of someone's body or walk in front of someone praying towards Mecca. Holding hands in public is acceptable only between members of the same sex and two young men with arms around each other are not homosexual. However, funnily enough, when I attempted to shake hands with a woman, my gesture was considered scandalous and embarrassing.

Torii gates at Fushimi Inari, Kyoto, Japan.

LEARN A LOCAL TRICK – FOLD A THOUSAND PAPER CRANES

A fun thing to do for anyone with an IQ greater than that of a five-year-old is to track down a kid and get them to teach you something. There are all kinds of games and tricks stored in a child's mind and although they can be a bit shy at first, once they realise that foreigners are people too, they make patient teachers. A child in Japan taught me that if I were to fold a thousand origami cranes, my deepest wish would come true. My deepest wish at the time was that my girlfriend's mother, a traditional Japanese oki san, would relent and allow me to stay overnight.

My tutor went on to explain that a thousand cranes had become a symbol for peace ever since Sadako Sasaki, a young girl exposed to the radiation from the Hiroshima atomic bomb, folded a thousand cranes for world peace and to end suffering as she lay dying in hospital from leukemia. Today the statues in Hiroshima's and Nagasaki's Peace Parks are smothered in crane garlands. By comparison my wish seemed somewhat self-serving.

 VISITING JAPAN OR KEEN FOR WORLD PEACE? Start your cranes now.
Origami crane instructions available at www.deanstarnes.com.

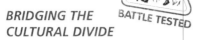

BRIDGING THE CULTURAL DIVIDE

Here are a few tips to help you get along with the locals. Who knows? Some of them may even work.

- *Instead of handing out lollies, money or pencils to the local children (which only encourages begging), take along a bottle of bubble mixture and blow bubbles for them. They love it, you'll love it and the world's a better place. Save the donation for their school.*

- *Read a novel set in the destination you are visiting.*

- *When you tire of the museums, cathedrals, temples and ruins, buy a ticket to whatever the locals are watching. Sport, even if you have no idea what's going on, is always fun. From the rodeo in America to sumo in Japan; they all offer subtle insights into a country's psyche. Local movies, like Indian Bollywood epics, are also a fun and insightful night out.*

- *Tip or not to tip? It doesn't matter what you do back home; do as the locals do. Tipping can drive up the prices for locals if it isn't the norm, and not tipping in places where it is expected can cause offence.*

- *Churches aren't tourist traps, they are spiritual places. Ask before whipping out the camera.*

Don't mention the war

There are certain subjects that you don't discuss, war being the classic example. Others, like national icons and small children, shouldn't be questioned either. While working as a kitchen hand in the small Austrian ski village of Hopfgarten, I managed to weave the two together. As it turns out, Austrian chefs regard kitchen hands to be only slightly above cockroaches in the kitchen hierarchical ladder and therefore my questions regarding the quality of their *wiener schnitzels* were seldom received with the enthusiasm in which they were delivered. My efforts to improve customer satisfaction, by critiquing the food, weren't appreciated either. Once, when I casually observed that the apple strudels were a bit crap, I was almost fired. At this point I let slip, almost in passing, that Hitler was Austrian and not German as most people believed. Unbeknown to me, the chef was even touchier about the war than he was about his flaky pastries and took this innocent war reference to mean that I saw certain similarities between his kitchen and Nazi-run concentration camps. The discussion kind of went downhill from there.

Who's your daddy?

Many topics that are deemed private in the West are open for public debate in Asia. 'What's your name?' is quickly followed by 'How much do you make?' then 'How much does your father make?' and finally 'Are you married?' If the numbers stack up, your earning potential, the standard of living of your country and any immigration possibilities will all need to be discussed.

If you are single, they'll need to know why. If you are a woman and single they'll really need to know why. Clearly something has gone wrong and condolences may well be offered. If you are married, the whereabouts of your children will need to be ascertained and a childless couple will need to explain their inability to produce children. An English couple I met in Thailand was so fed up with the constant probing into their childless state that they had begun taking turns to make up outrageous explanations. There are now

THE TRIBE VIBE
If you would like to see more pictures of the Kenyan Samburu (like the lady pictured above), Turkanain, Rendilli and El Molo tribes, view the slideshow at www.deanstarnes.com.

THE WRITING ON THE WALL

Having shaken off the shackles of Soviet totalitarianism, Lithuania, barely two decades old, has had to come up with all kinds of national icons. There are national flowers to be chosen, animals to be selected, anthems to be played and some kind of constitution to be drafted. And since a country's constitution is inseparable from its cultural identity I was amused to see that in the bohemian heart of Vilnius, local artists have declared themselves independent and written their own founding document for their state – The Republic of Užupis. There are 41 articles in all, stamped in three languages on brass plaques for all to see on a crumbling Paupio wall. A few of my favourites are listed below:

- *Everyone has the right to live by the River Vilnele, while the River Vilnele has the right to flow by everyone.*

- *Everyone has the right to die, but it is not a duty.*

- *Everyone has the right to love and take care of a cat.*

- *A cat is not obliged to love its master, but it must help him in difficult times.*

- *Everyone shall remember his name.*

- *Everyone has the right to be of various nationalities.*

- *Everyone has the right to celebrate or not to celebrate his birthday.*

- *Everyone is responsible for his freedom.*

A man walks his bicycle in Užupis, a mock republic in Vilnius, Lithuania.

several villages in Northern Thailand who believe the English often lose their children in Bulgaria or sell them as slaves in Russia.

When Yes means No

We are all taught that 'no' means 'no' but in many places 'yes' can also mean 'no'. An Indian for example would rather answer 'yes' to a question than disappoint you, regardless of the correct answer, or whether they even know at all. Questions such as 'Is this the way to the town centre?' will typically be answered with a reassuring 'Yes!', even if you are pointing to the waterless wastelands of the Thar Desert. Instead avoid 'yes' or 'no' questions and re-phrase them so they require exact answers. 'Which way to the town centre?' is more likely to yield a beneficial, although less imaginative, answer.

A little about laws

Some countries have laws and cultural practices that many travellers find not only alienating, but morally wrong. Unless you are American and have an army to back it up, it's best to stay out of other people's business. In some Islamic countries women are expected to walk a respectful distance behind their men, adhere to a strict dress code and abide by rules that are exclusively to the advantage of men. If you travel to such countries, you have to accept that things are going to be different.

It gets worse. In Kenya, Female Genital Mutilation (FGM) is carried out for cultural and gender identity reasons and is an integral part of the tribal system. Clearly the practice, which leaves young girls with lifelong menstruation, urination, intercourse and childbirth complications, has little, beyond tribal beliefs of hygiene, aesthetics and health, to recommend it. Yet in East Africa, where social welfare is unheard of and tribal affiliations can be the difference between life and death, travellers should think twice before pressuring young girls to become a martyr for this cause. In such cases it is far better to lend your financial support to a group that is in a position to put pressure on community leaders and governments to change their ways, than browbeat an individual.

THEY'RE PLAYING OUR SONG

Every country has one, although many shouldn't. National anthems could well include some of the worst songs on the planet. Nonetheless, if you take the time to learn one, especially if it's in a foreign language, you will dumbfound the locals when you burst into their song. Norwegian babes don't expect a stirring rendition of 'Ja, vi elsker dette landet' from an otherwise linguistically challenged tourist. With such disarming tactics it's possible to make a powerful impression.

This doesn't work with everyone. Australians, for example, seem ambivalent about 'Advance Australia Fair' – and who could blame them – but sing a few lines of 'Waltzing Matilda' and you'll have a homesick Aussie blubbering like a schoolgirl.

Relaxing – Australian style.

©Dan Smith (Panoramica)

RULES OF ENGAGEMENT AT TOMATINA

For just over 60 minutes chaos reigns when every year 40,000 people descend on the small Spanish town of Buñol to turn truckloads of ripe tomatoes into bolognaise sauce by splattering them against each other in an event that brings new meaning to the expression 'playing with your food'. But like all fights, even food fights, there are rules.

- *You must squish your tomato before throwing it – whole ones hurt. You must not tear another's clothing and it is illegal to throw or even bring onto the streets any kind of bottle or object that could cause an injury.*

- *Accept the fact that you won't see a thing. Either your eyes will be stung shut from the tomato juice or your goggles will fog up. There are public showers to rinse off afterwards but obviously you'll need a change of clothing.*

- *You must give way to the lorries which carry the tomatoes.*

- *As soon as you hear the second banger you must end your reign of carnage, i.e. stop throwing and make nice.*

Every man and his band

It seems that at any given moment, somewhere, someone is celebrating and a traveller's party calender is getting rather full. You have your obligatory music festivals like Glastonbury which sold out in 1 hour and 45 minutes, forcing everyone else to scale the security fence in order to get to the mosh pits.

Religious festivals like Christmas and Ramadan are more seemly. They usually commemorate important holy dates (Christmas) or allow the pious to demonstrate their devotion (Ramadan). The world's largest festival is the Hindi Kumbh Mela which is held four times every 12 years in one of four holy locations. The Kumbh Mela of 2001 was attended by a staggering 70 million worshippers. The crowds which came to participate in the month of bathing and purifying rituals were so vast they could only be appreciated by satellite imagery. In some years armies of naked *sadhus* (holy men) clash, occasionally using their elephants and ceremonial weapons on each other.

Cultural festivals (like dragon boat racing in China) and patriotic celebrations (like the Irish's St Patrick's Day or the Netherlands' Queen's Birthday) are perhaps the most colourful of all the festive categories. You can expect outlandish costumes, crazy antics and vast quantities of alcohol. This heady mix usually attracts large numbers of Australians and New Zealanders, especially in Europe, where they travel from one drunken bash to the next with barely enough time to sober up in between. Honorary mention, however, is reserved for the Spaniards and Japanese, who have so many festivals (many involving crazy stunts performed while naked) it's a wonder they work at all.

I love festivals – not only do you get to watch the locals make fools of themselves, but the entertainment is free.

FESTIVAL TIPS

- *Looking for a weekend break? Festivals add extra colour to a weekend get-away, bringing the place alive with the added celebratory buzz.*

- *Book early. The whole city will be swamped with both international and domestic tourists, making accommodation scarce.*

- *If you can't arrange accommodation beforehand, rock up and try the cheaper places without an Internet presence or listing in a guide book.*

- *Don't try to outdrink the locals. If you do, carry a piece of paper with your name and hotel address on it. That way, when you have passed out in the gutter, anyone going through your pockets will know where you should be.*

- *Don't carry a lot of money when attending a large festival. While you're shaking your money maker others may be robbing it. Take a disposable camera instead of an expensive SLR.*

- *Find out beforehand which part of the festival will be the most colourful. Some religious festivals last for months.*

- *Photographers might want to go early and photograph the participants getting ready. These often make for great candid shots.*

BATTLE TESTED

So many parties … so little time

'The healthy being craves an occasional wildness, a jolt from normality, a sharpening of the edge of appetite, his own little festival of Saturnalia, a brief excursion from his way of life.'

– ROBERT MACIVER

Below is a quick overview of some of the best places on earth to kick off your shoes, throw yourself into the fray and shake your booty until your hips hurt. These days the gods of yore don't require the still-beating-heart sacrifices of virgins like they once did. Most seem happy with some kind of drunken dance party. That said, a cast-iron liver is a necessity for the habitual festival-goer and while you probably won't remember it, there is something quite special about sharing a drink, a dance and, in some cases, a social disease or common injury with a person whose name you can't pronounce.

JANUARY

HOGMANAY (31 DEC. – 1 JAN.), EDINBURGH, SCOTLAND To celebrate the arrival of the new year, the whole city drinks enough beer to guarantee that no one remembers the last one. If you find yourself singing 'Auld Lang Syne' on the steps of Edinburgh Castle, arm in arm with a big, hairy man wearing a skirt, you may well want to forget it too.

HADAKA MATSURI – THE NAKED FESTIVAL (13 JAN.), INAZAWA, JAPAN This rather peculiar Shinto festival is all about purifying the menfolk. Something that requires lots of saki, no clothing and way too much male bonding. The 10,000 or so strippers, I mean participants, strip down to their little *fundoshi* loin clothes at the coldest time of the year and line the streets waiting for their chance to touch the *Shin-otoko* (an entirely naked man, shaved of body hair and protected by bodyguards armed with freezing cold water) which brings certain luck. Meanwhile the 300,000 voyeurs, I mean spectators, wait for the arrival of the much man-handled *Shin-otoko* at the Konomiya Shrine where he is jostled again by men keen to get their hands on a little purity.

FEBRUARY

ELF STEDEN TOCHT (HELD WHEN THE ICE IS THICK ENOUGH), FRIESLAND PROVINCE, NETHERLANDS Sixteen thousand ice skaters take to the frozen lakes, ditches and canals in an attempt to skate through 11 cities in one night. In a kind of Tour-de-France on ice (but actually set in Holland) serious contestants cross farms, duck under bridges and shoot along city streets in the nationally televised event. The amateur contestants drink *jenever* which greatly assists their ability to perform lovely pirouettes.

YENSHUI FIREWORKS FESTIVAL (15 DAYS FROM CHINESE NEW YEAR, USUALLY FEB.), TAIWAN To commemorate the eviction of cholera with fireworks more than a century ago the citizens of Yenshui build tens of thousands of bottle rockets which are massed onto wooden frames the size of trucks. When one of these 'beehives' goes off Yenshui is turned into a war zone.

Thousands of rockets shoot horizontally into the crowd like tracer bullets, bouncing off houses and burning any exposed flesh. Don't even think about attending without a motorcycle helmet, gloves and two layers of fireproof clothing. Many wrap an old towel around their neck to stop rockets bouncing up into their helmet and setting fire to their face.

A devotee at Thaipusam attaches limes to the hooks embedded in his torso. Others will pierce their cheeks or tongues with metal skewers of up to a metre in length while in their trance-like state. Kids, don't try this at home – try it in Malaysia.

THAIPUSAM – FESTIVAL OF FAITH (DURING THE TAMIL MONTH OF THAI, JAN. OR FEB., ON THE DAY THE STAR PUSAM APPEARS), BATU CAVES, MALAYSIA Not for the squeamish and now banned in India, Thaipusam still attracts million-strong crowds in Malaysia. Hindi believers, many of whom have purified their bodies by spending the previous 40 days meditating, maintaining a strict vegetarian regime and abstaining from earthly pleasure, prepare themselves to make atonement for their sins. The climax occurs when deep

HOW TO SURVIVE RUNNING WITH THE BULLS

Before you tie a red bandana around your neck and jump in front of five tonnes of angry bovine you may want to consider the following.

- *Don't run on the first day – just watch. That way you'll know what you're in for. Then, if at all possible, run sober.*

- *Take the corners tight – the bulls go wide.*

- *Once you start you can't get out until the end. The crowd will push you back onto the street should you attempt to climb out.*

- *Take the whole thing seriously. The police don't allow nervous-looking foreigners to run.*

- *Don't run just behind the bulls – they sometimes turn and trample the tailgaters.*

- *If you go down, stay down. Curl up, protect your head and wait until you feel an onlooker tap you on the shoulder indicating the bulls have passed.*

in the caves *kavadi* (heavy birdcage-like wooden or metal accoutrements) are attached to the body of a devotee with chains, hooks and needles. In unnerving trances filled with vicious twists and twirls and accompanied with chanting of incoherent songs, the devotees shock the crowds with their demonstrations of devotion.

MARCH

MARDI GRAS (FAT TUESDAY, FEB. or MARCH), NEW ORLEANS, USA
Katrina has been and gone and New Orleans is once again turning up the heat. Inhibitions (and clothing) are tossed aside as the beautiful people shake their drunken booty and show their boobies to the sizzling beats of southern jazz and Latin American samba. The whole shebang threatens to self-combust during the Krewe du Vieux parade when people will do anything for a string of beads or cheap toy.

CARNIVÀLE (FEB. OR MARCH), RIO DE JANEIRO, BRAZIL
When the samba schools of Rio don their sequined g-strings and feathered finery to sashay their way through the streets, the only thing missing a few beats will be your heart. If you are wanting a more personal, hands-on experience, forget the purpose-built Sambadrome and head to any of the smaller carnivàles that are held all through Latin America.

HOLI – FESTIVAL OF COLOURS, (FEB. or MARCH), INDIA AND NEPAL
To celebrate the end of winter and the destruction of the evil demon *Holika*, arm yourself with coloured powders (*gulal*) and dyed water (*pitchkar*), take to the streets and pelt anyone who comes within throwing range. Sounds messy? It is. You'll end up coated from head to toe in a psychedelic concoction of fluorescent paint so bright it'll make your eyes water.

Throughout Central America, Semana Santa is celebrated by dancing, passion plays, feasting and parades that would cause our Easter bunny to hang its head in shame. Seen here, celebrations in Oaxaca, Mexico.

APRIL

SEMANA SANTA (HOLY WEEK – LAST WEEK OF LENT), ANTIGUA, GUATEMALA Each day extraordinarily detailed *alfombras* (carpets) of flower petals, coloured sawdust and sand are painstakingly created on the streets only to be destroyed by the shuffling feet of the holy processions. The best days are Palm Sunday, Holy Thursday and Good Friday although you will need watertight accommodation as Antigua gets booked solid every year.

HOUNEN MATSURI – PENIS FESTIVAL (15 MARCH), KOMAKI, JAPAN Ever wanted to stroke a three-metre long penis or suck on a penis lollipop? Well here's your big chance, and I mean big. Coming in at just on three metres the wooden dong of the Tagata temple is the main draw here. Locals love to get their wanger out and parade it around town to protect them against STDs and promote fertility. No one goes home empty handed; the temple does a brisk trade in smaller penises

BOATING WITHOUT WATER

HENLEY-ON-TODD REGATTA (A SATURDAY IN LATE AUG.), ALICE SPRINGS, AUSTRALIA

Seemingly all you need is a few drunken mates and anything that can be vaguely construed as a boat. No water required. The event is open to everyone and all you have to do is cut a hole in your craft and run down the dry river bed towards the cold beer. Cheating is encouraged. Registrations are taken on the day and some of the events include:

- *Classic multi-crewed boat races such as the Bring Your Own Boat race, the Mixed Maxi Yacht and Rowing Fours.*
- *The technically difficult Oxford Tubs, during which boats (carts on rails) are paddled (shovelled) along the river course.*
- *During the Bath Tub Derby (pictured below), four crew carry a bath and a bathing beauty to a market buoy where it is filled with a bucket of water and then back to the start line for a wet T-shirt finish. Very gruelling.*
- *Battle Boat Spectacular – three battle boats, powered by four-wheel drives, fight it out with flour mortars and high-powered water cannons.*

although they never look as good on your mantelpiece as you might have hoped.

FESTA NACIONAL DO ÍNDIO (APRIL), BERTIOGA, BRAZIL When Europeans first arrived in Brazil, there were an estimated 1000 indigenous groups. Today, only 227 tribes survive. A resurgence in the value placed on ethnic diversity now sees indigenous peoples from deep in the Amazon and as far afield as the United States gather to celebrate cultural traditions and ritualistic performances in an event that has more feathers than *Carnivàle* and more flesh on display than a Rio beach in a heatwave.

SONGKRAN (START OF BUDDHIST NEW YEAR, 13–15 APRIL), CHIANG MAI, THAILAND What may have began as a purifying sprinkling has turned into a no-punches-pulled water fight. Bring some kind of weaponry; a bucket will do but super-soakers are better. Be careful of the kids, they're relentless little water-bombers, and avoid the roadside at all cost. Drive-by squirtings are commonplace.

LE FESTIVAL DE CANNES (MAY), CANNES, FRANCE Unless you're Christina Aguilera who once asked 'So, where is the Cannes Film Festival being held this year?', this cinematic event needs no introduction. The official screenings are only open to industry members which means the riffraff like you and me have to be content with celebrity spotting and the limited public beach screenings.

COOPER'S HILL ANNUAL CHEESE ROLLING (LAST MONDAY IN MAY), GLOUCESTER, ENGLAND Life just doesn't get any more fun than chasing a wheel of cheese full tilt down a hill. Sound easy? It ain't. The cheese is very fast and the hill very steep. Serious contenders fortify

MAY

PRETTY AS A FLOWER

HANAMI – CHERRY BLOSSOM VIEWING (25–31 MARCH), JAPAN
The samurai said that life, like a cherry blossom, is fleeting and each year, during the brief time when the sakura (cherry) trees shower the parks with petals, the Japanese, millions of them – possibly all of them – go out to play.

Every night sake-guzzling, karaoke-singing picnickers set up camp under the cherry trees and attempt to drink the country dry. TV stations feature nightly updates on the blossoming trees as one city after the next is swept up in springtime euphoria. Banzai!

©mostlymozart | www.1stockphoto.com

HIGHLAND SHOW SLIDESHOW. See all the tribes, not just the Skeleton Men from Chimu, shake their birds-of-paradise tail feathers in a gallery of images from my visit to the Mt Hagen Show.
www.deanstarnes.com

A HIGHLAND FLING

Strap on your best money belt and be prepared to be swept away by a thousand Papua New Guinean highland warriors adorned in birds-of-paradise feathers, shells, boar's tusk, body paint and loincloths in one of the world's last great gatherings of ethnic tribes.

Historically when the tribes met, they were prone to warring and eating each other and while these cannibalistic traditions have vanished, other, more colourful but less violent, antics remain.

Who would have thought that these shows, started by missionaries in the 1960s to promote goodwill, would be frequently credited as one of the most impressive anthropological displays on the planet, prompting the Chicago Tribune to name it as 'one of the 12 travel wonders of the world'.

The two principal shows are held at Mt Hagen (third weekend in August) and Goroka (mid-September), Papua New Guinea.

their courage with alcohol and sprint headlong after the Stilton. When they fall, as they invariably do, you can almost hear their bones breaking. The crowd loves it. No former training required.

JUNE

DRAGON BOAT RACING OR TUEN NG (JUNE or FIFTH DAY OF FIFTH MONTH OF CHINESE CALENDAR), STANLEY MAIN BEACH, HONG KONG, CHINA Teams gather from around the world to race their long boats, decorated as, you guessed it, dragons. Dragon boating is the only sport to be celebrated as a national holiday and it is taken very seriously by the teams competing. Rhythmic drumming provides the 'heartbeat' of the dragon and keeps the paddlers in sync.

FESTIVAL OF SAN FERMÍN (7–14 JULY), PAMPLONA, SPAIN Home to the 'Running with the Bulls' in which locals and drunk Australians run through the streets of Pamplona chased by a pack of cows. Animal activists stage the 'Running of the Nudes' a few days prior in which locals and drunk Australians run through the streets dressed only in cow horns. It's important not to get the two confused.

FESTA DE SÃO JOÃO (23–24 JUNE), PORTO, PORTUGAL Arm yourself with a wilted leek or plastic hammer and take to the streets for a midsummer night of madness. The aim is to bang a babe. If you spot someone attractive amidst the street stalls, fireworks and bonfires give them a whack on the head with your leek. Why? Not sure; presumably it's a Portuguese thing.

INTI RAYMI – THE FESTIVAL OF THE SUN (24 JUNE), CUZCO, PERU On the day of the winter solstice (as measured by the Incan sun dial the *pacha unachaq*), at the fortress of Sacsayhuamán huge crowds gather to watch the re-enactment of this ancient Inca ritual. The whole production features hundreds of actors, two llamas (no longer sacrificed) and a week's worth of parties.

JULY

MOONING AMTRAK (JULY), LAGUNA NIGUEL, USA The sole purpose of this event is to line a chainlink fence in Orange County and reveal your arse to every passing train. Spectators are welcome and the Amtrak trains are filled to capacity with passengers eager to see the 'moon show' so get your train ticket early. According to their website, overweight butt-bearers are welcome for the extra-high-intensity mooning they provide.

THE LOVE PARADE (JULY), BERLIN, GERMANY If you ever wondered what 1.2 million sweaty German teenagers have in common, now you know. They all attend this, the world's largest rave, to dance their horny little butts off to trance, house and techno music broadcast from a parade of trucks. The police stand back and let them fight it out for the port-a-loos.

FIESTA DE MERENGUE (LAST WEEK JULY), SANTO DOMINGO, DOMINICAN REPUBLIC For Dominicans the Merengue isn't just a way to dance but a way to live. Each year, the rhythms get

Burning Man, the home of 'radical self-expression', encourages attendees to contribute in any way they can to the experience. Personal expression ranges from giant mutant vehicles to decorative body art. Get freaky here.

faster and the hip-grinding routines sexier. Don't expect to sit back and watch though; everyone is expected to dance or die trying.

AUGUST

BOG SNORKELLING CHAMPIONSHIP (BANK HOLIDAY, AUGUST), WAEN RHYDD PEAT BOG, WALES

Most people go to considerable lengths to avoid a dip in a peat bog. But in Wales, for a mere £12, you too can slide, kick and flounder your way through 120 yards of stinky, muddy bog-water in an attempt to beat the 1 min 35 sec world record. The only catch is you can't use any conventional swimming stroke to get you there. Instead, dog paddle your way to glory.

BURNING MAN (LATE AUGUST), BLACK ROCK DESERT, USA

Nobody quite knows what to make of this one, other than if it was any more edgy it would be a cliff. Once a year Black Rock City, the fourth-biggest city in Nevada, blossoms into life when thousands of blissed-out youths and aging hippies descend on the desert to weird each other out with strange art, individual expression and some serious drug-inspired dancing. At the end of it all, the towering

YOU CAN DANCE IF YOU WANT TO

Ever wanted to parade around in public wearing skimpy clothes and a ridiculous amount of feathers? Here's your chance.

Rio's carnivàle has evolved into something far more than a hedonistic street parade. Competition between the samba schools is fierce and preparation for the Samba Parade starts months in advance of the main event. Once the theme has been finalised, the song is written and the designers begin working on ideas for costumes and floats. By December, the rehearsals begin and the schools' annual samba songs are recorded and released to the record shops. By this time the production of costumes is well under way and thousands of supporters are already heavily involved in preparing for the big event.

The only criteria for joining a samba school is being able to afford a costume. www.rio-carnival.net details everything you need to know about buying a costume and choosing a samba school. Some of the advice they offer include the following:

• Expect to pay US$300–700 for a costume depending on whether you are happy to be on the ground or the top of a float.

• Some of the flamboyant costumes get heavy. A costume with a light headdress may be more comfortable if less glamorous.

• Buy your costume directly from the president of the wing within the school you wish to march for. It is their responsibility to ensure your costume is made correctly. Buying a costume through intermediaries or agencies only increases the price, not the service.

• Try to buy your costume in the first two weeks of January when most costumes are still available.

• There may be 4000 people in your team but the judges watch everyone. Take the time to learn the school's song as you will be expected to sing it! Other than that, try to ooze vitality.

• Cameras are not part of the costume and you will not be permitted to carry one.

Carnivàle dancers in the Sambadrome, Rio de Janeiro's purpose-built stadium – Brazil.

burning man effigy is set alight along with much of the art and the whole thing goes up in smoke in one big, hedonistic party. Burn baby burn!

EDINBURGH FRINGE FESTIVAL (AUG.), EDINBURGH, SCOTLAND I laughed, I cried, then I laughed some more. What may have started out as a small-scale alternative to the Edinburgh Film Festival has turned into the world's largest arts festival. With over 2000 acts playing at over 250 venues during three weeks of comedy, dance, drama and song, you'll be begging them to stop.

TOMATINA (WEDNESDAY, LATE AUG.), BUÑOL, SPAIN Modestly described as the world's largest tomato fight but more aptly likened to all hell breaking loose when 40,000 people and 130 tonnes of tomatoes collide.

SEPTEMBER

FROG FESTIVAL (LABOR DAY WEEKEND, SEPT.), RAYNE, LOUISIANA, USA To quote from the festival website: 'You can bring your own frog or rent one.' That's right, if you are too poor to own your own frog you can hire one on the spot. Then what? Entering it in a jumping or racing competition is popular but then again so is eating them with Cajun spices.

GEEREWOL (SEPT. END OF DRY SEASON), IN-GALL, NIGER The Wodaabe men are born beautiful and physical beauty is an attribute much admired by the Wodaabe people. Things aren't left to chance, however, and to become the perfect male you also need some *maagani* (secret potions), make-up and the ability to dance for seven days during the *yaake*. Facing the sun, so that the female judges can see them better, the men impress their women by performing intense – and I mean intense – facial expressions. The outlandish grimaces, grins, crossed eyes, skewed lips, puffed cheeks, and raised eyebrows either win them a bride or unrelenting scorn.

OCTOBER

OKTOBERFEST (LATE SEPT.), MUNICH, GERMANY The grand-daddy of beer festivals where drunken Australians throw up on each other – although that isn't the main attraction. It may have live music, big tents and great food but this festival isn't all beer and skittles – it's just beer.

FANTASY FEST (MID-OCT.), KEY WEST, USA It's a 10-day, rude, crude, rum-soaked extravaganza of hedonistic temptation. Mostly about booty, booze and outlandish costumes, blush-resistant punters head to the Dungeons & Dragons leather fetish party while others stick to the Hog's Breath Homemade Bikini contest and street parades. Warning: this festival features overweight, middle-aged Americans 'dressed' only in body paint and g-strings. Be brave.

NOVEMBER

DÍA DE MUERTOS (1–2 NOV.), MEXICAN GRAVEYARDS During the Day of the Dead, sugar skulls, favourite foods and chocolate coffins are offered to the dead as their souls return to visit the living. 'Skull' poems are read, altars built and graveside vigils maintained. Macabre? Not really; the graveside picnics are family, fun-filled times and what the dead don't eat and drink is consumed by the celebrants safe in the knowledge all the calories have already been absorbed by the spirits.

The best place to spend Christmas? Lapland with Santa? Bethlehem, home of the first Christmas? Listening to the Pope deliver his annual Christmas message in The Vatican City? Nope, none of those; for most, Christmas is best spent with friends and family (like my niece and nephew above). And while Bing Crosby may have been 'Dreaming of a White Christmas', in New Zealand, my home, Christmas marks the beginning of summer vacations, T-shirts and beach-side barbecues.

DECEMBER

CHRISTKINDLMÄRKTE – CHRISTMAS MARKETS (MID-NOV.–24 DEC.), VIENNA, AUSTRIA
Warm yourself with a hot mug of *glühwein* (mulled wine) and *kartoffelpuffer* (potato pancakes) as you wander between the Christmas street stalls and elaborately decorated trees. The thousands of fairy lights, handcrafted gifts and smells of sizzling onions would make a Grinch smile.

ABENE FESTIVALO (LATE DEC.), ABENE, SENEGAL Bring your rhythm! You'll need it if you are to keep up with the dancing to the drums at one of West Africa's newest festivals. Diverse ethnic groups promote traditional music and arts from the region and travellers often sign up for music or dance workshops that are held to perfect their hip-gyrating moves.

In Tibetan Buddhism, kata (scarves) are given as symbolic gestures of goodwill. Different occasions require different coloured scarves. In this case, the blue of the kata indicates that these were gifts from Mongolians.

No one gets out alive

There doesn't seem to be much left for us agnostics not to believe in.

– JED LARSON

10. RELIGION

Travel and religion have always gone together. Ever since the Pope sent his crusading armies to root out the Muslims and heretics in the Holy Land, Christians have been tramping around the globe 'saving' the savages from eternal damnation and nicking their gold in the process.

Even today many Christian denominations send out squads of bright-eyed youngsters to spread 'the truth', and if you enjoy a bit of proselytising this makes a great way to see (and save) the world. If Third World hellholes don't do it for you, you'll be pleased to know you can always become a Hare Krishna and dance around JFK airport, handing out flowers and hitting up naive travellers from the Eastern Bloc for a dollar. Otherwise your best bet for a cushy assignment is to sign up with the Mormons; they even send missionaries to Japan. Bible-beating doesn't get much easier than playing the Japanese circuit as the locals are too polite to slam the door on anyone – even Mormons.

Japan isn't the kind of place I expected to find missionaries. I guess Japanese souls are as good as the next guy's but they still caught me off guard when they came knocking on my door in Fukuoka. I don't want to harp on about the Mormons; they're certainly no worse than any other religion, but the weird thing about them is that they all look the same. It's not just the white shirt and tie but the way they all look so clean. I suspect the two that came banging on my door that day may have signed a pact with the devil because they arrived by bicycle during a 40°C heat wave and hadn't broken so much as a single drop of sweat. I don't know where The Church of Jesus Christ of Latter-day Saints stands on perspiration – maybe they banned it – but it freaks me out when they send sweat-proof teenagers, who've mastered Japanese in six months to the point they can argue Zen theology, knocking on your door. It scared the bejesus out of my girlfriend at the time; she thought I was getting drafted.

No one does churches like the Russians. This multi-domed stunner is The Church of the Saviour on Spilled Blood in St Petersburg.

It is Islam that produces the greatest religious travellers of all. Every Muslim capable of doing so is expected to perform the Hajj – a pilgrimage to Mecca – at least once in their life. These days, thanks to cheap air travel, the Hajj draws in excess of two million pilgrims every year. It is the largest annual pilgrimage in the world and no amount of frankincense can disguise the smell of four million sweaty armpits in the desert sun. Besides the BO problem, crowd-control techniques have become critical as hundreds of pilgrims are trampled in the crush, or killed as ramps collapse under the weight of the devout every year. Saudi Arabia's Ministry of Hajj publishes this message on its website: 'Be peaceful, orderly and kind. No crushing.'

The Jews too are great, although hardly enthusiastic, travellers. Historically they have been shunted from pillar to post, from one corner of Europe to the next as various empires and nations have expelled their Jewish citizenry or sought to eliminate them entirely. Anti-Semitism reached a peak when Hitler's Holocaust led to the 'Final Solution' in WWII. Understandably, most of the surviving Jews gave Europe the finger, packed up their *menorah* (candelabrum) and decamped to Israel and the United States.

The two great Eastern religions, Buddhism and Hinduism, haven't spread themselves around the world to the degree that Islam and Christianity have (probably because they aren't required to convert followers) but are the two that often fascinate travellers the most.

It is a sad fact that many travellers on reaching India suddenly realise they are vegetarian, join a sect and sign over all their worldly possessions to their guru. They then start justifying to all and sundry the importance of a multi-armed, blue-faced god in the modern Western world. Similarly, many travellers in Tibet have the annoying habit of continually 'connecting' with the locals. You can tell when they have 'connected' for a little too long; their brows become permanently knitted, their smile becomes permanently beatific and they have the annoying habit of nodding solemnly whenever a Buddhist person speaks. Under such circumstances the best thing for everyone involved is a quick, humane death followed by a few prayers for a less galling reincarnation.

Been a naughty traveller and need to be cleansed of a few sins? Fear not. Many religions provide on-the-spot services that will have you born again in no time.

In the picture below, all I had to do was crawl inside this Buddhist statue, spin around three times and crawl out a different hole to the one I had crawled in and voilà, my sins were gone; although my knees were scraped.

Cemeteries can also be surprisingly interesting places to visit. All kinds of people have died over the years and some of their graves, like Jim Morrison's (of The Doors) at the Père Lachaise cemetery, have become huge tourist attractions. My favourite tomb is this one pictured above – the Bibi-Khanym Mausoleum in Samarkand, Uzbekistan.

For God so loved the world, that he gave his only begotten Son, that whosoever believeth in him should not perish, but have everlasting life.

– JOHN 3:16, THE BIBLE

Babies waiting to be baptised into Catholicism, Estonia.

AVOIDING MASS HYSTERIA – HOW TO BEHAVE IN A CATHOLIC MASS

- *Dress conservatively and speak softly. Men should remove their hats.*

- *When you enter the church cross yourself with Holy Water.*

- *To make the Sign of the Cross, hold your thumb, index finger and middle finger of your right hand together. Touch your forehead as you pray mentally ('In the name of the Father …') then your breastbone ('and of the Son …') and finally your left then right shoulders ('and of the Holy Spirit. Amen').*

- *If you go to confession before Mass, let the priest know how long the queue is; if time is short, do the mortal sins first.*

- *It is very rude to loiter near the confessional, especially if it is in use.*

- *When you reach your pew, genuflect – kneel briefly on one knee – before sitting down. Repeat this when you leave.*

- *Do not receive the Eucharist (Body of Christ) unless you truly believe and have confessed your mortal sins.*

- *Never applaud in church for any reason.*

- *Have a small cash offering prepared for the Offertory at the beginning of Mass.*

- *You don't have to sing the hymns although you should stand when the congregation does. The page numbers of hymns for the Mass are usually posted at the front of the church. Hymn books are located in each pew.*

WHAT TO DO AT A THAI BUDDHIST WAT

- At a wat (Thai Buddhist temple or monastery) dress respectfully. This means no shorts for men or short skirts and clothing that leaves the shoulders exposed for women.

- Remove your shoes and hat at each building's entrance.

- Since there are no chairs, sit on the floor but be sure to keep your legs tucked under yourself and avoid pointing your feet at others.

- Your head should be lower than the Buddha's and any monks present.

- At every temple there is a place to buy offerings (usually candles, lotus flowers or incense sticks).

- When making an offering at the shrine in front of the Buddha do not smell the flower you have brought or extinguish the flame you used to light your incense stick by blowing it out (just flick your hand instead).

©Maureen Tan, ww.inorbit.us

'The thought manifests as the word. The word manifests as the deed. The deed develops into habit. And the habit hardens into character. So watch the thought and its ways with care. And let it spring from love, born out of concern for all beings.'

– BUDDHA

Boys studying the suttas (teachings) of Buddha.

HOW TO BEHAVE IN A TIBETAN BUDDHIST MONASTERY

BATTLE TESTED

- *The best time to visit a Tibetan monastery is between 9 and 11 a.m. during the chanting and prayers.*

- *While you may enter at this time, do not step in front of the monks. Instead move clockwise around the back to get to the altar.*

- *At the altar make a small cash offering and then bow.*

- *You may also choose to bow before a monk. If you do, they will probably touch your head with their prayer book to bless you.*

- *Do not photograph anyone or anything inside a temple without permission.*

- *Many temples and some entire monasteries are ringed with prayer wheels. Spend the day with the locals walking the circuit and spinning the wheels (clockwise).*

Pilgrims spinning prayer wheels.

TOP FIVE 'ALTERNATIVE' RELIGIOUS EXPERIENCES

A FETISH FOR MAGIC
Marche des Feticheurs, Lome, Togo
A one-stop shop for all things vudun (voodoo). Witch doctors here sell animal bones, dog heads, thunderstones, snake venom and endangered animal parts to those in need of a little black magic.

THE THIRD REVELATION
Cao Dai's Holy See, Tây Nin, Vietnam
Forget East meets West, Cao Dai manages to encompass The Big Bang, Buddha, 36 levels of heaven, 72 planets containing intelligent life, God and Victor Hugo together with some pretty weird Disney-esque architecture.

THE WITCHES OF THE ANDES
Mercado de Hechiceria, La Paz, Bolivia
Bowler-hat-wearing Bolivian witches are all smiles, and why wouldn't they be? Business is brisk – there is always someone in need of a toad talisman, medicinal amulet or magical potion.

SHAMANISM AMONG THE REINDEER
Russia Tuva / Mongolian Border
Visiting the Tsaatan Reindeer herders is difficult. Isolated beyond belief these people still rely on their Shaman to enter the Spirit World and mediate on their behalf.

CARGO CULT
John Frum Cult, Tanna Island, Vanuatu
Join the locals awaiting the return visit of John Frum, the legendary American GI who appeared in WWII. Only at this time will the material wealth of the white people be finally distributed among them.

Dried llama fetuses for sale at the Mercado de Hechiceria (Witches' Market) in La Paz, Bolivia.

Finding God

Once my friend told me that he had found Jesus. I thought to myself,
'Woohoo, we're rich!' It turns out he meant something quite different.

— EMO PHILIPS

It is while travelling that many people find God – usually whenever
air turbulence strikes or while flying with Aeroflot. These planes,
which are much like Venezuelan buses only with fewer chickens and
more vodka, can have the most strident atheist praying in the aisles
before they've finished taxiing to the runway. Once while flying with
Air Istanbul, the captain had the plane face Mecca in order for us to
pray. All I can say is that while I'm usually the one to question blind
faith, when the pilot asks you to pray, you pray.

Plane flights aside, travel represents a great opportunity to
get personally acquainted with a religion. The only problem is
that it doesn't take long to realise that behind the exotically
incomprehensible dogma and quaint robes is a person with the
same foibles, shortcomings and xenophobic fears as the rest of us.
A young and beautiful French couple I once met in China had been
totally turned off Buddhism on account of a monk who, keen for a
three-way, had propositioned them behind the monastery walls.

It is important to take care when discussing religion because it is very
easy to give offence. Just as you wouldn't walk into a Dublin pub,
bad-mouth Guinness and expect to come out alive, don't expect
a warm reception in Jordan if you have an axe to grind with the
Prophet Mohammed.

My advice, especially for missionaries, is never talk religion with the
locals. The reason is not because the locals aren't happy to explain
their faith; on the contrary, if you are respectful and curious, most
people are only too happy to explain the foundations of their belief,
but sooner or later you are going to spot a flaw. And once a flaw
has been spotted it's difficult to let it slide. 'Hey buddy, don't you
think it's unlikely that Siva, being a God and all, couldn't recognise
his own son *before* he chopped his head off and replaced it with

*A Balinese girl performs in the
Ramayana – the epic Sanskrit poem of
Rama, the seventh incarnation of the
Hindu god Vishnu.*

*In the story, Rama's wife Sita is
abducted by the demon king of Lanka
from whom she is eventually rescued.*

*For Hindus, the Ramayana has become
an integral part of their faith, the
embodiment of morality and Rama the
representation of an ideal son, an ideal
husband and an ideal king.*

that of an elephant's?' Or 'I know it's a *really* big boat, but I still don't think it would fit two of all the animals in it'. Not convinced? Okay, do yourself a favour – if you are hell-bent on talking God with the locals, ask them about their faith but don't expect them to justify it. If you must say something critical use 'your religion' not 'you'. This also works well for Irish alcoholics – 'Your countrymen drink a lot of Guinness', not 'You are a pisshead'.

Visiting the houses of God

Judaism

There are three main sects of Judaism (Reformed, Conservative and Orthodox) but only the Orthodox tradition requires strict lifestyle changes. Jews are often called the 'People of the Book', and with good reason: Judaism revolves around the study and observance of God's laws and commandments as written in the Torah and expounded in the Talmud. Their most important belief is that of a single, omnipotent God who established a covenant with the Israelites, and revealed his laws and commandments to Moses on Mount Sinai in the form of the Torah.

Since 1948 Israel has been the homeland of the Jews and today 41 per cent of Jews live there while the remaining 59 per cent remain scattered in diaspora. The Temple Mount in Jerusalem is the holiest site in Judaism, as it was here that the First and Second Temples were built before their destruction. All that remains is the Western or Wailing Wall – a remnant of the wall encircling the Second Temple. Prayers here have extra zing and it's customary to write God a note and slip it into a crevice. Watch for water seeping through the cracks in the wall – this foretells the coming of the Messiah.

Unfortunately, Jews aren't the only ones with a claim to the Temple Mount.

HOW TO SHOW RESPECT IN A SYNAGOGUE

- *Dress as you would for church – respectfully and modestly. Men, Jewish or not, should wear a yarmulke (skullcap) out of respect and they are available at the entrance of the sanctuary for those who do not have one. Non-Jews should not, however, wear a tallit (prayer shawl) or tefillin.*

- *Be aware that men and women are seated separately in most synagogues.*

- *Jewish prayer services can be very long, especially on the Saturday Shabbat service – be prepared to stay for a while and eat something beforehand. Orthodox services are in Hebrew and you'll get more from it if you take the time to review Jewish liturgy before attending the service. If you just wish to observe bring something else to read to avoid standing out in the crowd.*

- *Generally sit and stand with the congregation although if you prefer you may stay seated apart from the times when the Ark (the cabinet containing the Torah) is opened – then stand.*

- *Stay in the sanctuary whenever the Ark has been opened. If you need to go to the toilet you should wait until the Ark is closed and the rabbi says it is okay to sit down.*

- *Keep prayer books on your lap or in the book holders provided by your seats. Do not put holy books on the floor.*

- *Don't take photos while inside a synagogue on the Jewish Shabbat (Friday evening prayers to Saturday evening prayers). Photography is prohibited during these times.*

- *Avoid speaking during the reading of scriptures and during silent prayers.*

BATTLE TESTED

In the shadow of the Wailing Wall (Jerusalem, Israel) a boy shoulders the heavy responsibility of the ark, the cabinet containing the Torah, as part of his Bar Mitzvah celebrations and passage into adulthood.

'All creatures are Allah's
children, and those dearest to
Allah are those who treat His
children kindly.'
– THE PROPHET MOHAMMED

*Men praying in an Esfahan
mosque, Iran.*

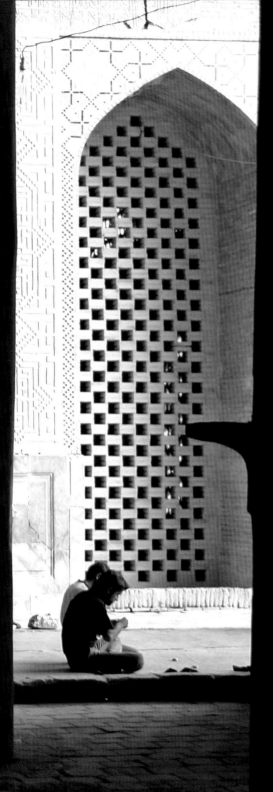

HOW TO ACT IN A MOSQUE

- *Many mosques are closed to visitors so seek permission first before strolling in. Many Muslims prefer travellers to visit outside of their prayer times (sunrise, noon, mid-afternoon, sunset, an hour-and-a-half after sunset and all day Fridays).*

- *Be aware that men and women often pray separately, either at different times or in different locations – there may even be separate entrances for males and females.*

- *Do not touch the* Qur'an *(holy book).*

- *Men should wear a long-sleeved shirt and a pair of long pants. Women should cover up with a loose-fitting tunic and head scarf. Take your cue from the other women attending the mosque.*

- *Perform* Wuzu *– the ceremonial washing before prayer. Most mosques offer facilities for this in the courtyard.*

- *Leave your shoes at the shoe storage area near the entrance – in summer the marble surfaces can be hot so bring socks.*

- *Step inside the* sahat al salah *(prayer hall) with your right foot first.*

- *The* mihrab *(the vaulted niche in the wall) indicates the direction of Mecca towards which Muslims must pray.*

- *To participate in* Namaz *(the ritual prayer of Islam), watch what the others are doing, although it is fine to observe quietly from the back of the mosque.*

BATTLE TESTED

'Know the self to be sitting in the chariot,
the body to be the chariot, the intellect the
charioteer, and the mind the reins.'
VEDA UPANISHADS

A Hindu pilgrim takes his early morning dip at
one of the many bathing ghats (steps leading
to water) at Varanasi, India.

WHAT TO DO IN A HINDU TEMPLE

- *Unlike the other major faiths, and in contrast to the generally tolerant Indian attitude, many Hindu temples and most innermost sanctums are only open to Hindu followers. Frustratingly, state tourist boards often publicise temples that are closed to travellers.*

- *As a general rule, you cannot convert to Hinduism. You are either born a Hindu or you are not. Painting a little red dot on your forehead won't get you in.*

- *Inside a temple complex behave sedately, respectfully and quietly. Turn off cellphones, extinguish cigarettes and refrain from eating or drinking.*

- *Dress conservatively and avoid showing too much flesh. Short pants, short skirts and low-cut tops are all inappropriate.*

- *Accept that it is unlikely that you will be given permission to photograph anything or anyone.*

- *Every temple is different, often with a unique set of rules. Some temples may require you to leave bags and outerwear at a security office before entering. Others require you to enter bare-footed.*

- *To improve your karma buy a garland of marigolds to offer, a candle to light or a caged bird to set free.*

- *There are an abundance of colourful Hindi festivals during which everyone is welcome as well at many significant holy places, like the bathing ghats in Varanasi, which all offer fascinating insights into this religion.*

- *Cows are holy, but if they are blocking your way, give them a whack.*

BATTLE TESTED

A family kneels to pay respect as they enter a church in Riga (Latvia).

Islam

Muslims too believe in one, all-powerful God – the same one as the Jews and Christians, but their take on it is that God revealed the Qur'an to Muhammed, God's final prophet, and it is this book and Muhammed's teachings that form the bedrock of Islam. Muslims do not see Muhammed as the founder of a new religion, but as the restorer of the original faith of Abraham, Moses, Jesus and the other prophets.

From the spice islands of Zanzibar to the marooned enclave of South America's Suriname, Islam is the second most widespread religion after Christianity. After the death of The Prophet, leadership squabbles eventually divided Islam into two main denominations; the Sunni and Shi'a.

The traveller needs to be aware that alcohol is forbidden, even to tourists in some countries, and during the month of Ramadan, from sunrise to sunset, it can be difficult to find food as all restaurants are closed and the taxi drivers crabby without their nicotine fix. The holiest Islamic destination, Mecca, is off limits to non-Muslims so instead visit the Dome of the Rock on the Temple Mount in Jerusalem. This is where the Angel Gabriel took the Prophet Muhammed on the Night Journey before accompanying him to heaven to meet Allah himself.

Christianity

Same story, different ending. Christians believe that Jesus Christ is not just a teacher, as the Muslims would have us believe, but the son of God who suffered, died and was resurrected for the salvation of us all. He was the Messiah prophesied in the Jewish Old Testament and his teachings can be found in the New Testament, the second half of the Bible. In the 2000 years since Christ was nailed to the cross his church has fractured into many denominations. The Vatican, a landlocked sovereign city-state in Rome (Italy), is home to the Catholic Church and the Holy See. It is also Christianity's largest tourist attraction and St Peter's Basilica and the Sistine Chapel draw 25 million devotees and tourists annually.

Buddhism

According to Buddhism, sometime in the fifth century, Siddhartha Gautama (Buddha), after meditating for 49 days, 'awoke' from the 'sleep of ignorance' when he realised the true nature of reality. Strictly speaking Buddhism isn't a religion, but a set of teachings, the core of which is the belief that somewhere between self-indulgence and self-mortification lies the 'Middle Way' – a path that breaks the cycle of reincarnation and suffering. Or to put it simply – life's a bitch, then you die, then life's a bitch again.

A common motif with Buddhist artists has been the carving of statues and you'll find them sitting, standing and reclining all through Asia (except for the ones in Afghanistan that the Taliban blew up in a moment of religious zealotry). The public face of Buddhism is the Dalai Lama, the spiritual head of Tibetan Buddhism, and he is to world peace what rock stars are to teenagers. Ever since his exile, the Dalai Lama has lived in Dharamsala (Northern India) and this has become the 'Mecca' for modern-day pilgrims, although it is the Tibetan capital of Lhasa that boasts the Potala Palace – the official residence of His Holiness. To visit

Tibet independently is difficult although not impossible. The Chinese, depending on their mood, only allow travellers to visit on officially sanctioned tours which mouth a lot of 'governmental policy' and little else. Most independent travellers either book on cheap tours and ditch their guides once in Tibet or cross from Nepal via the Friendship Highway.

Hinduism

Hinduism can be best described as kaleidoscopic in its diversity. At its heart it is similar to Buddhism in that your karma dictates whether you will be reborn closer to, or further from, spiritual salvation and the freedom from the otherwise continual cycle of rebirth. Add to the mix a whole battlefield of gods – each with multiple appearances during their different reincarnations and manifestations. Naturally each reincarnation requires at least one consort (the union to produce yet more gods) and an associated animal or 'vehicle' on which to ride. Vishnu, for example, when not appearing as himself also appears as a boar, Rama (the ideal man), Krishna, a man-lion and Buddha. Confused? I am. To top it all off, just when you are beginning to differentiate between Parvati as Durga and Parvati as Kali somebody says that for them (no one agrees on any of this) Hinduism is in fact monotheistic with one omnipresent god who has three major physical representations (Brahma the creator, Vishnu the preserver and Siva the destroyer and reproducer).

If you are in need of a little spiritual guidance then get yourself to India which has plenty of gurus who will, for a few dollars, soon set you on the correct path. You'll also see many *sadhus* (someone on a spiritual journey) wandering around India and Nepal half-naked, covered in dirt and sporting matted beards and hair. Some *sadhus* are merely beggars working an angle but many others are genuine and have forsaken careers, family and material possessions to undertake a spiritual search. The Indonesian island of Bali is also a Hindu stronghold.

Another fine mass

Mexico is famously Catholic; nearly 90 per cent of Mexicans profess Catholicism, but in San Juan Chamula in the State of Chiapas the locals have grafted old Mayan beliefs and new doctrines together, creating a brand of Catholicism unlike any other I have seen and one I'm not sure the Pope and the higher echelons of the Catholic faith would completely condone.

It all started during the 16th and 17th centuries when missionaries spliced Christianity onto the local pre-Hispanic religions – conversion through cohesion. But even though old gods were given new names and old festivals were appropriated by various saints, Christianity remains little more than a veneer. For some, everything from the trees, rain and Coca-Cola are believed to have supernatural powers. An innovative *curandero* (healer) starting prescribing Coca-Cola to his patients as a method of expelling evil spirits;

by all accounts his remedies found local favour and other faith healers soon started following suit. The key to a successful exorcism is getting the patient to burp out the offending spirit at the appropriate time in the treatment. The appropriate time as it turns out, is after a large gulp of Coca-Cola. Pepsi wasn't to be outdone, and in a stroke of innovative corporate endorsement, it sponsored another *curandero* to prescribe Pepsi instead of Coke as the evil-spirit-expeller of choice. Coke, never one to lose a marketing opportunity, followed suit with sponsorship deals of its own. The cola wars had arrived in the Mexican highlands and added a whole new dimension (a spiritual one) to their branding manoeuvring.

Lenesça and I visited San Juan on a Sunday when locals flock to the weekly market in the town's square. Stepping through the church doors was like stepping back in time into a different world. Outside was the clear mountain air along with a bustling highland market, noisy and colourful. Inside the air was thick and darkened by the smoke from the hundreds of burning candles all over the floor. No one was talking apart from the chanting *curanderos* performing their ministrations. People knelt on the pine-needle-encrusted floor praying and bringing offerings to whichever saint they were praying to. Lenesça and I had to tread carefully. With so many candles it was easy to imagine yourself accidentally brushing against one and setting yourself alight. The whole place was a fire hazard; I'm surprised it hadn't been shut down.

What heals the patient also pleases the saints. Six-packs of cola, along with more traditional offerings of candles and incense, were heaped around the feet of the saints that line the church's walls. The effigies are not easily recognisable under layers of decorative clothes. Every year the saints are fitted out with new threads without the older clothes being removed. The saints get fatter and their heads look ridiculously small. I suspect it is just a matter of time before the saints are swallowed up by their outfits.

The church may have been small but it was certainly memorable. It was also thirsty work – I had a Sprite.

The San Juan Chamula church has recently attracted so many tourists that the market in the town square is now a great place to pick up Mayan rugs and textiles. I found Lenesça deep in conversation with a young lady over the price of this bright orange tablecloth. I use the word 'conversation' in its broadest possible sense as neither were speaking but gesturing rapidly at one another. The indigenous people here speak Chol, Chuj, Lacandón, Mam, Tojolabal, Tzeltal, Tzotzil and Zogue. Lenesça speaks English.

Meeting the locals at a Fergana valley market, Uzbekistan.

Places to go … things to do

Watching Argentinians samba isn't the same as kicking off your shoes, throwing yourself into the fray and dancing until your hips hurt. To get the most out of your travel experience, concentrate less on the 'seeing' and focus more on the 'doing'.

Trust me, while some tourists may be gushing over the Islamic architecture in Esfahan (Iran), there's more fun to be had sipping tea under the arches of the Si o Sé Pol bridge than gawking at yet another mosque in 40° heat. If you take my advice, you'll forget the laser light show, befriend a local and instead of dutifully feigning interest in yet another museum, get involved in whatever it is that really interests you. Don't get me wrong: sightseeing most definitely has its place; it's just that tourists tend to go overboard on the seeing, whereas travellers have as much time for the people as tourists have for the places.

Cultural fallout syndrome

This is most prevalent among those who have been on the road for a long time. Early symptoms are the inability to remember the names of where you have been and what you have seen; one church blends into the next and all the temples start to look the same. Before you know it, the only thing interesting at the Acropolis is the stall selling cold drinks. If left untreated, this condition can trigger a severe bout of 'Extreme Cultural Apathy'.

Extreme cultural apathy

You'll know you have this when the highlight of the day isn't seeing the seventh wonder of the world, but discovering that your hotel has an English-language TV channel. If you catch yourself more enamoured by the pyramids on the Discovery channel than by the ones you've just seen, then things are really bad; you may need a holiday from your holiday.

The first step on the road to recovery is recognising that you just really aren't that interested in seeing every Roman ruin this side of

'He who has seen one cathedral ten times has seen something; he who has seen ten cathedrals once has seen but little; and he who has spent half an hour in each of a hundred cathedrals has seen nothing at all.'

– SINCLAIR LEWIS on sightseeing

'… a disease of the mind, [whose] germ is the idea that one may learn that which is valuable, or in any way acquire virtue, by the process of being shown things.'

– KINGSLEY MARTIN on modern tourism

BATTLE TESTED

Bronwyn on a bike in Kenya.

Athens. There are only so many museums anyone can see before they become 'museumed out'. It is far better to pick two or three you think you'll enjoy and see those. Remember, the purpose of the trip to Europe isn't to snap as many photos of yourself in front of famous architecture as humanly possible, but to – and try to follow me here – enjoy yourself.

Fortunately this is easy; interests that you have at home are just as interesting abroad. Fancy yourself a bit of an artist? Why not forget the Tate and sign up for one of London's life-drawing classes. An outdoor enthusiast? You lucky sod, the world is mostly made up of outdoors; there are mountains to be climbed, rivers to be rafted and trails to be hiked.

Thrills and spills

The world's an exciting place and nothing makes you feel more alive than when you are on the verge of death.

White-water rafting

In my view, white-water rafting is always excellent value. As far as I know, no one has ever fallen asleep while plunging head first down a waterfall. And it's not all about near-death experiences; rafting is an excellent way to see inaccessible scenery. Take Costa Rica's Pacuare River for example; the Pacuare is a river in a hurry, late for a very important date with a larger body of water. But what makes this river so special isn't the thrills and spills, although there are plenty of these; it's the stunning scenery. Rio Pacuare plunges down to the Caribbean through tree-encrusted canyons and swirls around bends that lead to breathtaking vistas of waterfalls cascading down near-vertical walls.

However, it was neither the rafting nor the beautiful scenery that made me gasp. It was the snake.

I had always been told that wildlife is shy – you'd be lucky to see anything in a rainforest except trees and rain. I was under the

ON YA BIKE

Renting a cycle is well worth the effort. From zooming along country back roads (like those pictured here in Estonia) to weaving through congested streets in Beijing, you're able to stop whenever you please and set your own pace.

I first rented a bicycle in China 10 years ago, to avoid the buses and taxis. At that time there were an estimated 250 million bicycles on the roads. The traffic rules were simple – there were none. You could cycle everywhere; down the off ramp of a motorway seemed popular. Slowing down for major intersections was considered cowardly. Everyone sounded his or her horn, or rung his or her bell continuously while in motion. The only safe thing about such a system was that in the resulting chaos and confusion, no one ever reached truly dangerous speeds.

It was all going splendidly until someone stole my bicycle. Bicycle theft is an everyday occurrence in China and by all accounts if you can't find your own bicycle it is acceptable to steal someone else's. The same goes in Japan. I've had four bicycles stolen there and nicked two myself. Outside department stores and train stations are huge parking lots of bicycles from which people generally help themselves. Some bicycles are clearly abandoned, presumably nicked from someplace else on a one-time joy ride. Oddly the same is true for umbrellas – Japan's a hard place to retain ownership of bicycles and umbrellas.

impression that animals didn't attack unless cornered and I felt confident that since we were in the middle of a river we hadn't cornered anything. I was wrong.

Swimming across the river, in fact making a direct course towards us, was a small but determined bright green snake. Whenever I raft I always pay strict attention to 'paddle instructions', because I don't want to die. No one has ever drilled me on the appropriate response to an attack by a small persistent reptile. Our guide, who looked like a young Bob Marley, was clearly unsure as to what to do, but assured us that it probably wasn't venomous. This was of no comfort, because 'probably wasn't', as we all know, is the same as 'possibly is', and as far as I knew there was no anti-venom on the raft.

In the end it came down to a mad paddle. At home I had dutifully read the *National Geographic* articles at my dentist and not one of them had ever mentioned that snakes sometimes attack rafts. I had been misinformed on the average snake's swimming abilities. I knew that sea snakes could swim (obviously) and anacondas lurked in the backwaters of the Amazon, but I was unprepared for how fast tiny green snakes could get from a river bank to us. Faster, say, than six adults could paddle.

Not able to out-run the snake, it was evident that a plan B was called for, because this snake was determined, its intention was clear – it wanted in. My only real source of instruction was from The Crocodile Hunter Steve Irwin – the man who made a habit of prodding dangerous animals with sticks until one eventually killed him. I told the snake to 'seettle down lettle fella' and gave it a few whacks with my paddle.

Now I know all animals are protected within a national park, but surely there are exceptions. For my part, I was all for using my paddle as a club and bashing the living snot out of it if it got any closer. Others were screaming and making signs that they were preparing to abandon ship and yet others were still paddling. The snake was having a hard time getting over the smooth rounded sides of the raft and kept sliding back into the water. To further compound the problem the next set of rapids was fast approaching.

The snake eventually gave up, never quite being able to negotiate the raft's slippery rubber sides, and swam away. After that everything kind of paled in comparison; the rapids, as fun as they were, didn't hold the excitement or adrenalin rush that one tiny snake had caused.

All of this just goes to prove what I have long maintained – ultimately your fondest recollections will not be the time when everything ran like clockwork, but will be those times when the unexpected blindsided you: the time you got lost, the time you ended up on the wrong bus or the time you were attacked by a snake. And, nine times out of ten, it is more likely to happen while you're actively involved in doing something, rather than passively watching. Of course there are exceptions; some activities inherently contain all the excitement that you will ever need. For example there is bungy jumping.

Rafting the Rio Pacuare in Costa Rica.

©Debbie Starnes

New Zealand's Tongariro Crossing is one of the finest one-day walks in the world. Follow the other Hobbits up the same route used by Frodo and Sam in their mission to destroy the ring. Shuttle buses ferry walkers to the trail head every morning and collect them, six hours later, on the other side of the mountain. The highlight is the crossing itself, a snowy trail between two volcanic cones, besprinkled with tiny aqua-blue crater lakes.

Bungy jumping

If something unexpectedly happened during bungy jumping, I doubt it would be good. I suspect it would be brown and smelly and rather embarrassing. Bungy jumping is a simple concept: throw yourself off something really high attached to a slightly shorter cord and try not to shit yourself. No great skill is required – all you need to know is how to fall with aplomb.

Bungy jumping has been around for centuries. Islanders of Vanuatu have long been throwing themselves off wooden towers; dislocating legs, knocking themselves out and occasionally killing themselves, in an effort to impress the local ladies. Only relatively recently did a crafty New Zealander (A.J. Hackett) see the commercial opportunities in what, until then, had been seen as glorified suicide.

Walking

'Anywhere is walking distance, if you've got the time.'

– STEPHEN WRIGHT

One of the best things you can do while travelling is take a walk – it's free, you get to work off some of that cheap Italian pasta you've been surviving on, and it's a great way to meet the locals once you're lost and have to ask for directions.

The best walkers are undoubtedly the Australian Aborigines who 'go walkabout' for six months as a rite of passage into adulthood. They re-walk the Songlines (ceremonial paths) of their forefathers, following the exact route their ancestors took and, in a fashion, imitating their heroic deeds. And while I'm not suggesting that you launch into the Appalachian Trail (USA's seven-month, 3500 km hike across 14 states), I am advising you to ditch the tour bus in favour of a walking tour. It's a sad fact that over 90 per cent of visitors to American national parks don't venture more than 500 yards from their cars. That's fine by me – it leaves all those waterfalls and mountain tops uncrowded for those of us who take the time to see them.

Not all walks need to be through the wilderness. Some of the best are historic rather than rugged.

Walking on the Great Wall of China is both, although you do need to pick your spot to see the wall at its best. I like the roller-coaster-like Simatai section with its 35 watchtowers, but it's no place for acrophobiacs.

Horse trekking in Mongolia

Most people associate day walks with national parks, and while parks do offer unparalleled opportunities for day-walkers there is also plenty of scope within the city confines. Many tourist information centres have free walking-tour maps and in some places you can even join 'walking-buses'. I once signed up for a free walking tour of Greenwich, staffed by elderly volunteers. I was the only one on my 'bus' and the best thing about spending two hours alone with someone's grandmother was that after I got the skinny on the Royal Naval College and the National Maritime Museum, she told me the 'real' reasons for the fall of the British Empire. According to Joan, it's the fault of the Indian and Pakistani immigrants.

Animal trekking

Many people believe that riding a horse will be a softer option than walking. They're wrong. It's all too easy to underestimate the strain on your inner thighs and the pain in your arse that comes with having your legs wrapped around a barrel-chested pony for five straight hours. And it's not just that. Horses can sense – God only knows how – if there's a beginner amongst the group, and when they do, they turn savage. Maybe it's the way you walk – not

enough splay-legged swagger in your gait for their liking. Once these schizophrenic little demons are onto the fact that you don't know your reins from your stirrup, you're in for a bumpy ride. If you're riding in the developed world, no problem – there's so many health and safety regulations, you'll be lucky if you even get to touch the reins. But in the Third World – and farmstays in New Zealand's East Cape – you'll be lucky to get a saddle.

I once rented a horse from a Tibetan farmer in Xiahe, China. I had decided to go to Xiahe because I wanted to visit the Labrang Monastery – one of the more colourful of the Tibetan Buddhist towns to survive the Cultural Revolution. It was here I learnt of the nearby Sangke Grasslands where Tibetans graze their yaks on flower-filled pastures.

The farmer ran through the basics for me in a language that may have been Chinese, hoisted me onto the saddle and left me to it. It was the first time I had ever ridden a horse and while it looked easy enough, I quickly learnt that there's no accounting for horse personality. Horses generally are psychotic to the point of paranoia and this one was no exception. One moment we would be casually trotting along, the next I would be sailing over its head because

Camel trekking in India's Thar Desert, Rajastan.

it had suddenly 'frozen' on the spot, believing it had seen something, a crouching tiger or hidden dragon perhaps, in the grass. I spent the afternoon stop-starting my way over the grasslands.

If horses don't appeal, then for those with a taste for the exotic, there are the ever-popular elephant treks in Northern Thailand. My elephant was a lovely old thing which came with her own squadron of horse flies who, after years of biting through elephant hide, soon learnt that they could sink their proboscis clean through a pair of jeans to the bone. Most of my three-day trek was spent running around on top of the elephant's back warding off these flies.

If that wasn't enough, during my camel trek in the Thar Desert in Rajastan (India), my camel developed a taste for naan bread and spent most of its time harassing me out of mine. Camels are cunning creatures – every time we encountered a thorny bush or cactus, it would walk right through it in an attempt to dislodge me and run off with my naan bread.

Sightseeing

'The traveller sees what he sees. The tourist sees what he has come to see.'

– G.K. CHESTERTON

Travel agents specialise in making arrangements for tourists; they often have little travel experience themselves apart from a few free junkets to whatever resort is in need of more business. The moment you sign up on an all-inclusive package holiday is the moment you mutate from an active traveller into a passive tourist. There is a difference. Your voyage of adventure and discovery turns into two weeks by the pool eating lobster and sipping cocktails, which I must admit, when I say it like that, can't be all bad. Where do I sign?

My advice is to organise things yourself, as you go. Not only will your money go directly to the local community, but you'll be able to meet the guide, inspect the vehicles and negotiate a discount directly with the manager. In fairness, travel agents can be a useful resource, particularly when time is short and a pre-booked tour provides a degree of security that you would be uncomfortable without. If that is the case, who am I to persuade you otherwise. Seriously though, where are your balls?

It may seem daunting to fly directly to some exotic destination, clutching a guide book, with nothing pre-planned, but believe me: once you arrive you'll be swamped for choice. Yes, safaris are easily arranged in Tanzania. Yes, you can hire a jeep once you reach Mongolia. Yes, there are plenty of city tours on hand in Vienna. Yes, yes, yes, the answer is always yes.

If you don't believe me, jump on the Internet – Lonely Planet's Thorntree forum (www.lonelyplanet.com) is a discussion board in which thousands of travellers across the globe swap stories, share ideas and give advice. Post a question, it's free.

Walt and Mickey stand proudly in front of Cinderella's Castle at the original Disneyland in Los Angeles (USA). Since then Mickey has set up residence in France (Euro Disney), Florida (Disney World), Japan (Disneyland Tokyo) and now China (Hong Kong Disneyland).

But the Mouse is not alone. Amusement parks can be found throughout the world, some are excellent (6 flags in LA). Some are ill inspired (Holland world in Fukuoka, Japan) and others, believe it or not, are free (like Jerudong Park in Brunei).

Tours

Having reached your destination, invariably the time will come when you'll want to fork out for some professional help and sign up on a tour or with a guide. Don't worry, the touts will find you. It's a little disappointing to be so easily recognised as a tourist.

In Costa Rica's Reserva Santa Elena, wishing to see more, I signed on a tour with a leading female naturalist. Apparently a 'naturalist' is not a fit nudist chick (that's a naturist), but an older, fully clothed lady, who knows lots about wildlife – disappointing.

I tried to mime what I wanted to see with a practical demonstration, but either my miming skills have deteriorated or *Ticos* (Costa Ricans like to be called this, I don't know why) have no tolerance for public nudity, because things got a bit weird thereafter.

The tour, however, was great (although chilly) and well worth the expense. Even though it was the middle of their rainy season (it had been raining pretty much non-stop for 40 days and 40 nights), we managed to see two quetzals, two poison arrow frogs, two capuchin monkeys, two sloths and two … just a sec …

Guides

In Guatemala, at the magnificent Mayan ruins of Tikal, I forked out for a guide who brought the place alive with tales of gruesome human sacrifice and the antics of local jaguars.

He had an exhaustive knowledge of the region's history, flora and fauna. He even had a sense of humour, identifying a chicken with a sore leg as a 'red-crested knock-kneed hummingbird'.

I also slipped over once, and this was used as a reference point when he gave directions – 'Turn right where the tall skinny guy fell over', or 'Straight past the spot where that guy landed on … what do you call this?' (Pointing to his arse.) Talk about funny.

Needless to say, a good guide can make all the difference and it's worth asking other travellers for their recommendations.

Brides in a line. Adjoining the Winter Palace, the Hermitage complex with its Atlas-style sculptors holding up the portico's roof is a popular spot for newly-weds to be photographed.

CITY LIFE

'A great city is not to be confounded with a populous one.'

– ARISTOTLE

Some cities have it all – culture, art and enough of a seedy underbelly to give the place an edge. When visiting a city try to experience all three.

Steph and I started our day's sightseeing in St Petersburg (Russia) with the Hermitage, one of the world's great art museums. With over a thousand rooms, it's best to focus on what interests you. Steph checked out the Impressionists while I wandered about counting how many of the female guards had moustaches – 19 out of 37, which made me suspect they recruit from the Chernobyl area.

For something different we then went to St Petersburg prison. I think any tour where the guide wears a balaclava, carries a semi-automatic and has to radio in our location every ten minutes is always good value. There are 10,000 inmates in St Petersburg prison but we only saw their hands sticking out of windows and a few exercising in a yard. Steph kept asking when visiting times were, because I had forged a registration stamp in my passport and she said she wanted to visit me in jail when I got caught.

We finished the day off with a ballet – Swan Lake, which is about duck shooting – ostensibly to experience Russian culture, but mainly so Steph could check out the size of Russian men's packages.

Steph shares her photos with a Mongolian family. A great thing about digital photography is that you can instantly share your pictures and everyone is curious to see how they look on camera.

SEE THE LIGHT. Photography has been made needlessly complicated over the years. When you strip aside all the bullshit, photography is based on a few simple principles. All the rest is just 'bells and whistles'. In photography, like other art forms, it is important to understand the medium in which you are working. The medium is light. Download the PDF file 'I See The Light' from www.deanstarnes.com for a free tutorial on photography and PhotoShop.

Shooting people

For me, one of the most enjoyable experiences while travelling is photographing what I see. Some people argue that with a camera constantly glued to my face, peering through a view finder, I forget to enjoy myself. They tell me the camera acts as a barrier and that people resent having a lens thrust in their face and by doing so I treat their communities as human zoos. I say 'Bollocks'.

Photography helps me look harder, irrespective of whether I take the shot or not. My memories are therefore more vivid. By studying every face, peering around every corner, I learn more. I travel better. For me, photography brings markets and busy streets alive.

With the advent of digital cameras I can instantly share (and erase) photos, allowing me to cut through language barriers and make friends. A picture speaks a thousand words in anyone's language.

Ask first, shoot later
Ask someone before photographing them. If they don't wish to be photographed or obviously look uncomfortable, respect that. There will be another shot around the corner and you'll feel better for it.

Paying for posers
In many places, locals charge to have their photo taken and this really irks some travellers. After all – they're just standing there right? In one village I went to in Kenya, you had to pay up front for the photos. You couldn't even enter the compound without paying the 'photography fee', regardless of whether you took many pictures or not – consequently many tourists stayed on the bus.

Before you begrudge the locals their dollar, keep in mind how poor they are and how few opportunities they have to earn money. And no, they aren't just standing there in all their traditional regalia; they are, in their own way, busking. In the case of the Kenyan village, the scheme was set up to discourage begging and to allow the cash to be pooled for the collective benefit of the whole village. The money was used to buy medicines and employ a teacher for the school.

TIPS FOR DIGITAL CAMERA USERS   BATTLE TESTED

- *If you are prone to getting lost and can't pronounce the hotel you are staying at, take a picture of it or the street sign to show the taxi driver later on.*

- *If you promise to send someone a print, make sure you do.*

- *Photograph your bag, just in case the airline loses it. That way you'll have something to show them when they ask what it looks like.*

- *Travelling with a friend? Consider using one camera and sharing the files. That way you can enjoy yourself without the temptation to photograph everything you see – and you won't have to argue later about who is the better photographer.*

- *Document the people and the 'now' of a place – not just the landmarks and the history. Often it's the taxi drivers, police, sidewalk cafés and locals that are more interesting (photographically) than the museum cases and architecture.*

- *When you switch to digital save your empty film canisters – they make ideal watertight pill bottles.*

- *Give your friends a break. Sort through your photos and keep the top 10 per cent and show only half of these.*

©rhyman007 www.iStockphoto.com

THE WORLD'S TOP FIVE ICONIC SPORTING EVENTS

FOR EIGHT SECONDS OF GLORY AND TWO WEEKS OF BRUISES – Calgary Stampede, Calgary, Canada
The draw here is fun with angry livestock. Besides bull-riding, the rodeo hosts chuckwagon racing, tie-down roping and steer wrestling. Dressing as a cowboy and listening to country and westen music is mandatory – enjoy!

THE LAST 'STREET COURSE' ON THE CIRCUIT – Monaco Grand Prix, Monaco
Pack your platinum and break out the bling-bling for the sexiest Formula One race on the calendar. Here petrol-heads get so close to the screaming engines and smoking tyres that they're able to taste the burnt rubber in the air.

BAREBACK ON AN ITALIAN STALLION – Il Palio, Bareback Horse Racing, Siena, Tuscany, Italy
Forget the Kentucky Derby and Melbourne Cup; riders here take incredible risks as they race through the twisty, slippery streets to the Piazza del Campo. Jockeys frequently whip other competitors, and riderless horses occasionally win.

A TOUR DE FORCE FOR THE TOUR DE FRANCE – Tour de France bicycle race, France
Started as a publicity stunt to promote a sports newspaper, the event is now the world's most prestigious bicycle race, attracting 15 million specatators and 189 male cyclists battling it out over 3000 kilometres of French countryside.

A JOG TO THE PARK – New York Marathon, New York City, USA
Since 1970, 700,000 runners have crossed the finishing line in Central Park in this, the world's largest marathon. Due to its popularity, numbers are now restricted to 37,000 largely lottery-chosen entrants. Kenyans usually clean up.

And the winner is …

'You can discover more about a person in an hour of play than in a year of conversation.'

– PLATO

Sport is great; it breaks down all the old cultural barriers and replaces them with a whole lot of new ones. Nothing brings out your one-eyed patriotism more than the sight of a mob of your countrymen chasing a tiny ball around an enormous field for an hour or so, and if they get into a bit of biffo with the opposition, so much the better. Indeed, most sport, even ping-pong, is only one bad referee call away from becoming a boxing match.

From sumo wrestling in Japan to camel racing in Saudi Arabia, there is always something to bet on. Any effort by the traveller to see, or better yet, get involved in, the local sport is richly rewarded. Forget your tickets to Broadway and get yourself tickets to Yankee stadium. And while Andrew Lloyd Webber may be hot in London's West End, sizeable crowds can also be found at Wembley, Wimbledon, Lord's and Ascot.

Sporting events

Sporting events are often reasons in themselves to travel and major sporting events attract some serious crowds, so it's important to book your tickets and accommodation early. Unfortunately, the earlier you book, the more likely it is that whatever team you have travelled to support will lose in the semis, leaving you stranded with two tickets to a final that you're too depressed to see. Americans cleverly avoid this by having a 'world series' in baseball in which the only teams competing are North American. The Olympics of course are open to everyone, and everyone, along with their synchronised swimming team, usually shows up. Don't visit a soon-to-be-host city the year before, however – anything worth seeing will be closed for refurbishment, and all the derelict bums won't be booted out of town yet. It's better to wait until just after the whole thing winds up. There will be plenty of accommodation still on offer and the locals won't have wised up to the fact that they'll spend the next four years paying off all those valedromes and never-to-be-used-again stadiums.

Football

No matter where you go, it's possible to spend hours with the locals arguing over the merits of whatever soccer team they happen to support. If the conversation flags just mutter, 'I hear [insert neighbouring country's name here] is pretty good' and everyone will spring back to life with more intensity than a cocoa-fuelled Bolivian bus driver let loose on the autobahn. But be careful. For some, football isn't just a sport, it's more a religion. In Colombia, eight pro players have been murdered in the last 10 years, making this the world's most dangerous pro circuit.

EAGLE HUNTING

Hunting bunnies with eagles is not for everyone because generally speaking, things turn out pretty poorly for the bunnies.

Steph and I met the eagle hunter pictured opposite in Kyrgyzstan. The deal we struck was that we would provide a cute, little rabbit, and he would provide a killing bird of prey.

We found that the key to enjoying a good eagle hunt is not to make friends with the rabbit. Once you have bought it, just pop it in a sack and forget about it. The moment you start getting it out, playing with it and feeding it carrots you're not going to be thrilled about seeing it ripped apart by some guy's eagle.

Of course the eagle has to feed and if they don't eat live food they lose their killer instinct. You can't be much of an eagle hunter if your eagle is a pacifist.

Our rabbit initially made a great dash for freedom but judged the situation poorly when it decided to 'freeze' on the spot. It probably didn't realise that hurtling arrow-like towards it was a hungry ball of feathers and claws. When the eagle hit you could literally see the fur fly.

The rabbit did a couple of somersaults in the air then took off as fast as it could – which wasn't fast enough. The eagle doubled back and this time she landed right on our rabbit, pinning it to the ground, with its talons around its neck. The eagle was fairly excited and it was explained to us that we would have to wait a bit for her to calm down before she would finish off our bunny and start to feed.

The eagle with the remains of our rabbit in Kyrgyzstan. Eagle hunting in central Asia has been popular for the last 2000 years and in times of great hardship the Kyrgyz have used eagles to help catch food for their families.

Attending a soccer game is a lot of fun, but ask around to see what the local hooligans are up to, in case they mistake you for a visiting supporter and kick seven different kinds of shit out of you. The risk is slight; tougher security measures mean that soccer hooliganism is often confined to fields far away from the main game and people at the fights have to post their commentaries on the Internet.

But, I'm just here to watch

Right, whatever you say. Everyone knows that some sporting events, especially motor racing, are quite boring and most of the crowd are actually just watching each other watch each other. They know that sooner or later some girl will get drunk enough to flash her tits at the cars. When this happens, all the guys – and at motor racing events, it's mostly guys – get really excited. There seems to be something about the smell of high octane fuel combined with the sight of a girl's nipples that really gets their motor running – so to speak. Not for me though. My advice, if you are after some cheap thrills under the pretext of sport, is that you can't go past the Brazilian women's beach volleyball team. It's part of the rules that the participants must wear bikinis; how good is that?

Extreme sports

Extreme sports are those likely to result in death. Some of these are nothing more than stylised suicide attempts involving some kind of steep incline and the use of monosyllabic sentences – a bad combination at the best of times. Usually the steep incline (like a wave, ramp or mountain) is tackled on a board, bike or skateboard until someone dies or says, 'Man, that nooseslide was sick.' Whatever comes first.

Skiing and snowboarding

Skiing and snowboarding are the most extreme of the sports habitually undertaken by travellers. The climatic conditions alone are treacherous, and assuming you survive the hypothermia and difficult chairlift dismount, the act of balancing on a brake-less board while careering down a mountainside at eye-watering speeds over frictionless ice and snow can make a grown man cry. Not only will you be expected to dodge beanie-wearing teenagers and European yuppies still spinning from their last line of charlie, you are expected to thread your way between the rocks and trees. And, to top it all off, if you do survive an impact with a tree you'll probably fall into the tree-well, die during the night and not be discovered until the spring thaw. Gnarly.

Only those of great testicular fortitude survive to endure numerous shots of *Jägermeister* in the huge piss-up (correctly referred to as *après-skiing*) afterwards. Death by alcohol poisoning soon follows. It usually comes as a relief.

Batter up

Joining a local sports team is an excellent way to get into the national psyche. Of course it can be disappointing to learn that sports fans in other countries are also ill-tempered, one-eyed, egotistical racists. Nonetheless, provided the sport in question isn't Thai kick-boxing you really have nothing to lose but your dignity. Before you challenge anyone to anything, remember that in the Third World, people don't sit around all day watching MTV and drinking beer. They may be skinny but I'm telling you, they are strong, wiry, nimble little bastards who will show no mercy on a sports field.

Chapati the naughty camel

In an effort to follow my own misguided advice about joining in whenever possible, I once entered the Maralal International Camel Derby in Kenya.

The $108 cost of entering the amateur camel race includes the hiring of the camel and the services of its handler, but it is left to you to select your camel and find a handler. I wandered around where the camels were corralled behind makeshift fences or hobbled to one another in small herds, searching for an animal that looked placid.

I met a local tribesman named Larangli, who agreed to rent me a camel and act as its handler for the upcoming derby. I had never had a camel, let alone a camel handler, at my disposal before, so I jumped at the offer. That was my first mistake – that and believing that racing camels would come naturally.

Larangli took me to the most unremarkable herd of camels he had and showed me a camel that was more unremarkable than the rest. When people met my camel, they were impressed with how unimpressive this camel was. It was that kind of camel.

There are two schools of wisdom when it comes to selecting a camel. One train of thought involves inspecting camel teeth. The only insights I gained using this method were insights into camel diet (green, slimy stuff) and the quality of camel breath. Instead I opted for the spiritual connection method. After looking deep into this camel's eyes I soon felt a bond – he was cheap and so am I. I asked the camel's name but was told an unpronounceable

Chapati's breath wasn't exactly floral.

name which I later learnt meant 'bollocks'. I refused to represent New Zealand on a camel named Bollocks and become the laughing stock of the entire derby before even starting, so I renamed him 'Chapati'.

Chapati as it turned out was an unorthodox camel with quite particular views on how a camel derby should be raced. Things began well when Chapati pushed his way to the front of the starting line but, despite the best efforts of my handler, insisted on facing in the wrong direction. Despite this, the race began and I had a great view of the other 55 entrants galloping at full tilt straight for me. I had been so busy trying to turn my camel around that I didn't have time to secure a firm grip on my reins and was unprepared for his sudden acceleration. Chapati may have not been much to look at, but he was surprisingly nimble.

My contribution to the race was to throw away my reins and yell at the top of my lungs 'whoaaa Chapati whoaaaa' as we galloped off. When I finally opened my eyes I was sitting back to front, clinging to Chapati's hump and coming fourth. My handler had been left

Me at the starting gate on Chapati. You can tell by the smile on his face that this camel would be nothing but trouble.

far behind and Chapati was showing no signs of slowing; in fact we were gaining on the first three camels. The crowd was stunned.

Unfortunately Chapati was an excitable beast and as we approached the front of the pack he was so out of control (not that there had been any control to begin with) he galloped into another competitor's camel, lost his footing and fell. I don't know if any of you have ever found yourself on the wrong side of a toppling camel, but it is quite frightening. When you climb aboard a camel, the beast is sitting down. As it stands, it's like a deckchair unfolding and you are raised to a dizzy height in a series of lurching movements. Well, when they fall, it's more like a beach umbrella getting turned inside out. My feet got tangled in the stirrups so I couldn't jump clear, but I did manage to cushion Chapati's fall with my body. By this time my handler had appeared and got the camel off me, and even though I was bleeding and bruised I was mostly unhurt so I remounted Chapati and set off once again. I was no longer fourth.

About six kilometres into the race, Chapati lost interest and sat down in the shade of a shop. My handler laid into my camel with a whip and a crowd of about 20 Turkana warriors appeared and began pushing, pulling and kicking my camel to get him back in the race. Chapati was quite okay though; he sat there happily chewing his cud, watching the other camels trot by.

I gave up and went off to buy a cold beer to settle my nerves. As I sat on Chapati's back contemplating a second beer, an old chief poked a stick up his arse which did the trick and once again we were back in the race, setting off at a brisk trot. Even though it was strictly against the rules (which I viewed more as suggestions), I employed a few young boys to follow behind me and tickle Chapati with sticks if he slowed down and thus I began passing other camels (whose riders had, I should point out, all employed small boys with sticks of their own).

I even got the knack of steering and no longer had detours through the mud huts, scattering chickens and children before me, and I finished in what can only be described as a truly unspectacular fashion. Chapati walked the last 100 m and slowly ambled over the finish line a respectable 14th of a field of 55.

Later that night at the bar, many people congratulated me on racing such an entertaining race, but I'm not exactly sure this was complimentary. However, the more I drank, the more I realised that I knew quite a bit about camel racing after all and I found myself in deep conversation with a wizened Samburu chief, who spoke neither Swahili or English (by this time neither did I), about the finer points of camel handling. He was a great listener and showed much delight at my backwards start and looked very grave as I related how I got trapped under my camel. He asked if it was usual to drink beer during the race where I came from and I assured him that in New Zealand, not only is it not unusual, but it is the preferred way to race camels. He was greatly impressed.

Boys practise wrestling in Mongolia. I too had a go against some older lads. I started off well, right up to the part where I got lifted off my feet and slammed into the sand.

THE THREE MANLY SPORTS

Genghis Khan kicked off the Naadam Games in the 12th century as a way of sorting out the men from the boys, and today, over eight centuries later, the nine tribes of Mongolia still gather in what is the oldest sporting festival on earth.

Steph (keen to see the Mongolians in tiny tights) and I (keen not to) attended Naadam to watch the participants (not all men) go head to head for top honours in the three manly sports.

Wrestling: *Dressed in little more than a pair of shiny knickers, cowboy boots and a waistcoat, huge Mongolian nomads grapple with one another for prizes and titles. One guy was given the title, 'Eye-Pleasing Nationally Famous Mighty and Invincible Giant'. Quite a mouthful.*

Archery: *My favourite on account that this sport seemed popular with guys so old I doubted they could see either the target or the judges who stood nonchalantly chatting next to the bull's eye under a rain of arrows.*

Horse Racing: *Boys as young as five and six race their horses over 30 km of open countryside. For much of the race all you can see is the approaching cloud of dust from the hundreds of galloping hooves, but when the winner crosses the finish line all hell breaks out as the whole drunken audience runs to comb the sweat from the winning horse. Steph and I ran too, but we didn't know what for at the time. I thought Russia had invaded.*

Men playing the African Bao game in Uganda. Cheating is common as they flick their seeds from one hole to the next in speeds purposely fast to confound their opponent.

BEAT THE LOCALS AT THEIR OWN BOARD GAME

'There is not enough time to do all the nothing we want to do.'

– BILL WATTERSON

It seems that old men in parks all around the world have nothing better to do than play board games with one another. You'll find them in parks and cafés – usually under a cloud of cigarette smoke, rolled-up newspaper in one hand and a chess board in the other.

They love to be challenged by foreigners so don't be surprised if a crowd gathers or expect any mercy. For some it's a matter of national pride and they'll try to thrash you in as few moves as possible.

Similarly, in backpackers and pubs the world over there are board games stashed behind the bar and an ample supply of fellow travellers nearby to play against.

If you know these five strategy-based board games – chess, backgammon, igo, mahjong and the African bao game – you'll never be without friends – especially if you're really bad at them, for in board games, everyone loves a loser.

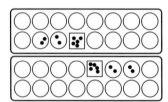

 DOWNLOAD THE RULES for chess, backgammon, igo, mahjong and the bao game at www.deanstarnes.com.

Getting the drift of things

A week later, following on from my success as a camel racer, I had the opportunity to crew in the annual *East African Shelia Dhow Race* off the Kenyan Island of Lamu. A *dhow* is an East African boat that uses tatty blankets as sails and rotten planks for a hull. I had been off to get some juice when someone told me they had space for an extra crew member and asked if I would like to participate. I tried to explain that I had nothing to do and it usually took me all day in which to do it, so I didn't really have the time, but they would have none of it. Before I could say, 'Hey, I don't think this thing is seaworthy', I found myself the seventh crew member in one of the boats.

The captain, who for reasons unexplained was called Captain Flower, asked if I had any sailing experience and I quickly assured him that I did. Captain Flower didn't believe me until I mentioned New Zealand, which he recognised as a sailing nation. I assured him that within our short history, New Zealand had a long history of almost winning sailing races. As recently as 2003, some of our best sailors had lost the America's Cup, and what is more, they had lost the races in a very convincing manner. I promised him that as a crew member, I could almost certainly guarantee to lose as many races as New Zealand's finest. I could, I told Captain Flower, snatch defeat from the jaws of victory as well as the next New Zealander and I would do it in a very convincing manner.

Donkeys trotting beside the stone buildings on the island of Lamu. I too was about to make an ass of myself.

An important part of *dhow* racing is smoking Bob Marley cigarettes, which turned out to be a lot of fun. The more puffs I had, the funnier it seemed to me that only last week I was racing camels and here I was racing *dhow*s – a word I wasn't even sure I could spell, let alone race. I'm not sure why I thought this so funny, but I sat in the bottom of the boat chortling merrily to myself until the race started. The rest of the crew had been gesticulating and waving their arms around violently at opposing crews, but since I could only gesticulate in English I didn't bother.

The race started suddenly. Captain Flower issued a number of instructions to me in Swahili, which was all Greek to me, and suddenly our sail was up and we were off. It was all very good fun. I wanted to hoist a protest flag because if there is one thing I know about sailing, hoisting a protest flag early on is vital if you want to dispute the outcome later on in court. There was no protest flag, so I then wanted to protest about the lack of protest flags. This also struck me as rather funny and the more I puffed on the Bob Marley cigarettes, the funnier it got.

Even though I was in the race, I had trouble actually following it. All the boats took off in what I'm pretty sure were different directions. Some sailed off right, some left, some tacked this way and that. We passed boats that were headed in the wrong direction. I decided the best thing I could do was to give any rope that came my way a mighty heave-ho until someone wrestled it from me. Sometimes my mighty heave-hos were a good thing and sometimes they were not. I viewed it as the crew's responsibility to keep ropes that didn't require mighty heave-hos outside my sphere of influence.

A lot of water came into the boat from between the wooden planks, and when I pointed this out to Captain Flower, I was told the boat was 'sweating' from the strain of the race. I told him that I was pretty sure the correct sailing term was 'leaking' and if the situation got worse it was called 'sinking'. We finished the race fourth out of a field of 13 – even Captain Flower was surprised, but maintained, rather unreasonably, that my sailing prowess left a lot to be desired.

Me on the dhow *during the East African Shelia Dhow Race. I'm the white guy.*

BLOOD ON THE SAND

Bullfighting isn't for the faint-hearted and, some would argue, shouldn't be for the stout-hearted either. Lenesça and I saw our first (and only) corrida de toros in Oaxaca, Mexico, and even though we knew the bulls died we weren't really prepared for how much blood was going to be shed in the process. After the death of the first bull – there's usually six – my stomach had that slippery, sliding sensation that suggested that my Corona and I might soon be parting company. Lenesça, the sensitive soul that she is, turned white and couldn't even finish hers!

It began benignly and thrillingly enough with the bull galloping into the bull-ring and tearing around trying to impale the cape-waving toreros on its horns. After a few minutes of this carry-on, two picadores entered on heavily padded and blind-folded horses. This is the most gruesome of the three suertes (acts). The picadores jab at the bull's shoulder muscles with their long lances (picas), opening wounds that pulsate blood with every heartbeat and soon the bull is drenched with its own blood. Once significantly weakened the banderilleros appear and stab three banderillas (the blue darts in the photo above) into its back. Finally the matador enters and after exactly 16 minutes of artistic, fancy footwork and cape-twirling bravado delivers the lethal estocada – the act in which a sword is buried to its hilt into the bull's body, piercing its heart and, all going to plan, dramatically killing the beast. ¡Ole!

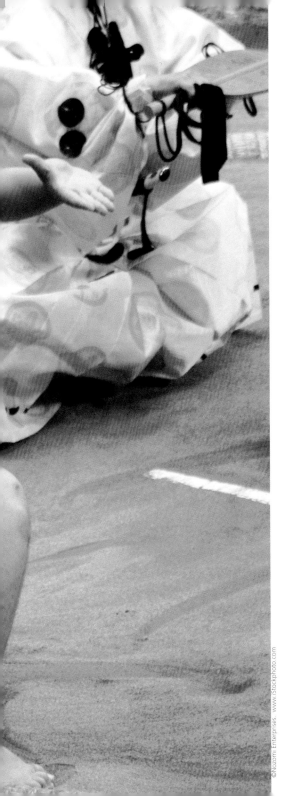

©Nozomi Enterprises www.iStockphoto.com

THE WORLD'S TOP FIVE ICONIC SPORTS

SUMO WRESTLING, JAPAN

If you want to feel thin without going on a diet then sumo is the sport for you to watch. Large men wearing little more than a pair of nappies attempt to push, jostle or shove one another outside of the ring or to the ground. The last man standing wins.

BULLFIGHTING, Spain

'If you have fought well and killed perfectly and swiftly – que maravilla. They cut the ears for you and it's the best feeling in the world. Other times luck isn't with you on the sword and, even though you follow all the rules, you hit bone and then – madre mia, you've wasted it all. Lost the ears. Lost everything. Even the crowd can turn against you.'
– Jesús Millán, bullfighter

MUAY THAI, KICKBOXING, Thailand

With roundhouse kicks to the head, elbow thrusts to the face and quick knee-hooks to the ribs, Thai kickboxing is one of the few combative sports to use all the parts of the body (excluding the head) as weapons. Tourists keen to have the snot beaten out of them are welcome to join in the training camps in Bangkok. Who's the ladyboy now?

RUGBY, New Zealand

Ever since the New Zealand rugby team in 1884 performed 'a Maori war cry' before their match, the New Zealand All Blacks have become synonymous with the sport of rugby. Unlike American football, rugby players don't need helmets or pads – just balls.

BUZKASHI, Afghanistan and Central Asia

Buzkashi resembles an all-out brawl on horseback. All you need is a beheaded and disemboweled goat and a pony with a death wish. The highlight? When an adrenalin-crazed horseman manages to make off with the headless carcass only to be run down by a mass of angry riders.

Wearing only their elaborate mawashi *loincloths and heavy belts of braided rope these sumo wrestlers prepare themselves to fight by performing a series of slow dance-like manoeuvres and symbolically purifying themselves by throwing salt.*

It's better when it's wetter

Swimming and surfing

The world is 70 per cent water, so if you don't swim you are, statistically speaking, rather limiting yourself. Everyone has their favourite beach, lake or swimming hole and mine are the *cenotes* of Mexico's Yucatán Peninsula. *Cenotes* are divine swimming holes that have formed in collapsed limestone sinkholes underground.

Swallows usually nest in their hundreds on the cavern roofs, making bird shit a real hazard as you drift below them in your inner tube. My friend Lenesça was so upset when one shat on her shoulder; I didn't have the heart to tell her about the five in her hair. They remained there until the following Friday (our appointed hair-washing day), allowing me to point them out to everyone we met.

Kayaking

In theory it's a fairly straightforward prospect. Sit in your little boat and paddle. In a river it's even simpler (provided you are heading downstream): just go with the flow. Sometimes the flow can get excessive; this is called white-water kayaking.

Most people are natural white-water paddlers, instinctively able to pull off the first half of an Eskimo roll without any training whatsoever.

Drinking

Strictly speaking, drinking isn't a water-based activity, although in some places you'd be forgiven for thinking it's an Olympic sport. Nearly every country has an associated alcoholic drink; from Jamaican rum to Portuguese port, there is a barstool somewhere with your name on it.

Drinking alcohol while travelling can be dangerous of course – Lenesça almost snuffed it when sitting under a coconut tree in Mexico. A huge palm frond gave up the ghost and came crashing

Lenesça drifts under a beam of light and dangling tree roots at cenote Dzitnup just out of Valladolid, Mexico. Cenotes are limestone sinkholes filled with crystal-clear water and freaky, toe-nibbling fish.

PIRANHA FISHING

How hard could it really be? Bait your hook with a hunk of bloody meat, toss your line into the deceptively placid waters of the Amazon and wait for the river to explode in a feeding frenzy, as a hundred thousand starving piranhas tear themselves apart.

I don't know what went wrong the day I went fishing for piranha near Rurrenabaque in Bolivia. Maybe the piranha were full, maybe their dietary habits were more discretionary than I had supposed. What I do know is that eventually, overcome by boredom, we went swimming. It was excellent fun staging fake, but horrific, piranha attacks. That is, until I saw my fishing line suddenly go taut. I had to stand on the heads of several friends to clamber, screaming, into the canoe. Pictured below is me with that sole, panic-inducing fish.

to the ground, bouncing off her head and sending her sunnies flying. Luckily she was pissed at the time and didn't seem to mind. The concussion symptoms were hard to distinguish from the hangover so, once she had relocated the straw for her piña colada (it was breakfast so we were trying to include some fruit in our alcohol), we assumed things were fine.

Scuba diving and snorkelling

Thanks to a proliferation of dive shops around the world, it's quite possible for the traveller to see as much of what is going on below the waves as on shore. If you can't afford to dive there's always snorkelling; which is just like diving but with a slimmer chance of drowning – for that kind of fun you have to pay extra.

A 'PADI Open Water' dive certificate requires a four-day commitment. Standards are reasonable, but there's usually a hard sell to 'upgrade' your qualification. Options include the obligatory 'Advanced Open Water' – same shit, only deeper; 'Night Diver' – same shit, only darker; the 'Underwater Naturalist' – learn the difference between sharks and guppies; and 'Underwater Photographer' – take the guppies' photo. You can follow that with the 'Wreck Diver' (the boat is the wreck, not you), 'Search and Rescue', 'Dive Master' and 'Ice Diver', even more impressive if you are learning in the Caribbean.

These courses don't compensate for common sense and experience. Scuba diving is potentially dangerous so adequate training is essential, but to be proficient takes hours of underwater diving to hone your skills. The most interesting thing I learnt? If you throw up underwater, the fish will eat it.

For an adrenalin rush with teeth, forget the dolphins and swim with sharks (great whites) off Dyer Island, South Africa. There's nothing like being trapped in a cage as it's lowered into a feeding frenzy of aquatic carnivores. PADI may want to bring out a course, 'Death by Being Eaten by Ravenous Killers' perhaps.

Me, arriving back to the Honduran island of Utila. Arguably the world's cheapest place in the world to learn scuba diving, the Bay Islands of Honduras's reefs are a continuation of the Belize Barrier Reef, the world's second largest after Australia's Great Barrier Reef. The water teems with fish, lobster, coral and, in October, whale sharks.

Don't know your warp from your weft? It doesn't matter. Buying a Persian carpet is all about cunning, good-humoured negotiation. They start ridiculously high, you start insultingly low and everyone drinks apple tea until, many hours later, a price is finally agreed on. These boys here in Bukhara, Uzbekistan, kill time between customers with a game of chess.

Who's haggling now?

'People who say money can't buy you happiness just don't know where to shop.'

– TARA PALMER-TOMKINSON

One of the best things about heading off to far-flung places is that you get to buy tacky, cheaply made souvenirs that serve no discernable purpose once you get them back home. A souvenir, like a scar, is something that acts as a reminder of all the fun you had while on vacation. They also make excellent gifts – my mum loves the way her snow dome from Paris offsets her Congonese death mask – who wouldn't?

Of course, what makes a good souvenir for one person is largely a matter of taste. I have a penchant for ethnic art; that stuff is like cocaine. I've tried to give it up, but sooner or later I find myself caught at customs, trying to convince the officials that the termites inhabiting my wooden masks are the good kind and not about to eat their way through the country's agricultural industry. My partner likes to make a list of things I'm not allowed to buy before I head off. This list is under constant revision but currently I'm banned from soapstone elephants, tribal masks, Japanese swords, Persian carpets, chess boards of any description and those really good textiles you get in Guatemala. She, on the other hand, only has to steer clear of ethnic clothing and getting her hair braided in Bali; it's hardly fair.

With so many shops and so little money, it's important to shop wisely. Excessive shopping also adds unwelcome weight and bulk to your backpack, so be judicious in your choices. I once bought – I'm not sure why – 15 brass door handles in India. They were too expensive to post and too heavy to carry. I have also learnt the hard way that those fake Rolexes you buy in dodgy places like Korea, Vietnam and London inevitably stop working the moment the seller disappears around the corner with your cash. The same is generally true for other pirated goods. Those Calvin Klein undies you get in Turkey stretch to twice their original size once they're washed and the Turkish belts shrink to half their length the moment it rains. The pirated software from Russia won't boot up and the cheap DVD you picked up in Hanoi comes complete with head shots of the people who sat in the front row of whatever cinema it was filmed in.

Post haste

The option of posting things home often costs more than the item's original purchase price, which doesn't seem right. Most countries no longer offer 'surface mail' (by sea) and insist on sending everything by air. Gone are the days when you could haul your excess baggage to the local post office, shove it in a carton, have it stitched closed in sacking and entrust it to the bureaucracy of the mail service. Gone too is the thrill

SHOPPING TIPS

- *No price tag? Good. That means you get to haggle. Hell, in some places you haggle even when there is a price tag.*

- *Try to find some flaws on the article as an excuse to depreciate its value.*

- *Be stubborn and persistent when bargaining – but keep smiling.*

- *Remember, what you buy, you have to carry. Life-size terracotta soldier statues do not travel lightly.*

- *Sometimes sellers endeavour to embarrass or bully you into closing a sale by implying you're too stingy or racist to do business with them. Prove them right and walk out.*

- *Check if prices include the VAT or GST. It's also worth finding out about any tax or duty-free refunds you may be entitled to on departure.*

- *Check carefully that your warranty is valid internationally, has been endorsed with the retailer's stamp and is for the correct product.*

- *Be aware that many antiques are not allowed to be exported or require a special licence to do so. Without this certificate, airport officials will confiscate them.*

- *Once the stall keeper has accepted your price, do not try and beat them down again. That's not how it works.*

of unwrapping it if it actually arrives and gluing all the pieces back together. A crucial reason for mandatory 'air mail' rates is that without this price hike, it's hardly worth the effort for the local post office employee to steam off your postage stamps and resell them.

The longest I waited for any parcel to arrive was a year. I posted a wooden statue of a Masaii warrior to myself from Mombassa. Judging from the post marks on the outside of the box, that statue is better travelled than I am. I think it spent three months touring Europe and at least six months travelling in South East Asia. I believe it even went to Burma which makes me mad because I have always wanted to go there.

That said, my favourite countries to post things from are still India and Iran. Packages from here are usually stitched in cloth and finished with a wax seal. Receiving these battered parcels in the post, wallpapered in strange stamps and covered in scrawled re-directions is like receiving a gift not just from somewhere wonderfully exotic but from some primitive time long ago – like the '80s. It's better when the parcel has taken ages to arrive because by then you have forgotten what you bought – it's very exciting.

In Iran you have to fill out multiple forms and have your carpets inspected by the official 'carpet inspector' at the post office. His job is to make sure you aren't exporting any national treasures and he is the guy to give you an honest appraisal of the quality and value of your purchase. According to Key-khosrow of the Tehran post office, my four rugs were astute buys. I'm not recommending buying four Persian rugs though. I was once given a book called *The Carpet Wars* (by Christopher Kremmer) and was unduly influenced by the author's enthusiasm for carpets and mistook that for my own. Persian rugs are difficult to backpack with and in the end I had to fork out to send them home. Christopher Kremmer may be a talented writer, but he owes me $150. The Iranians, however, were very helpful, but sadly unsure where New Zealand was, so everyone agreed it was better to send my consignment to Hawaii and let the Americans sort it out. Surprisingly, this worked.

Russian traders share a smoke at Moscow's weekend Vernisazh market. Besides fur hats, this is a great place to pick up matryoshka *(traditional nesting dolls), Soviet memorabilia and handmade crafts.*

THE WORLD'S TOP FIVE SHOPPING DESTINATIONS

These places all have more shops than Bill Gates has money – a highlight from each city then.

London, United Kingdom – HARRODS
A department store like no other – Harrods covers 4.5 acres; operates 40 lifts and answers 7000 calls a day. Incidentally, the famous facade is lit up by 12,000 light bulbs – of which 300 a day are changed by the store's electrical engineers.

Tokyo, Japan – TSUKIJI FISH MARKET
Give your wallet a break. Get up at the crack of dawn for this frenzied fish market. Buyers have been known to wear wetsuits to better inspect the octopi, sea urchins, tuna and occasional whale on offer here.

Paris, France – 8TH ARRONDISSEMENT
Forget the sad, now tourist-clogged Champs-Elysées; the glitterati head straight to the haute couture shops found on Rue du Faubourg Saint-Honoré and Avenue Montaigne in the 8th arrondissement. 'Oh this? It's Cartier darling.'

New York, USA – 5TH AVE VS MADISON AVE?
Two streets, two styles; 5th Avenue, home to some of the city's most famous department stores (Bergdorf's, Bendel's and Saks) squares off against Madison with its boutique fashion houses full of designer Italian shoes. Many a woman has come undone here. Me? I opt for the Apple Store in SoHo.

Hong Kong, China – THE GOLDEN MILE
'You buy now … show me your money.' Take your chances along Nathan Road's Golden Mile, where cheap designer-wear is flogged along with dodgy electronics. Watch out for the old 'bait and switch' con, in which one model is exchanged for an inferior, cheaper one.

Nathan Road, Hong Kong.

A stall owner re-hangs a bag after a hard day of haggling. The Anjuna flea market in Goa, India.

A THOUSAND BEAUTIFUL THINGS

The Wednesday Anjuna flea market in Goa is like you have died and gone to the great, sequinned, hippy store in the sky. Within the time it took me to purchase a can of Coke, I had attracted a crowd of street merchants and an ever-expanding entourage. There were three children wanting bakeesh, a persistent wooden-snake seller, a cow, the Coke seller from whom I had bought my drink – who was now keen to reclaim my empty bottle, a rickshaw wallah trying to secure my fare back to the beach, a fortune teller trying to read my palm, a professional ear cleaner claiming he could see wax in need of removal, a Gujarati woman selling saris and, trailing towards the rear, four sweaty and dancing Hare Krishnas after a donation. Once I got out of the car park it got worse.

Ready, steady … shop

Before you strap on that money belt and plunge head first into that den of thieves commonly referred to as the 'local market', you might want to sort out a few tactical ploys. Suss out your code words, that kind of thing. Admittedly I'm not the world's best shopper. I've probably been ripped off more times than Britney Spears has worn a thong, but having been ripped off more than most, I feel qualified to offer some hard-won advice.

Firstly, it's not as easy as you would think – these guys are good, they do it day in and day out, year after year, and by virtue of the fact they are still in business, it's safe to say that they'll be able to fleece any loose change off you before you can say 'I don't need another authentic Mayan cellphone cover'. Secondly, just because that tea-towel you got from Mt Rushmore is the very embodiment of the American spirit, doesn't mean it wasn't made in Taiwan. This is also true for antiques. Looking old and being old are too different things and you'd be surprised how many antiques a Cambodian 12-year-old can turn out with a smoky blow-torch and some soot. Thirdly, some things – ground rhino horns, elephant-foot waste paper bins, a kilo of hash – just aren't worth buying no matter how cheap they are. I find any souvenir that requires transportation home in a body cavity should be avoided.

Now that we have covered the basics, it's time to get down to the nitty-gritty of it. Here are a few basic rules and some tried and trusted techniques that can help level the playing field, if not the shopping cart.

Money talks

Remember that right up to the point where you hand over your cash, the power resides with you. Once you realise the seller wants your money more than you need his papyrus painting, you'll see how strong a negotiating position you're actually in. Unfortunately there is a dark side. I was once offered a carved wooden Buddha in Indonesia for $75. I really liked it and offered the guy $5. He countered at $20, then I with $6. This went on until I was at $9 and he was at $10. Neither of us would budge. He had so dramatically inflated his initial price that I hung out for the $9, even though he seemed desperately to want $10. The trouble was – and I didn't realise it at the time – his poverty was such that he would have sold it to me for any price. For me it was only a trinket; for him it was food on the family table. It's a cold-hearted traveller who knowingly takes advantage of another's misfortune in order to save a dollar. Bargaining can become so ingrained and you can become so accustomed to the hard sells, it's difficult to see when you are the one being unreasonable. In my case, I had to find the guy and give him the extra dollar that he had initially wanted. He was overjoyed and I got this weird mushy feeling deep inside. Remember that bargaining isn't a matter of life and death (at least not for you) so stay good humoured and don't get worked up about it. If money talks – let it say something nice.

A dog lies sleeping under a stall at the Pisac market, Peru.

The enemy within

So how do you know when a fair price has been reached? You don't. The trouble is that typically the reverse is true. The prices are so inflated, with the vendors all pleading poverty, it's safe to say that whatever price you agree on will be more than fair to the local vendor. In fact it's the tourists who are prepared to pay inflated prices who drive up the costs for other travellers and locals. By accepting the fact that tourists can be overcharged you aren't doing anyone any favours. You only create a greedy, money-worshipping marketplace, skewing the local economy and leaving the locals with the impression that all Westerners are money-laden, easy targets. If you like paying exorbitant prices, go to Switzerland.

Don't be a tease – the follow-through rule

There is one rule for bargaining that everyone must observe and to break this can lead to a lot of ill will. If you offer a price, even in passing, and the vendor agrees on it, then you should buy it. If you are not sure that you really want a stuffed blowfish, don't enter into negotiations. By all means, ask how much stuffed blowfishes go for, but leave it there. If you offer any kind of price to 'get an idea' of its value, you should be prepared to pay it, if accepted. The opposite is also true. Once a price is stated by the vendor don't let them raise it.

Go low, stay low

The standard advice you often hear is to halve any figure the vendor starts off with. If they say the rug is worth $200 you offer $100. This is crap advice. They know you are going to halve whatever they offer and the clever weasels have inflated their price beyond double. But the tables have been turned; now you know they know, you can offer less than half. Of course it is only a matter of time before they know you know they know, in which case they will quadruple the starting price. It's like an arms race, it's very exciting. My advice is start really low and stay low. If they say the rug is worth $200, offer $20. You won't get it for $20, but if you start low and stay low for as long as you can, you have a better chance of paying local prices.

Been a bad boy or a naughty girl? Fear not. Small religious markets often spring up around holy places full of not just tacky memorabilia but offerings for the Gods. This Mumbai (India) flower seller makes her livelihood from selling long strings of marigolds to devotees who toss them into the ocean to improve their karma.

EXCHANGE THIS

- *The best exchange rates are often through credit cards and drawing money out of ATM machines.*

- *Ensure that your PIN number is only four digits long. ATM machines in some countries do not accept longer codes.*

- *Visa, followed by Mastercard, are the best credit cards. Diner's Club and American Express are not widely accepted. Bring a spare and carry them in separate places.*

- *When carrying cash, the rule is: lots of change, in lots of places.*

- *Carry a small calculator to help with tricky conversions and to aid when bargaining across language barriers.*

- *If exchanging currency on the street or on the black market – count it carefully before handing over your cash, to avoid being short-changed.*

- *Traveller's cheques are a dying breed and not as easily replaced as the TV adverts would have you believe.*

Money made from inscribed banana leaves, Trobriand Islands.

Talk then walk

This is my personal favourite. Shop keepers can't leave their stalls. If you walk, then they run the risk of losing a sale. They have to close the deal before you disappear; otherwise you may end up buying someone else's tablecloth. Of course they hear this all the time and are unlikely to give you their best price if they suspect you'll just use that information to leverage a better deal down the street. It's like a game of chess – you have to convince the shop owner that you will, if the deal is right, buy something then and there.

The good shopper, bad shopper routine

Just like the 'good cop, bad cop' routine in the movies, this requires two people. The good shopper openly admits that they want to buy the African throwing spears and names a fair price (which will invariably be refused, but nonetheless needs to be fair for this ploy to work). Frustrated good shopper then enlists the help of their buddy, hereafter referred to as the 'bad shopper'. It is the job of the bad shopper to hate the aforementioned African throwing spears and tell everyone loudly and rudely that no matter how cheap they were, they would rather die than see these things hanging above their telly. Bad shopper tells good shopper that even if the shop owner were to meet the initial price, no deal is possible. Good shopper shrugs and allows themself to be dragged away from the shop (if you are a thespian type some dramatic sobbing, kicking and screaming can be productive). Faced with the prospect of immediately losing an otherwise easy sale, the retailer will usually offer to meet your price, saving hours of protracted negotiations. High-five each other out of sight.

The 'ole switch-em-at-the-last-minute ploy

This is an excellent ploy to use with carpet sellers. I have a Turkish friend who used to sell carpets in Istanbul and confided that he once sold a door mat – an old, tatty carpet of no value – to a Japanese tourist for a thousand dollars as an antique. Unscrupulous? Not really, it's all part of the game; the value of any item is always a perceived value. It's no one's fault if your

Women dressed in huipiles *at the Chichicastenango markets.*

500 YEARS OF BARGAINS

Before the conquistadors brought disease, pestilence and Christianity to Guatemala; before the town was even given the tongue-twisting name of Chichicastenango (Chichi to the locals) and long before mass tourism, there has been a market here. For the last 500 years, Mayan traders have been spreading their blankets and setting up their stalls in one of the biggest indigenous markets in Central America. Every Sunday and Wednesday they still do.

The stalls around the market edge sell tourist-oriented items – wooden masks, embroidered textiles and local crafts – while the stalls deeper in the market cater to locals, with vegetables, fruits, clothing, household items and spices. Prices are cheapest in the early afternoon, as traders prefer to sell off excess stock rather than carry it back to their outlying villages. Beside the great buys on offer, Chichi is strong in shamanistic traditions and pre-Christianity beliefs. It is not uncommon to see cofradias (religious brotherhoods) leading processions and burning incense near the church of Santo Tomás and throughout the town square.

average tourist wouldn't know an antique carpet if they were pissing on it; we only know what they tell us, and they only tell us what they want us to know. Usually they are very forthcoming with knot density, vegetable versus chemical dyes and the relative merits of individual carpets. At times things are more subjective: the age of the piece, how long it took to make, the originality of the design. At other times you may be simply misinformed: silk is not necessarily better than wool, other towns and other shops are not necessarily more expensive and you are likely not the lucky first customer of the day.

It doesn't matter if they tell you the truth or not; two can play at that game and it's possible to use their lies to your advantage. You have to rely on your own judgement, which is probably better than you think. I once bet a salesman that I could order all of his 15 rugs, from the most expensive piece to the least. I won the bet even though I knew nothing about rugs.

When you have found a carpet you like, don't indicate any interest in it. Instead, begin negotiations on a different but slightly inferior piece. Most salesmen will sing the praises of an inferior rug beyond its true

Fresh fruit for sale at the Damnoen Saduak Floating Market (Thailand), 110 km west of Bangkok. These days it is somewhat commercialised and draws as many tourists as it does local shoppers.

worth, making it easy for you to suddenly say you can't afford such a high-quality piece as has been described and switch your attention to the better rug simultaneously lowering your price. Suddenly the shop owner finds himself going backwards on the basis of the information he supplied – cunning.

'But I'm a poor student' gambit

Don't even waste your time with this. In their eyes you are rich; after all you're on a holiday that they could only dream of. Even if you are a poor student, the level of poverty you claim to be a hardship doesn't approach what they endure. Instead, say that you aren't an American and therefore can't afford 'American' prices – claim to be from New Zealand with a crap exchange rate.

Get help?

Get help – local help? Are you mad? This is fraught with danger. Whenever you step foot into any kind of market, you will almost certainly be befriended by all manner of locals dying to help you spend your money. Art students inviting you to their exhibition, English students who, as luck would have it, know someone selling exactly what you are after for half the price. Others likely to help you spend your money may include the hotel receptionist where you stay, the children hanging out on the street and the taxi driver who will, at no extra charge, take you to your destination via his uncle's, friend's, hairdresser's gem shop. It's all a racket because whenever one of these fellows follows you into a store, you'll be paying a commission regardless of whether they actually brought you or followed you. In Zanzibar (Tanzania) they're referred to as *papoosi* (lice), such is their determination to stay stuck to you and the fact that they are not easily dislodged. The most effective technique to thwart commission-hungry 'guides' is to shop in pairs, ducking into neighbouring shops. The *papoosi* can't follow you both. That or return later under the cover of darkness.

THE WORLD'S TOP FIVE MARKETS

ON THE EDGE OF COMMUNISM
Sunday Market – Kashgar, China
Step back in time a thousand years. Camels are still traded here, as are the pelts of endangered snow leopards, bicycles and pipe-like devices for affixing to a baby boy's penis in place of nappies – weird.

THE AFRICAN TRADER
Masaii Market – Nairobi, Kenya
They'll take the shirt off your back and the shoes off your feet – but you'll get a carved mask and a pair of elephant bookends for them.

1001 ARABIAN NIGHTS
Night Market – Marrakech, Morocco
Find yourself a balcony above the unfolding drama in the Djamaa el Fna square below. People-watching is unsurpassed here – water-sellers, jugglers, snake charmers, acrobats, storytellers and pickpockets – sit back and enjoy the show.

A LITTLE OF EVERYTHING
Camden Market – London, UK
Six markets in one and now open every day. Bring plenty of money and your most comfortable shoes.

'YOU BUY BIG'
Chatuchak Market – Bangkok, Thailand
Every weekend 15,000 stalls, selling anything from handicrafts to singing birds, fight it out to attract the attention of passers-by. Tactics employed include shouting, making odd noises, playing music and wearing outlandish clothes.

PEOPLE WATCHING

'People travel to faraway places to watch, in fascination, the kind of people they ignore at home.'
– DAGOBERT D. RUNES

Most people back home are a bit dull. People on telly are more exciting, obviously because they're celebrities.

This is not true for overseas people. Overseas people are very weird. They do weird things, say weird things and dress in weird clothes. They are enthralling and there is no better place for some serious people watching than spying on those going about their daily lives in their local market.

In many countries, markets are the heart of the town and a great day out – even if you aren't interested in shopping – is to visit the local market.

Just look at this fellow opposite in a Mumbai (India) market. I can't even name all the vegetables, let alone explain the dress he appears to be in, and where are his shoes?

ANIMAL MARKETS

These phenomenon usually occur on Sundays in towns throughout Central Asia and the resulting mishmash of people and their beasts is a photographer's dream. Grab your camera and throw yourself in; just watch your step, for where there is livestock, there is also livestock shit.

Get up early; the action normally kicks off at about 6 a.m. I can't see why you can't buy your bovine at 10 a.m. or, better still, just after lunch, but it's normally all over by morning tea.

If you happen to be in the market for a small goat (and who isn't?), inspect its teeth (good molars and you're onto a winner) and feel free to 'test-drive' the donkeys – a lot of fun until you're kicked in the head.

Animal markets are surprisingly addictive and before long you'll want a sheep of your own, or possibly a matching flock.

Making way for sheep

By the time Marco Polo gatecrashed Kashgar 900 years ago, it was already one of the great trading towns on the fabled Silk Road. Legendarily remote, surrounded by the Karakoram branch of the Himalayas and the giant wasteland of the Taklimakan Desert to the east, this city is the furthest from Beijing you can get and still be in China. It is also home to Asia's most exotic and eclectic market.

Before the first call to prayer from the minarets and before the first glimmer of sunlight, hundreds of donkey carts, horses, sheep, goats, pedestrians and camels thunder into town. As they arrive everyone (including the animals), yell 'Boish boish', which translates as 'Coming through, coming through'. It's a shambles.

By ten in the morning it has turned into a bargaining bonanza and sub-markets have formed in different areas, each specialising in a certain style of goods. In the livestock section, two humped camels are traded whilst men recklessly gallop horses through crowds as they test-drive various sway-backed beasts. Meanwhile in the vegetable arena, donkeys all but disappear under colossal burdens of carrots and melons. Over in the household goods area, knives, babies' cots and snow leopard pelts freshly poached from the Himalayas are haggled over.

Beijing may be the tail that wags the dog, but the capital is remote and foreign to the local Islamic Uigur and other tribal people who live in the surrounding districts.

By early afternoon the crowds are beginning to thin, the best bargains are gone and there is growing unrest. Merchants load their unsold goods and recently acquired purchases, and soon the whole crowd is once again moving. This time, however, it's out of town and back into the barren desert or unforgiving mountains and as they go, they all yell *'Boish boish'*.

The infamous Kashgar Sunday market, a weekly extravaganza that turns the eastern fringe of town into a labyrinth of impromptu stalls and informal huddles haggling over produce and livestock. The market reaches a frenzied climax of 200,000 shoppers, hawkers and thieves by 8.30 a.m. Bring it on.

How bazaar

I have became addicted to *kilms* (woven rugs) and whenever I'm in a country that produces them, I spend many happy hours foraging around bazaars, unfurling carpets one after the other.

An ideal place to start is the Tabriz bazaar (Iran), which has 35 km of covered walkways, 7000 shops and numerous 15th century caravanserais (domed halls) where caravans of camels were once watered and fed. However, for sheer magnitude, check out the giant Tehran bazaar; it's a city within a city and has its own mosques, guesthouses, banks, a fire station and somewhere between 200,000 and 300,000 shops. The daily shopping population swells to three million during peak hours.

A madman with a chicken told me all of this, so my facts may be a bit shoddy. He only knew about five phrases in English but made impressive, if somewhat repetitive, use of them. One of the phrases was 'to pay the chicken no mind', which of course makes you wonder what the chicken was going to do. And while I was wondering this he scarpered, leaving me alone with his chook, which was fairly irresponsible. The Tehran bazaar's bustling alleys are daunting to negotiate at the best of times and even more so with a chicken. Chickens are difficult to herd effectively.

To get from one side of the bazaar to the other, do not attempt to walk. You (or your chook) will be lost within minutes and probably run over by some kind of haulage trolley. Instead make your way out of the nearest gate and jump on a motorbike taxi.

Motorbike taxi drivers think nothing of doing a u-turn in the face of four lanes of oncoming traffic and taking to the footpath on occasion. Sometimes other motorcyclists would ask my nationality as they zoomed past. If you want even more excitement, tell the driver you are in a hurry then hang on. It's a fantastic adrenalin rush and yes, the madman and his chicken were happily reunited.

Eerily quiet, the combination of Ramadan (the month-long Islamic fast) and a downturn in tourism (thanks to being included in the axis of evil) empties out this bazaar in Estafan. In Iran, cash is king. Credit cards and traveller's cheques are not accepted and there are no ATM machines in the country that will accept foreign cards.

African safaris are the quintessential wildlife experience. The animals are so used to Land Rovers and minivans tearing around the place that they barely acknowledge your presence. The jeeps must stay on the trails at all times to help prevent erosion but apart from that there seemed to be few rules. It was great.

Where the wild things are

It's funny: the first time you see a new animal, you're like, 'All hail the majestic wildebeest!' The second time, you say, 'Look honey, another wildebeest.' The third time, it's 'Get the damn wildebeest off the road.'

But that said, animals in the wild aren't the same as those you've seen in the zoo. For a start they are far skinnier, but that is not what I'm getting at. Wild animals are more thrilling, but I'm not sure why. Maybe it's all the extra effort that is required to see an animal in its natural environment that makes it so rewarding when you actually do. Who knows? What I do know is that before I travelled I wasn't much of a tree-hugger. I once ate whale in Japan (I thought it was dolphin at the time) and it took constant vigilance by my girlfriend to ensure our trash was free from recyclables. I didn't always put the scraps in the compost bin. Sometimes I just hid them under other rubbish.

Not now though. Now that I've seen the great outdoors, I'm all for protecting it. I now believe that some of the earth's most interesting inhabitants aren't human. Nor am I alone on this. The 'green' dollar is a currency on the rise. From watching game on an African safari to frolicking with rays in the crystal-clear waters of Moorea (Tahiti) eco-tourism is a growing trend.

In Costa Rica from the late 1980s to the mid-1990s the annual number of tourists doubled, surpassing bananas and coffee to become the nation's largest industry. Today Costa Rica gets over a million tourists annually with over 70 per cent of foreign travellers visiting at least one nature destination. Sometimes I wonder if there is any room left in the parks for the animals.

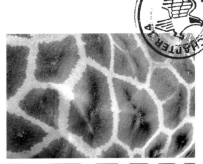

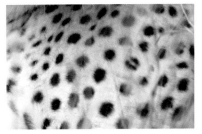

Top to bottom are the hides of a Masai giraffe, Burchell's zebra, Thomson's gazelle and a cheetah.

Gorillas in our midst

'The trick is,' explained our guide, 'don't show any fear. If they sense you are afraid it only makes it worse. If the silverback charges, stand there looking submissive and unafraid.' Submissive and unafraid weren't two expressions I previously had any reasons to deploy together. I wondered if I could get it right. I'm a terrible actor and now it appeared my lack of thespian skills might get me savaged by a gorilla.

The worst part was that trekking to see Uganda's mountain gorillas hadn't even been my idea. It had been Bronwyn's. To me, the cost seemed prohibitively expensive, the transport to the park almost impossibly complicated to arrange and I had lingering security concerns about the area where the apes live. I suggested we go to the zoo instead and tell everyone we saw wild ones. I also pointed out that gorillas weren't the only primates to be spotted in Uganda and we had already seen black and white Columbus monkeys, baboons, vervet monkeys and chimpanzees. I was getting quite good at identifying the rear ends of monkeys as they disappeared into the undergrowth, so I was a little reluctant to pay to see an ape's backside vanish into a bush no matter how endangered and singular its particular backside might be.

Only days before we had been on a chimp trek in Kibale Forest National Park in southwestern Uganda and it had been a lot of fun. What happens is a whole group of tourists who have previously shown no interest in wildlife back home trek all day through forests whispering (it's uncool to talk loudly or even normally on wildlife treks as the animals don't like it) about any monkey rear ends they had seen. We didn't actually see the chimps at first but we did stand around some chimp crap whispering excitedly about the quality and texture of it. Eventually the guide asked everyone to remain completely quiet because the chimps were only a few hundred kilometres away – possibly in a neighbouring country. When asked to fill in the comment book I wrote, 'I saw crap' and didn't get in trouble for it even though we did in the end actually see some chimps. One even urinated on Bronwyn, but that's another story.

The 700 or so remaining mountain gorillas live in a small mountainous area of the Virunga volcanoes that straddle Uganda, Rwanda and the Congo. There are three habituated families in Bwindi and each are visited by a group of six tourists along with an entourage of armed guards, trackers and guides. The trackers had been out since 6 a.m. locating our group which was unimaginatively called 'Group M' and they radioed back coordinates to our guide. The machine-gun-toting guards are standard procedure since rebels attacked and killed tourists and rangers in 1999, bringing gorilla tourism to its knees.

Group M, as it turned out, seemed to like to live on the top of what I'm sure must have been the steepest volcano in an area renowned for steep volcanoes. Frequent rest stops were called for; some of our group looked like a couple of shots of oxygen wouldn't have gone amiss. Patches of sweat blossomed under our arms and spread over our backs until we were a dripping, damp mess. I was contemplating asking our guide if there happened to be any lowland gorillas about nearby when he called a halt. 'They are nearby,' he said

The silverback, just after he woke and walked over to our group cowering behind a bush. He studied us with intelligent curiosity until satisfied that we were all wimps and posed no discernible threat.

Our group of six, making the long, steep trek through Uganda's aptly named Bwindi Impenetrable National Park in search of Group M.

vaguely signalling to a viney mess of overgrown bushes that looked in no way different from all the other tangled bushes we had been pushing our way through. 'Remember, don't run. If the silverback approaches look down and SLOWLY move back and don't talk or make any sudden movements.'

It was exciting. All I could see at this stage was a shrub and already my heart was beating uncontrollably. Every time the guide mentioned a new rule – don't stare at them, don't cough in their direction, don't use a flash, don't be tempted to touch them (I wasn't) especially the cute babies (still wasn't), my heart skipped a beat and lurched into a series of thrilling palpitations. 'This is very exciting,' I shouted enthusiastically to Bronwyn while jostling for safety near the back of the group and simultaneously breaking several rules in the process.

Slowly we advanced forward pushing the branches aside as we squeezed into the dense undergrowth. The gorillas were all asleep. They looked like fake-fur-covered bean bags you might get in someone's trendy apartment. There was no sign of life; you couldn't see their faces, there was no movement and no detectable trace of breathing. There was certainly no chest beating, no charges, no baring of fangs. 'This is great,' I thought, then moments later, 'This is boring.' I signalled to the ranger to poke them with a stick.

Once the gorillas have been located you get exactly one hour with them, and if they sleep for that hour then that's just bad luck. There are no guarantees of what you will see, or indeed if you will even see them which is what also makes the experience so magical when you do.

Gorillas, unlike chimps, are total vegetarians; they live off bamboo shoots, giant thistles, wild celery and other leafy herbs. One side effect of their diet is that they produce a lot of gas and the first sign that these were indeed gorillas, as opposed to fake-fur-covered bean bags, was the frequency in which they started to fart. Unfortunately we were downwind of them which proved to be a tactical error on the guide's part. The farts were the heavy substantial kind that seemed to enjoy our company and lingered around us for ages. They were hard to ignore, so I pinched my nose and fluttered my hand in front of my face and mimed gagging. Maybe this woke them, maybe they were already awake, it is hard to say, but what was clear is that they were no longer asleep. In fact they were all suddenly up and about and walking in a decidedly nonchalant way straight for us. Behind the family, but looking unreasonably large and muscular was the largest silverback (well actually the only silverback) I had ever seen. I immediately endeavoured to look both unafraid and submissive. 'Wow look at him,' whispered Bronwyn. 'Shhhh!' I shrieked. The silverback looked us up and down and started meandering in an unconcerned but slightly aggressive manner towards us.

He had the look about him that suggested if you raised your voice above a whisper he'd rip your arm off and hit you with its soggy end. I stood behind Bronwyn and tried to get her to go closer to see what would happen. The silverback was clearly a force to be reckoned with. In a show of utter contempt he plonked himself down in front of us, turned so his back was to us and folded his arms across a chest so muscular it made Arnold Schwarzenegger look wimpy and malnourished.

Now that the gorillas were up and about there was a lot of action. There were ants to be sucked off twigs, grooming to be done, youngsters to be swatted when they bounded over older siblings and plants to be eaten. Our cameras clicked away happily. I even worked my way towards the front now that all signs of danger had passed.

The expense, the hard trek and my earlier reluctance were forgotten as there are few experiences in the world more magical than coming face to face with a wild gorilla. Watching them is not like watching any other animal. Recognisable emotions flicker over their faces and there is something familiar about them, some common ground. I hope they enjoyed our visit as much as I did.

SPUNKY MONKEY

I've met wild orangutans twice. The first time (where the picture below was taken) was in Bukit Lawang on the Indonesian island of Sumatra.

The second time was floating down a nearby river in an inner tube. Tyre inner tubes are difficult to paddle and the more frantically you paddle, the less inclined they are to do anything but go where the current takes them.

Oddly, the current took me to a huge orangutan that was hanging from a branch and slapping the water with his hand. I wasn't sure how the orangutan would react to a semi-naked tourist floating on his river so I attempted to flatten myself down as much as possible. I had my arse shoved so far down that tube that my body concertinaed in such a way that my legs thrust skyward and I almost wiped my toes on his face as I went bobbing past.

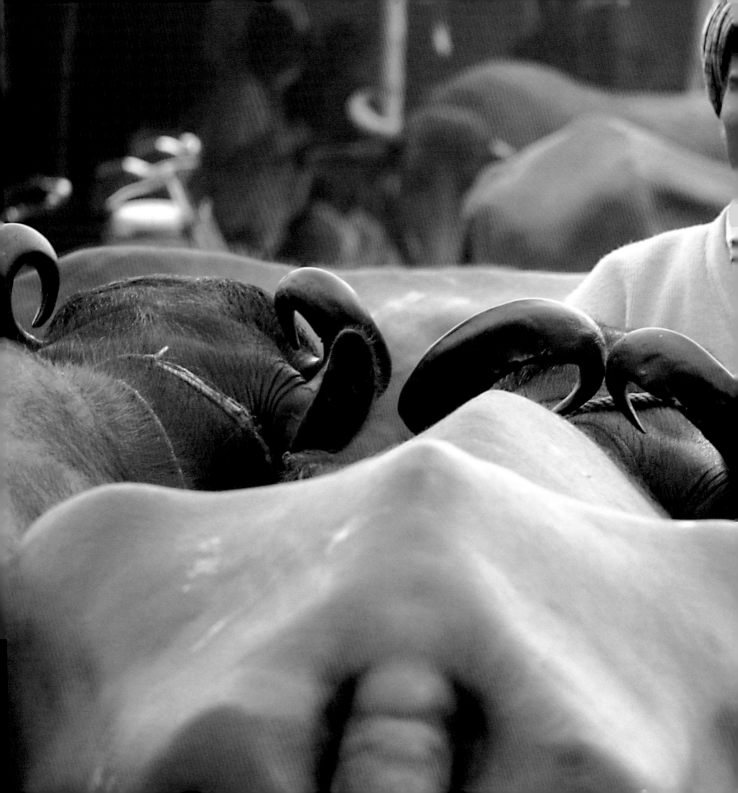

HOLY COW

In India cows are sacred and are seen as symbolic for abundance, nurturing, gentleness and the sanctity of all life. Most Indians do not like to eat them on hamburgers like everyone else does.

Many Hindus respect the cow, and in honour of their exalted status, cows roam freely in major cities. Even along the busy streets of Delhi you will find cows foraging through the trash for edible rubbish, while all around them cars swerve to avoid them. In places where there is a ban on cow slaughter, a person can be sent to jail for killing or injuring a cow. In only two provinces (West Bengal and Kerala) can cows be legally slaughtered and their meat exported.

Milk, however, is drunk on a daily basis and traditionally there were cows in every household. Because cows have long been seen as providers they are often regarded with the same endearment that Westerners regard dogs. Just as we would find eating our pet distasteful, Indians find the thought of eating beef unappetising.

Water buffalo for sale at Sonepur Fair (Patna, India). Although this is the largest cattle fair in Asia, all kinds of animals are sold here. Farmers, circus entertainers and traders get great deals on dogs, camels, donkeys, horses, monkeys, chimps, sheep, rabbits, bears, cats, guinea pigs and elephants. Birds, poultry and fish are also available.

THE WORLD'S TOP FIVE BIRDING SPOTS

For those who have trouble identifying a chicken, except when it's quartered, roasted and served with a side of chips, these spots will have you singing like a lark. No craning of necks, no fowl silhouettes and no no-shows in this lot.

ALL DRESSED UP WITH NO PLACE TO GO – King Penguins at South Georgia Island, Antarctica
You'll smell them before you see them and hear them before you smell them. Bring nose pegs and ear plugs.

DRAG QUEENS OF THE PACIFIC – Birds of Paradise, Kiunga, Papua New Guinea
Vividly coloured feathers, impossibly long tail feathers, iridescent breast shields, flashy capes, head ribbons, fleshy neck wattles, intricate dance routines and immaculately prepared stages are all part of their outlandish, campy costumes.

AN IMPROBABLE PINK TIDE – Flamingos, Lake Nakuru, Kenya
As seen in the movies (Out of Africa, The Constant Gardener), the vast flamingo flocks of East Africa's soda lakes.

ALL A-FLUTTER – Hummingbirds in Monteverde, Costa Rica
Visit the hummingbird gallery, stand among the nectar feeders and you practically have to swat these things away.

SOARING THE UPDRAUGHTS – Andean Condors, Canón del Colca, Peru
From the Cruz del Cóndor lookout, with the Rio Colca flowing 1200 m below, condors with 3 m wing spans glide past.

Pretty in pink

For days Bronwyn and I had been hearing about Lake Nakuru, one of Kenya's most accessible national parks and home to in excess of a million flamingos. It was a 'must see' and according to my guide book 'the world's greatest ornithological spectacle'. Even that description didn't really prepare me for the magnitude of the hundreds of flocks, each comprising tens of thousands of birds, that stretched into a distant bubble-gum-coloured blur along Lake Nakuru's shores.

It takes a special kind of naturalist to be a dedicated bird watcher and, let's face it, a bit of a nerd. To me every small brown bird is a sparrow and everything else a duck. Birds, quite frankly, just aren't that interesting, and in a country like Kenya, when it comes to interesting wildlife, competition is fairly brisk. For example, there are lions that rip things apart – birds simply suffer by comparison. I prefer animals with teeth, claws and an insatiable appetite. The only pink and white feathers I wanted to see were those in the jaws of some voracious predator. I couldn't have been more mistaken because flamingos are anything but dull. It's true, singular flamingos are somewhat ridiculous with their straw-thin legs, knobbly knees and strangely hooked beak through which they filter food. Their legs bend backwards and they eat upside down. It's fair to say that as a species they lack credibility.

Flamingos at Lake Nakuru where they gather to feed by swinging their upside-down heads from side to side, filtering out algae with their specially adapted bills.

Unlike herons, they fly with their neck fully extended as if peering uncertainly before them. Getting airborne doesn't seem natural to them either – they run, heads thrust forward, wings beating madly and gangly legs pumping manically in what appears a gigantic effort and expenditure of energy. Every time some took off I felt obliged to clap as a show of encouragement.

However, as ridiculous as they are, en masse flamingos have no equal. Through sheer numbers they can turn a lake pink and fill the air with a hundred thousand cries. They are transformed into a spectacle that the word 'flock' simply doesn't convey and so when flamingos gather, the resulting group is called a 'pat'. The name 'flamingo' comes from the Latin word for flame.

They are even fun to watch. Flamingos are social – they would have to be – but only to a point. Apparently not all flamingos are equal; there is a pecking order to be observed. Rules are to be obeyed, distances are to be maintained. There is a lot going on, and to see all of this you need to get close. Walking in the national park is not permitted other than at the lake's edge where it is possible to wander along the foreshore, stepping over the odd dead flamingo and gingerly tiptoeing over the guano. The birds are mindful of you and keep their distance but if you walk slowly and quietly you can get within 75 metres of them.

It is like bird watching for the attention-span challenged. Bring extra film; you only need to wave your camera in the general vicinity of the lake to take the kind of photos that make you consider taking up wildlife photography as a profession.

Lake Nakuru National Park was established in 1961 to protect the hundreds of thousands of flamingos and other birds that live within its borders. Like most other rift valley lakes, it is a shallow soda lake whose water depths fluctuate from one season to the next. During the mid-1990s the lake almost dried up completely, forcing the flocks to seek pinker pastures on Lake Bogoria. Since then, and with the aid of a couple of El Nino rains, conditions have improved and the birds are back in all their feathered glory.

©hibbolten   www.iStockphoto.com

PICK OF THE BUNCH ★ FIVE TOP SPOTS

THE WORLD'S TOP FIVE WILDLIFE ENCOUNTERS

IN FOR THE KRILL – Snorkelling with whale sharks in Belize

In late April, the usually elusive whale shark and less elusive European tourist congregate off Belize's coast to swim together. Whale sharks get big; then again so do European tourists.

LIKE A CAT OUT OF HELL – Watching cheetah run at the De Widt Cheetah and Wildlife Centre, South Africa

See the world's coolest cat go from zero to the nearest impala in less time than it would take a Lamborghini.

WILDLIFE ON THE HOOF – View the annual barren-ground caribou migration at Lutsel K'e, Canada

In spring 1.2 million caribou head north to their Arctic calving grounds in one of nature's most inspiring migrations.

KINGDOM OF THE MONARCHS – The Monarch butterfly migration to Santuario Mariposa Monarca, Mexico

Every year around 300 million monarch butterflies migrate 4000 km from Canada and northeastern United States to their Mexican wintering grounds, blanketing the ground and smothering the trees. Try not to step on them.

GONE FISHING – Viewing Alaskan brown bears fishing for salmon at McNeil River, United States

During July, when the river is leaping with migrating salmon, the world's largest gathering of bears takes place. As many as 40 bears can be seen lining the river's falls swiping at the fish. Visitation permits are obtained by lottery.

Game on

The Swahili word *'safiri'* means 'to travel' whilst the English version 'safari' refers to travelling around looking at animals which, for me, is the principal reason to visit Africa. Africa is a wildlife lover's idea of paradise. You don't have to spend hours in hides, and you get to zoom around in jeeps with your head thrust through the roof, from one herd of animals to the next. Bronwyn and I went to the Tanzanian town of Arusha (which is a bit of a dump) to book on a safari heading to the Ngorongoro Crater Conservation Area and the Serengeti National Park.

Most safaris in Tanzania leave from Arusha so if you hunt around you can get last-minute discounts from operators keen to fill any empty seats. There are heaps of touts selling safaris and they pester you night and day to join whatever trip they are commissioned to sell. Bronwyn was horrified at how cheap I was prepared to go. We eventually signed on with an outfit whose cook looked so sickly we were worried he may have leprosy and parts of him would drop off into our nightly stew.

The safari was fantastic, although we got off to a rocky start. We had only been in the Serengeti for a few minutes when we were attacked by some baboons. In the time it took us to unwrap our sandwiches a troop of baboons launched a military-style attack for our lunch. You could tell they had done it before; it was the

A hippo at Ngorongoro Crater.

kind of operation that called for split-second timing. They surrounded us and charged. I ran, screaming like a girl, possibly right over several other tourists, into the safety of the park office. To add insult to injury, while the baboons had us cornered, another cunning little monkey, a vervet I believe, mounted a secretive foray into our jeep and stole the following day's rations as well. Bronwyn managed to save her banana cake but left her passport and valuables in the territory controlled by the apes which clearly illustrated an unnatural cake dependency that did not bode well for our 'roughing it'. I was quick to point this out to her from behind the closed door of the park office. When the Masaii guard, armed with a *runga* (a long throwing stick), eventually showed up to rescue Bronwyn's bag from those beady-eyed, bare-arsed little mongrels she wanted him to try his luck with a semi-automatic.

We had timed our visit to coincide with the famous wildebeest migration. The migration is a natural event that occurs at the same time every year and thousands of tourists hire jeeps and chase all the animals north out of Tanzania's Serengeti into Kenya's Masai Mara National Park. Caught up amongst all those wildebeests are about a hundred thousand zebra, and following behind this smorgasbord on legs are whole prides of lions and other carnivores who keep the whole mob looking trim and terrific by eating all the weak and infirm.

TIPS FOR SAFARIS ON THE SPOT

There are many advantages to booking a safari on the spot. Firstly, your money goes directly to the local tour operator and not into the bank accounts of the middlemen in between. Secondly, you might be able to fill up an otherwise empty seat at a reduced rate. Finally, you'll be on hand to check that all suitable arrangements have been made and the equipment is up to standard. Here are a few points to keep in mind as you shop around the various operators:

- *Base yourself in a town where safaris leave from. Don't be pressured into signing up with the first tout who tells you that there is a one-off chance to join a safari that leaves tomorrow. Allow some extra days to arrange things.*

- *Every game drive is different but most people find that bouncing around in a jeep for two or three days is more than enough time to see plenty of animals.*

- *Generally the range in safari prices reflects the quality of accommodation and food offered. In some ways the budget tented accommodation can be more fun, especially if the animals come to visit, but the luxury options have superior food and transport. All should include daily game drives, fuel, meals, guides, drivers and tent rental. Bring your own water.*

- *A big component of a safari's cost is the park admission fees which are fixed and cover a 24-hour period. To maximise value, enter the park around noon which will allow an evening and morning game drive within your allotted period.*

- *The quality of the vehicles ranges wildly. Four-wheel drive jeeps are preferable to minivans which occasionally become stuck.*

- *Guides impact greatly on the experience. A knowledgeable, friendly guide is invaluable, so it is worth taking the time to meet the guides and inspect the vehicles if you are booking directly in Africa.*

- *If you are short on time or have a specific interest like bird watching, the Internet is an invaluable tool in pre-arranging a trip.*

BATTLE TESTED

SAFARI SLIDESHOW. There's more to the migration than wildebeest and zebra. Visit www.deanstarnes.com to see a slideshow featuring a bevy of animals from East Africa's Masai Mara and Serengeti National Parks.

Approximately a million wildebeest migrate annually into the 'Mari' and we saw all of them. In fact I think we saw some of them twice.

Everyone has their favourite animal and there was a certain amount of pressure on the guides to deliver the goods. Frequent none-too-subtle comments made it clear that the size of the tip was directly proportionate to the number of animals that were seen. This is unfortunate because it places unfair pressure on guides over events that they have absolutely no control over and encourages them to leave the trails in search of the more elusive animals. 'It's a park,' explained Isaac our guide, 'not a zoo. I can't guarantee where the animals will be.'

Bronwyn was hell-bent on seeing elephants which was fine because elephants, as we all know, are large and easily spotted. At one stage we were surrounded by a large herd and practically all we could see were elephants. I on the other hand was keen to see a cheetah because when I was in primary school I had belonged to a gang called the 'Cheetahs' in what I believed to be an incredibly clever play on words that alluded to our roguish and devil-may-care dispositions. I offered Isaac an extra tip.

We didn't see any cheetahs that day, nor the next. We did, however, see lions. Lions are a dime a dozen. The game drives typically started at 5 or 6 a.m. when the animals were the most active and returned at about 10 a.m. for a late breakfast. Usually there would be free time until dusk when we would set off again.

What impressed me the most was the sheer number of animals; often our jeep would be surrounded by herds numbering in their thousands. If I attempted to list all the species that make the Serengeti their home it would be enormous. The main attraction is undoubtedly the wildebeest migration, purely for the spectacle of it, but we also saw lions, gazelles, elands, impalas, klipspringers, warthogs, antelopes, hyenas, elephants, hippos, zebras, giraffes as well as diverse bird life. Our guide, Isaac, a Kikuyu man, was a wealth of information not only about animals, but politics, cultures and traditions, and deserved his tip. He even found me a cheetah. Just when I had given up hope, we came across two resting in the shade of a bush half an hour from our camp on the last drive of the last day of our safari. Way to go, Isaac.

The cheetah that we finally found at Serengeti National Park.

A crocodile in Botswana's Okavango Delta.

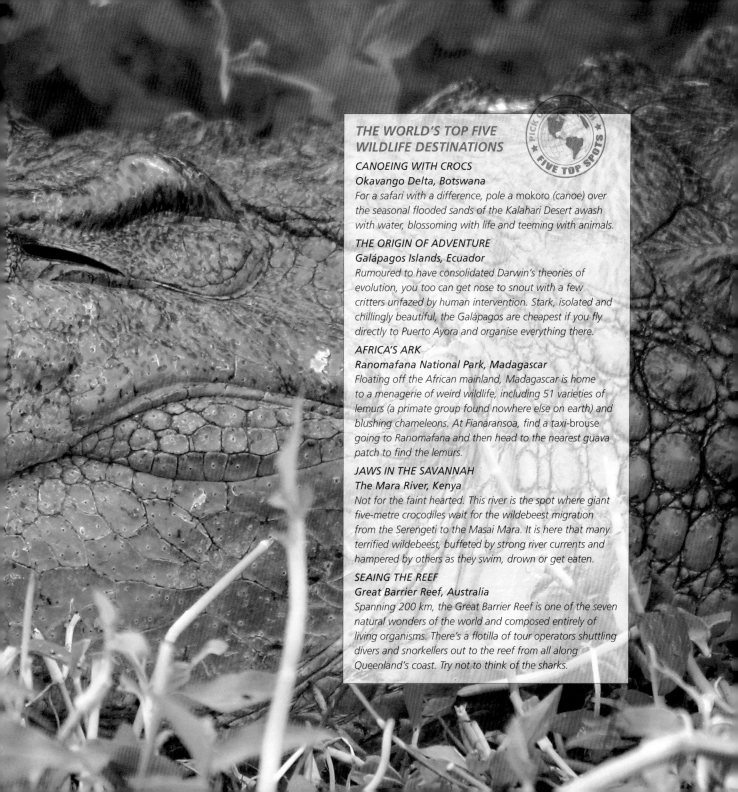

THE WORLD'S TOP FIVE WILDLIFE DESTINATIONS

CANOEING WITH CROCS
Okavango Delta, Botswana
For a safari with a difference, pole a mokoro (canoe) over the seasonal flooded sands of the Kalahari Desert awash with water, blossoming with life and teeming with animals.

THE ORIGIN OF ADVENTURE
Galápagos Islands, Ecuador
Rumoured to have consolidated Darwin's theories of evolution, you too can get nose to snout with a few critters unfazed by human intervention. Stark, isolated and chillingly beautiful, the Galápagos are cheapest if you fly directly to Puerto Ayora and organise everything there.

AFRICA'S ARK
Ranomafana National Park, Madagascar
Floating off the African mainland, Madagascar is home to a menagerie of weird wildlife, including 51 varieties of lemurs (a primate group found nowhere else on earth) and blushing chameleons. At Fianaransoa, find a taxi-brouse going to Ranomafana and then head to the nearest guava patch to find the lemurs.

JAWS IN THE SAVANNAH
The Mara River, Kenya
Not for the faint hearted. This river is the spot where giant five-metre crocodiles wait for the wildebeest migration from the Serengeti to the Masai Mara. It is here that many terrified wildebeest, buffeted by strong river currents and hampered by others as they swim, drown or get eaten.

SEAING THE REEF
Great Barrier Reef, Australia
Spanning 200 km, the Great Barrier Reef is one of the seven natural wonders of the world and composed entirely of living organisms. There's a flotilla of tour operators shuttling divers and snorkellers out to the reef from all along Queenland's coast. Try not to think of the sharks.

PICK OUR FIVE TOP SPOTS

It's a jungle out there

Turtle nesting isn't a thrilling spectator sport. It's not the most fast-paced adrenalin-laced action that the animal world has ever produced, but in Costa Rica's Parque Nacional Tortuguero it is oddly fascinating.

I had seen a turtle once before – in Belize. But since that particular turtle wasn't long for this world I didn't rate the experience as an enjoyable wildlife encounter. Standing on a street corner in Punta Gorda, I saw a baby hatchling drop out of a Mayan lady's pocket and make a mad dash for freedom, but being a turtle it wasn't much of a dash nor was it particularly mad. It was also in the wrong direction. Unfortunately the Mayan lady saw me pick it up and my Spanish wasn't up to lecturing her on turtles being a protected species and that she shouldn't really eat their babies. I know that Belizeans speak English, but this lady – she was about 90, old and frail, with the same beady look in her remaining eye that my mate Andy gets when he's looking for a scrap – wasn't having a bar of it and I'm ashamed to admit I was bullied into giving her back the turtle.

Back in Costa Rica, the villagers at Tortuguero have climbed aboard the 'green' bandwagon and make good money from the tourists who come to see the turtles nest on the Caribbean coastline. They have even posted some rules on a dilapidated notice board at the park headquarters. Most of which dealt with lighting concerns. Turtles apparently use star and beach lights to orientate themselves and these help them to return year after year to the same stretch of beach to lay their eggs. The notice board informed me that any additional lights I might carry would only confuse the returning turtles and disrupt the nesting cycle. The hardest part was leaving my camera behind (because of the flash) and I suggested to the park ranger that we cover the turtle's eyes with a blindfold that I had scored from the airline while we took pictures. He wasn't amused.

Because I had seen a Discovery documentary on turtles the year before, I wasn't expecting any surprises. I was confident that turtles were basically medicine balls with flippers and that they would emerge on cue from the thundering surf and scuttle up the beach to dig a hole and lay some eggs. I imagined it was all very straightforward. I planned to be back in the bar by ten at the latest.

I was unprepared for when I did actually come across Tortuguero's namesake. Firstly turtles are huge, far bigger than I thought turtles ever grew. I'm still not sure that what we actually saw that night wasn't in fact some long-lost prehistoric turtle and that I haven't let some monumental scientific discovery pass humanity by. Prior to sighting a real turtle, we had spent an absorbing half-hour watching a coconut bobbing in the surf, convinced it was a shy turtle bravely battling through the sharks we were told patrolled the beach for such arriving and departing delicacies. As the coconut grew closer we even took turns at shushing each other. I'm pleased to report that the coconut did safely reach the beach but under such intense scrutiny from our group it didn't lay any eggs.

Our English-speaking guide only knew a smattering of English phrases so most of the behavioural information in this article was gleaned by the collective input of the people in my turtle-viewing group. Unfortunately the closest thing we had to a naturalist in the group was a couple from California that liked to go to nudist camps and they knew practically nothing about the mating habits of marine turtles. My only input had been earlier in the day when I identified every bird, even a seagull as a 'yellow bird high up in banana tree'. I maintained that the song had a certain Latin American feel about it and was therefore likely rooted in fact.

We had stumbled through the dark for several hundred metres without so much as a glimpse of any of the turtle species that frequent this stretch of coast when we came across some tractor-like tracks leading from the water's edge. Where the tractor tracks stopped was what appeared to be a large overturned bath. 'Turtle,' said the guide.

When the guide shone his red light across her great, barnacle-encrusted back, we could see that the hole she had been digging was already at least three feet deep, and judging from the sounds of exertion she was making, it was tiring work. I feared for her health and a sudden heart attack. Turtles dig with their back flippers methodically resting between bouts of activity when they kick up huge clouds of sand with either their left or right flipper. Her progress slowed to such a mind-numbingly tedious speed that I feared my passport would expire before I actually saw her lay any eggs.

So there we were. A group of eight gathered around the rear end of a pregnant turtle trying hard not just to see her private parts but waiting for her to complete the intimate act of laying her eggs. There was complete silence except for the surf and a kind of grunt that the turtle made after each flipper kick. Frankly, it was a little embarrassing.

Eventually the turtle stopped. 'Now we watch, lay the eggs,' said the guide quietly and, as if in some well-rehearsed play, that is what happened. You had to be positioned in just the right way to see what appeared to be squishy ping-pong balls plop softly into the sand beneath her. Some were large, some were small and they just kept on coming until there were perhaps 60 to 75 eggs in the hole, quivering like a mass of fresh white eyeballs. Eventually we retraced our steps away from the snorting hulk who was now intent on covering the eggs with sand.

After seeing the effort that turtles expend to lay their eggs, battling through surf and sharks, dragging their huge bodies up the beach and slowly, almost painfully, methodically digging their nests it made me wish that I hadn't returned that baby to the old lady back in Belize. Instead I wish I had returned it to the sea – where it belonged.

These giant sequoias aren't the tallest trees in the world (that would be the 112 m 'Stratosphere Giant', a coast redwood) but sequoias are arguably the more impressive.

THE WORLD'S TOP TREE-HUGGING SPOTS

PICK OF THE BUNCH ★ FIVE TOP SPOTS

WITH THEIR HEADS IN THE CLOUDS
The Giant Sequoia, Sierra Nevada, USA
Stand in awe of 'General Sherman,' the 83.5 m high, 1500 tonne giant sequoia whose branches are bigger than any tree east of the Mississippi.

PLANTED BY A GOD
The Montezuma Cypress at Tule, Mexico
According to Zapotec legend, El Árbol, the largest living biomass on earth (with a 58 m girth), was planted in the Mexican town of Tule by a servant of Ehecatl (storm-god of the Aztecs), 1400 years ago.

WHERE BUDDHA SAT
The Bo tree at Anuradhapura, Sri Lanka
The original fig tree under which Buddha found enlightenment in northern India has died, but its descendant, a cutting taken to Sri Lanka in the 2nd century, lives on. This tree, the most revered on earth, isn't that impressive. It's neither big, grand, nor beautiful – how aptly Buddhist.

THE DEAD AND THE DYING
Bristlecone Pines, White Mountains, USA
The exact location of 'Methuselah', the world's oldest organism (at 4838 years old) is currently kept secret to protect it from vandals. Its trunk died several thousand years ago (about the time of Jesus's birth) but it lives on in its tips and roots.

LEAF PEEPING IN AUTUMN
Although all deciduous leaves turn, to witness this spectacle in its full autumnal glory, you'll need to head to one of these locations – Canada, Northern USA, Northern Europe or Eastern Asia (particularly China, Korea and Japan).

Lenesça and I met El Árbol in 2005 and the water crisis of 1994 had long passed. Back then, she had been close to death, starved for water according to the experts from the Royal Botanic Gardens at Kew. But on the day we met, she was in a green flush of health and impossibly wide to photograph.

'Tall and tanned and young and lovely' – a girl from Ipanema Beach, Rio de Janeiro. Rio has 37 beaches and seemingly more than enough babes and boys to fill them. Take a voleibol (volleyball) class on Ipanema in the day and head out to a baile (dance) with a new friend at night. You lucky dog.

Looking for love in all the right places

We've all heard the stories – that in some countries, women – gorgeous women – throw caution and their knickers to the wind the moment they hear a foreign accent. It's true, but what the stories fail to mention is that these women are called prostitutes and they're likely to leave you with an embarrassing social disease afterwards.

Nonetheless, a decent holiday romance may be all that is required to get you through that 'dry spell' – after all, there is nothing like being halfway around the world, far from disapproving eyes and surrounded by a mob of randy backpackers, to bring out your inner Casanova. Unfortunately, your charming accent will only get you so far and, traditionally, backpackers rely on alcohol to get them the rest of the way. However, there are other ways. With a little foresight and a few more showers, the average backpacker can become their country's very own ambassador of love.

Location, location, location

Like real estate, your romantic prospects vary from location to location. Back home, you may be dull and boring with a big honker, but in Japan you may find yourself to be a blue-eyed, fair-headed *ikemen*. Nor do you have to be particularly erudite or witty. Chances are, whoever you're hitting on doesn't understand a word you are saying. If they do, they probably haven't heard English for so long that anything you say will seem riveting. But be warned, choose your holiday fling carefully – especially if you are a guy. Just because you have a not-so-soft spot for Brazilian girls, it doesn't

---

KEEPING YOUR EYE ON THE BALL – PICK-UP LINES FROM AROUND THE WORLD

Yes, it's time to come clean and talk dirty. I can't guarantee any of these lines will actually work – they haven't so far – but good luck.

- *Tar anseo, mo chushla, agus tabhair póg dom.* (Irish Gaelic – Come here, my darling, and give me a kiss.)

- *Vill du bli med hem och slicka på min frimärkssamling?* (Swedish – Do you want to come home with me and lick my stamp collection?)

- *Rainen no kono hi mo issho ni waratteiyoh.* (Japanese – This time next year, let's be laughing together.)

- *Dè th'ort fo d'fhèileadh?* (Scottish – What are you wearing under your kilt?)

- *Fuck me if I'm wrong, but I think I want to kiss you.* (Australian)

- *¿Hace calor aqui, o eres tù?* (Spanish – Is it hot in here, or is it just you?)

And, just in case you need it, let's not forget –

- *Non dormo sulla chiazza bagnata.* (Italian – I'm not sleeping on the wet spot.)

necessarily follow that Brazilian girls are equally enamoured by unwashed and unshaven travellers. Statistically, you would expect reasonable success where there is a favourable male to female ratio (or vice versa). The Northern Mariana Islands have the highest female ratio with 0.77 males to every female and Qatar has the highest male ratio with 1.87 males for every female. But before your rush to your atlas to figure out where the Northern Mariana Islands are, remember that statistics aren't all they're cracked up to be.

If you are a girl, your chances of success are doubled. Not only has your accent suddenly become sexy but there is something hot about girls in pig tails and bandanas. One friend of mine met her husband backpacking in South America and a friend of hers met her husband standing outside the Colosseum in Rome. The only trouble with such exotic pairings is that invariably your newly found love will live on the other side of the planet.

Furthermore, travellers' personalities can change significantly when they hang up their backpack – that carefree, bohemian hippy you snogged at a Koh Samui dance party may actually turn out to be a stressed-out corporate banker fixated on the stock market when he gets back home.

Love is in the air

You can claim membership to the 'mile-high club' only when you have had sex a mile above the earth's surface, which usually means in the toilet cubicle of an aeroplane. This is widely considered to be quite an achievement and many randy travellers go to considerable trouble to arrange a 'rendezvous' halfway across the Atlantic. I'm not sure why they bother, because when all is said and done, sex in a public toilet, let alone sex in a tiny public toilet with a planeload of people outside waiting to go for a piss, just isn't that romantic.

Not so for public monuments. Nothing is more fun than shagging on top of a historical antiquity. Unfortunately, any proclivity you may harbour for getting your rocks off on top of the pyramids is unlikely to be shared by the authorities. It's one thing for pigeons to crap all over the Eiffel Tower; it's quite another for horny backpackers to bonk on top of it.

THE MANE EVENT

The mane thing (get it – it's a pun, it took me two months to actually think of it, so I don't want it to go undetected) about lions is their ability to shag. Not that I consider myself a connoisseur of animal fornication or anything, but lions have an active sex life. I mean really active – 72 times over a 24-hour period. That's more than I get in a year. That's more than some people get in five years.

Most people regard safaris as ideal 'kid friendly' vacations and I'm not saying that they aren't. I just want to point out that unless junior knows all about the 'birds and bees' they might get a little freaked out by the 'rhinos and giraffes'. The corkscrew monstrosity that passes for a stiffy on a rhino could emotionally scar a porn star. Parents need to know that springtime on the savannah is not so much a petting zoo as a heavy-petting playground.

I remember well the first 'bridal couple' Bronwyn and I saw in the Ngorongoro Crater in Tanzania. The term 'bridal couple' rather euphemistically, but mistakenly, implies that the lions had made some kind of commitment to each other, perhaps even exchanged little lion vows or something. Kids need to know The Lion King *is not a documentary. Simba's mum and dad were probably not very faithful – in fact it would not be slanderous to describe them as wanton sex fiends. If Simba's dad was anything like what we saw, he probably led Simba's mum away from the pride once he realised she was in season and pounced on the poor woman once every 15 minutes.*

It didn't take our guy long; a few thrusts and it was over – I was embarrassed for him. To make matters worse, watching all of this (along with the four or five jeeps full of tourists) were two or three more males ready to step into the breech should our guy's enthusiasm (amongst other things) begin to wane. Talk about pressure. Talk about performance anxiety. To add insult to injury, we were all taking pictures. Well not all of us; the girls maintained we should give them some privacy – it was a loving, intimate moment, maybe a little Barry White on the car radio would be more than enough. The guys on the other hand were high-fiving each other and swapping email addresses in case their photos didn't turn out. Fortunately, but now in hindsight, a little creepily, mine did.

HOT SPOTS

Looking for love or an overnight meaningful relationship? Then look no further.

- *Paris, France – très romantique. Those in need of a quiet place to practise their French kissing should head to* **Le Vert Galant,** *a quiet park at the western end of Île de la Cité, where locals say 'sweethearts love to linger'.*

- *Forget the carriage ride through Central Park and arrange your rendezvous at the libido-improving Oyster Bar in the recently restored and rather romantic* **Grand Central Station,** *New York (USA).*

- *From cybersex to Siberia, see the hotties at* **www.russianbrides.com.** *Need I say more? There are pictures on the Internet.*

- *For a rush of blood straight to the heart take a 43 m lover's leap at* **Queenstown,** *New Zealand. Tandem bungy jumping – it's either love or stupidity; maybe both.*

- *Been through the wringer? Take a stroll along a Tahitian beach one tropical night and see why French Polynesia would be a great place to be emotionally shipwrecked. Of course all the bare-breasted island maidens were converted to Christianity 200 years ago.*

- *Got a big hunk o' burnin' love? Get thee to the Elvis Wedding Chapel. No booking required but expect delays on Saturdays. 'Viva Las Vegas!'*

Young love canoodling outside St Antipy-by-the-Carriagehouse in Moscow (Russia).

Hot 'n' spicy in India

The world's a big place and when you start poking around you soon come across all kinds of sexual taboos and practices. I'm not going to get into specifics – you'll have to go to the Love Museum in Amsterdam for that – but I am going to bang on a bit about some of the freaky shit I saw in India. Before I do, I just want it noted and before I offend a billion-plus people, that India isn't even kinky; that'd be the French.

The 'free love' ashrams of India

It seems that you can't set foot on the sub-continent without hearing rumours of 'free love' in the *ashrams* of India. Apparently they promote a heady mix of spiritual enlightenment and sexual freedom. The theory goes that tantric sex and the gratification of the baser instincts is a sure way to block out the evils of this world and to achieve final deliverance. *Bhoga* (physical enjoyment) and yoga (spiritual exercise) are seen as equally valid in this quest for Nirvana and offer a direct route (no pun intended) to heaven. The stories go that after an initial AIDS test, you're free to shag your way around the commune, however and with whomever you choose – much like a night out clubbing in Ibiza.

Maybe *ashrams* like this existed in the 1960s, when the spaced-out hippies were doing the rounds – who knows? But what I can tell you is that no such ashrams exist nowadays – I've looked. When you press the storyteller for specifics – an address, GPS coordinates, that kind of thing – it soon becomes apparent that the *ashram* in question was a place a friend of a friend visited. Disappointed? Me too.

Sex and the city

The Taj may be trumpeted as the world's finest monument to love, but it's the temples of Khajuraho that embrace all that is erotic in India. Today, despite taking a considerable effort to get to, Khajuraho is one of India's major tourist attractions. It was here, 1000 years ago, that Chandella sculptors carved a city of temples, all embellished with stone *apsaras* (celestial maidens) and *mithuna* (erotic figures engaged in various acts of provocative posturing) for reasons that are no longer known. There are many theories; one of them is that the carved figures are a kind of *Kama Sutra* in stone, a how-to-do-it manual for adolescent boys, documenting the human race's unparalleled appetite for sexual diversity. Another story I was told is that the Goddess of Lightning is a shy virgin who, given the erotic nature of the temples, would be too embarrassed to strike such a place. Another relates that the rain god Indra was in fact a bit of a pervert and had a vested interest in the protection of these temples.

Whatever the reason for the carvings, they continue to cause shock, laughter, smiles and smirks. To get all the smutty stories, Steph and I even went to the expense of hiring a guide. We saw a group of Japanese with a guide and they looked shocked, especially at the carvings of group sex and one of a guy having it off with his horse. Often they would burst out laughing at some incredibly rude joke. They were having a great time.

The stone temples of Khajuraho feature a whole Kama Sutra of erotic possibilities. Here a couple enjoy 'yoga sex' while two shy apsaras *(heavenly maidens) avert their gazes.*

'Man is divided into three classes: the hare man, the bull man, and the horse man, according to the size of his lingam.
Women also, according to the depth of her yoni, is either a female deer, a mare, or a female elephant.'

– KAMA SUTRA

Hold your horses.
Details of scenes depicted on Khajuraho's Lakshmana Temple.

We, on the other hand, ended up with the world's most boring guide. It takes considerable skill to make the orgy-encrusted temples of Khajuraho sound boring, but this guy excelled at it. To make matters worse, he also hated to use prepositions or conjunctions when he spoke, which made it hard to understand him and ogle at the carvings at the same time. 'Woman pinch nipple, excite, man excite, lingam big, beautiful kiss,' he would say as he gestured to a Kama Sutra-style orgy where there was far more going on than a few pinched nipples and a guy with a big *lingam*. Our guide even apologised for the ribald nature of his forefathers. All I was after were details. I was even prepared to take notes. The only thing I learnt from our guide was the eight categories of sex. They are:

1   Kama-sutra (yeah-baby-yeah! kind of sex).
2   Tantric (oral).
3   Teacher/student (outlawed in most countries).
4   Master/slave (outlawed everywhere – except the Middle East where it is mandatory).
5   Yoga (sex on one leg – I swear, I'm not making this up).
6   Husband/wife (our guide was a big promoter of the husband/wife category and impressed upon us that we should be too).
7   Excite (a solo pursuit).
8   Like an animal (woof woof style).

Khajuraho may be the best, but it's not the only place to see erotically carved temples. Many go unnoticed and it's only when you look closely do you get an eyeful. In Nepal, at Katmandu's Durbar square, the most erotic carvings are found on the roof struts. These carvings, not considered pornographic but of a very definite sexual nature, range from your fairly standard exhibitionism to scenes of couples engaged in quite athletic and rather impressive acts of gymnastic intercourse. More exotic carvings included *ménage à trois*, masturbation and scenes of oral and anal intercourse. And, for the real voyeurs, there are temples which depict couplings with demons and animals – something for everyone.

Weddings often offer a great opportunity to witness local traditions. If the wedding is held at a church, like this one in Vilnius (Lithuania), you don't even have to be invited. Churches are mostly open to the public and no one objects if you sit quietly at the back.

A day before her wedding, an Indian bride's wrists, palms and feet are decorated with Mehendi. *These reddish brown henna tattoos represent the prosperity that a bride is expected to bring to her new family and considered very auspicious in Hindu weddings.*

Boy seeks girl, but not just any girl

When Indian parents are choosing a partner for their son or daughter, a number of factors are taken into consideration: caste of course is pre-eminent, but other considerations are beauty and physical flaws; a favourable horoscope; dowry and virginity are also of vital importance. The matrimonial ads in the newspapers can seem brutally frank.

LIFE companion for 28-year-old good-looking boy, well settled in decent job, suffering from sexual disorder, i.e., acute premature ejaculation. Girl should either be suffering from same disease or is not interested in sex otherwise.

Wheatish complexioned, handsome youth, slightly damaged after industrial accident, limping on one leg but fully recoverable after operation. We are a very traditional family coming from the Dist. of Bankura (W.B.). We are poor but our family has high ethics and morals, which our children carries as well. Can still ride own motor cycle. Boy will bear himself all expenses of both sides. Inter-caste marriage welcome. No sub-caste Kayasth bar within Kayasth.

– INDIAN MATRIMONIAL ADS

Another idiosyncrasy of an Indian marriage, albeit a more loathsome one, can be the ruinous dowry demanded of the bride by her parents-in-law. Although the practice is officially outlawed, a dowry is still expected in most cases. For poorer families the dowry can become a huge financial burden. Many men must stage a lavish feast and borrow heavily to pay for their daughter's dowry, usually at outrageous interest rates resulting in them becoming bonded labourers or indebted to money lenders for the rest of their lives. The financial strain on a girl to keep up with her dowry payments can lead to suicide and the opprobrious practice of 'bride burning'.

Bride burning is the euphemism given to murdering one's daughter-in-law in the hope that your son will then remarry someone who is able to pay a larger dowry. The official line is that these women have accidentally burnt to death in kitchen fires from 'spilt' kerosene. Thankfully the practice is declining.

STEPPING OUT WHEN YOU'RE OUT – THE WORLD'S TOP GAY CITIES

IT'S HIP TO BE QUEER – San Francisco, USA

On the last Sunday in June, half a million people party at the Gay, Bisexual and Transgender Pride Parade. Bring a rainbow-coloured flag to wave at the marching boys.

IS THAT A BUDGIE IN YOUR SPEEDOS? – Sydney, Australia

The biggest event on Sydney's tourist calendar each year is the gay Mardi Gras where buff boys in speedos shake their money makers.

THE ONLY PLACE WHERE THE WORD DYKE ISN'T OFFENSIVE – Amsterdam, The Netherlands

The gay capital of Europe where anything goes. While you're there check out the Homomonument – the memorial to the gays persecuted by the Nazis during WWII.

LADY-BOYS UNITE – Bangkok, Thailand

The accepting culture of Thailand means that most Thais are fairly accepting of alternative lifestyles; they need to be considering some of the riffraff that visit here on sex tours.

©Eric Hood Photography, www.iStockphoto.com

Sex on the beach

The trouble when travelling on the cheap is your accommodation is not always private. It can be difficult to consummate even the most clandestine of rendezvous in a dormitory bunk bed. Even for those of more substantial means, it can be tempting to try horizontal folk dancing in a place other than their hotel room.

Ever since Burt Lancaster and Deborah Kerr entwined their bodies amid crashing waves in the movie *From Here to Eternity*, people have fantasised about getting down and dirty in the sand. I don't know if you have ever had sex on a beach, but I have; once. I'm not going to go into all the details – it's not that kind of book. I just want to illustrate the point that on the road you are bound to come across some very romantic settings and it is very tempting to get a little amorous with your loved one then and there. This can be a mistake. In some countries people will be offended by open displays of affection and even holding hands can cause shock and indignation. This of course doesn't apply to Argentina. Over there you'll be hard pressed to find a park bench to sit and eat your sandwich on that's not already in use by some randy teenagers.

Besides the fact that most beaches afford little privacy and the sand gets everywhere, I have discovered that sex outdoors is not good for the environment. Caught up in the moment it's all too easy to start bonking on an endangered species. Anu (my girlfriend at the time) and I almost wiped out one tenth of the world's population of New Zealand fairy terns in one night. Before you call Greenpeace, let me say that New Zealand fairy terns were battling extinction *before* Anu and I even met them. In 2005 there were only 35 of them left on the entire planet so the odds of us making out on one of their nesting sites would be extremely slight. Or so you would think.

But if someone should be blamed for the demise of the New Zealand fairy tern, it should be Anu. She is far more knowledgeable about endangered animals than I am; she even used to be a ranger in a Washington State National Park (USA), so you would think she would be more environmentally conscientious. I don't believe she fully considered all the ramifications of having late-night sex on the beach and in the future she should be more careful.

Because most New Zealand beaches are pretty empty during the day, let alone at night, it stands to reason that anyone taking a romantic stroll along the foreshore could expect a certain degree of privacy – apparently not. That night, half of the campground was out for a walk – it was a freaking highway. It is very hard to maintain the level of commitment required for the job when you fear being spotlighted by a family taking a late-night stroll. Nor does a family, in the middle of their summer vacation, want to be confronted by the sight of my white buttocks bobbing up and down in the moonlight. I can assure you, it's not as pretty as I have just made it sound. In the interest of modesty, Anu and I decided to try our luck in the sand dunes. Fumbling around in the dark we came across an area cordoned off with the kind of tape used to mark out crime scenes. Ducking under the tape we found a nice little spot, conveniently sectioned off – as if to keep people away.

It wasn't until the next morning that we learned that this spot had been reserved for a far more important couple. Apparently there are only 10 New Zealand fairy tern breeding pairs left and they are finicky fornicators. Apparently they don't like to be disturbed and are prone to deserting their nests if they become stressed. I know this because the Department of Conservation officer explained it to us the next day.

It is easy to see why these birds are close to extinction. They make no effort at all. For starters they don't build proper nests, but lay their eggs directly on the sand next to a bit of driftwood or something. They don't consider tides, or storms, or the fact that there may be others who are also feeling amorous. If they are so easily discouraged in their own breeding endeavours, you'd think they would fly to the other end of the beach – the end without any people. But no, one of the last few pairs of these terns left in existence had to nest just below our tent site. I believe it is this lack of forethought on the terns' part that has gotten these birds to where they are today.

Thankfully, however, this story does have a happy ending. Not only did Anu and I enjoy ourselves thoroughly in that secluded spot, but the birds were fine too. When we looked through the ranger's binoculars, we saw that both chicks and parent birds were doing well and both Anu and I felt very relieved. The ranger thought that the birds may have been disturbed by a dog or cat during the night but everything seemed fine; he said nothing about shags.

Anu rinses the salt water off after swimming the next day, New Zealand.

Tourist traps

If you are to believe the media, the world is little more than a den of thieves whose inhabitants' sole purpose in life is to separate you from your belongings. The press mentions nothing of the more positive, life-affirming aspects of being robbed.

For starters, there's the initial thrill of surviving. Crime against travellers is nearly always non-violent. Sure there are plenty of exceptions and these are well publicised, but if you do fall foul of a crime, chances are it will be a relatively painless experience. Most criminals want neither your life nor any trouble; just cash. The easiest solution if you are mugged is to hand over whatever it is they want. Think of these petty crimes as 'atmospheric'. For example, there is little 'atmosphere' in Orange County (California, USA), but lots of 'atmosphere' in Washington. See? It hurts less already. And as for organised crime – they aren't interested in tourists. Colombian drug runners, Japanese *Yakuza* and Italian Mafia all have greater crimes planned than stealing the 20 bucks out of your back pocket.

Furthermore it's a cheap thrill at that. All things considered, getting mugged in a Third World country is less expensive than a coffee in Switzerland. I know which is more memorable. Scams are great fun too. For starters they are very entertaining and often quite imaginative. Nothing will bring a group of backpackers closer together than a night on the skids retelling tales of stupidity and bravado. Chances are, if you have never been robbed, you'll be wishing you had been.

To be successfully robbed, beyond the few dollars you should keep in your back pocket for that purpose, requires your cooperation. To make it worth their while, scammers have to gain access to your traveller's cheques, bank account or the wads of cash they believe you have stashed back at your hotel or down the front of your shorts. To further complicate matters for the thieves, most travellers avoid loitering in back alleys and choose to congregate at (surprise, surprise) very public and well-policed tourist attractions. In short, scammers require two things to disentangle you from your cash: a convincing con and a gullible patsy.

Like candy from a baby

Although I have been pick-pocketed twice and beaten up once (I was drunk at the time so it hardly counts as I never felt a thing), I have never been successfully mugged or conned. I have come close a couple of times but I have always managed to walk away, kidneys intact.

Here then are some popular scams from around the world, the first of which is the most convincing and is my all-time favourite.

A young Syrian shepherd tends his sheep in the shadow of desert ruins.

'Here [the tourist] is still an aberration. If you can come from London to Syria on business, you must be rich. If you can come so far without business, you must be very rich. No one cares if you like the place, or hate it, or why. You are simply a tourist, as a skunk is a skunk, a parasitic variation of the human species, which exists to be tapped like a milk cow or a gum tree.'

– ROBERT BYRON on travelling in Syria

The stranded Baptist pastor debacle

What made this scam such a winner was its simplicity and Oscar-deserving performance. There was no hard sell, no get-rich-quick scheme to appeal to one's greed, just a heartfelt appeal for help. Lenesça and I met an American Baptist Pastor in the Mexican border town of Chetumal, a short bus ride from the Belize border from where we had just come. The American Pastor had just been ripped off himself and was visibly distraught. Apparently this was his first trip abroad (a thank-you gift from his Chicago parish) and he had managed to lose his family's entire luggage while transferring buses in Mexico City. His family was stranded in an out-of-the-way village with no money, food, cash or even passports. His embassy didn't want to know him until 72 hours had passed and his parish were praying for him, but what he really needed was cash – ours if we could spare it. I'm an atheist so initially I was all for keeping my cash and taking my chance with hell, but this guy was visibly shaking, scared and close to losing it. Lenesça was adamant that we couldn't just leave him. Chetumal was a shit-hole, it wouldn't be right.

So we bought his story, hook, line and sinker. We withdrew $200 (which he promised to reimburse once he returned home) and were about to hand it over when, just to be safe, I decided we should check out his story with a few phone calls to Chicago. He supplied us with his brother's phone number and his church's address, neither of which proved to exist. By the time we returned to confront him he had scarpered and we spent the money on pineapples and tequila.

- Any con man worth his salt will have a plausible answer for every conceivable question. It is virtually impossible to distinguish a fellow traveller-in-need from a professional confidence trickster. Don't bother; instead attempt to verify their story from a third party.
- If you are convinced they are for real then by all means help. You never know when the boot will be on the other foot. The Indians call this karma.

The Russian bad cop, bad cop routine

Oh please, not the 'Russian bad cop, bad cop routine' (there is no good cop). This one is a real bummer because the cops are real and difficult to avoid.

Wherever you go in Russia, you are required to register with the PVU (the Interior Ministry's passport and visa agency) without exception. If you are staying in a state-approved five-star hotel, all this paperwork will be taken care of for you, but if you are staying with a friend or in a local hostel this becomes a bureaucratic nightmare. It is tempting to skip the odd registration or two. Don't.

Russian cops spend a lot of their time hanging around tourist attractions (especially those in Red Square) pouncing on tourists, finding fault with their paperwork and levying 'instant fines'. Woe betide any tourist caught with an unregistered visa or, worse still, without their passport. Even if your paperwork is in order, chances are they will still find fault. They are creative and unscrupulous.

- To mitigate costly fines, avoid the police, especially in Moscow. They are uniformed and easily avoided. Spot them before they spot you, then hide. Try not to giggle and give yourself away while hiding.
- Always carry a photocopy of your documentation. Never surrender your passport – if you do they will wander down an alley, out of the eye of public scrutiny, where it is easier to extort money from you. You'll be forced to follow.
- Stay in a public place. What they are doing is illegal. Better still, try to enlist the help of a passerby to act as a translator (witness).
- Produce a mobile phone and tell everyone within earshot you're phoning your embassy. Russian for 'I'd like to call my embassy' is *'Ya khotel by pozvonit v posolstvo moyey strany'*. Good luck with that mouthful but it works wonders.

Another popular scam involving Russian police is the Trans Siberian Paper Chase. When entering Russia you may or may not be given a Custom's Declaration Form on which you should itemise everything of value, especially your cash and traveller's cheques. The Mongolia/Russia border is infamous for neglecting to hand out these forms. Insist upon it and then ensure that the form is officially stamped. Otherwise when you leave, everything that is unlisted will be confiscated. Goodbye camera, goodbye iPod, and if you have any cash, goodbye money.

The fake Russian bad cop, bad cop routine

This is the same as the scam detailed above except the cops aren't real. Some enterprising locals, having seen how lucrative ripping off tourists can be, are giving it a go themselves.

- Simply ignore them. If they are not in uniform and don't have a police car, just push past. Undercover cops don't harass tourists.
- Unsure? Write down the officer's seven-digit identification number. Make sure he sees you doing this and then produce a mobile phone. Watch him run.
- Ask him to arrest you or tell him you want to pay at the station.

'On the other hand, there is a certain advantage in travelling with someone who has a reputation for shooting rather than being shot: as Keram said, in a self-satisfied way, they might kill me, but they would know that, if I was with him, there would be unpleasantness afterwards.'

– FREYA STARK,
on her native guide in Persia

A statue of Marshal Zhukov at the northern end of Moscow's Red Square (Russia).

PASSING THE BUCK

If you travel extensively in developing nations or Italy, sooner or later you are going to need to pass a bribe. In some countries, like Morocco and India, the hopeful recipients of your largesse will ask directly for 'baksheesh' and, as much as I hate to admit it, a few dollars across the right palm can cut through hours of hassle.

In other countries, the bribe is nothing more than a fee exhorted by corrupt officials abusing their power. In Kyrgyzstan, the drivers of the marshrutka (minibuses) really get hammered. Our driver was philosophical about the whole deal but his patience was wearing thin by the third 'fine' in 10 minutes. When a policeman signalled him to pull over for the fourth time, he motored on. 'I paid that one yesterday,' he shrugged. Individually the bribes were only US$0.50 but over the course of the day they mounted to several dollars and a sizeable part of his income. I offered to pay the next few and received expert instruction on how I was to do it.

1. At no stage show the official all your money or blatantly refer to the bribe. If you must refer to it, call it a 'donation' or 'on-the-spot fine'. Remain pleasant and calm throughout the proceedings and try to deal with only one, the most senior, of the officials. Stay in a public space and discreetly pass the cash in the open.

2. Fold the note(s) into a thin strip.

3. Anchor the strip of money between two fingers in the palm of your hand.

4. Shake hands, allowing the other guy to palm the cash.

STEP 3

STEP 4

Me in Kyrgyzstan – a great country to perfect your bribe-passing skills.

The Guatemalan quick grab

Pick-pockets, purse-snatchers, snatch and grabs, call them what you will – petty thieves are a problem the world over. Sometimes you see it coming and other times you don't.

The first time I was pick-pocketed was by an obliging Guatemalan who took it upon him/herself to carry all of my cash, which they removed from my pocket on a crowded chicken bus.

At the time I was travelling with Lenesça and, having lost all my money and ATM cards, found myself having to be really nice as she had money, whereas I had none.

To cut a long story short I adjusted to my new life as one of the many homeless there. I had a particularly nice hovel under a bridge that I decorated with discarded Coke and Pepsi cans. I shared the bridge with a couple of stray dogs and a drunk (Lenesça). Obviously I'm kidding; things worked out fine, I borrowed money from Lenesça and told her the exchange rate was 700 quezals to the dollar (its really 70), so in a strange-quantum-physics-inverted-mathematical-way the more I spent the more I made. All I had to do was keep her away from the banks and any other place displaying exchange rates.

Be careful of Morrocan snake charmers. Having your photo taken with their snake draped over your shoulders is free. Getting them to remove it can be costly.

- Don't keep all your cash and credit cards in an easily accessible place. Instead leave your passport, airline tickets and traveller's cheques locked in a safe back at the hotel (get a signed receipt) and carry a photocopy. Keep just enough cash in a wallet or purse for that day. If you are robbed it's no great loss.
- Don't be forever dipping in and out of your 'secret' money belt. Not only will it no longer be a secret, you won't make many friends by thrusting your hand down your trousers every five minutes.
- Pick-pockets love to operate in crowds. Be especially vigilant at bus and train stations, markets, congested streets and brothels. Yes, brothels; many young backpackers have lost more than their virginity when their pants have been conveniently pulled down.

HOW TO WIN FREE DRINKS

To even the odds, it's worth knowing a trick or two of your own.

1. *Shuffle the pack, secretly remembering the bottom card.*

2. *Ask your patsy to cut the deck into three piles then select, memorise and return a card to the top of any of the three piles.*

3. *Reassemble the piles into a full deck so the 'bottom card' you sighted at the beginning is placed on top of your victim's chosen card.*

4. *If their card is placed on the pile containing the 'bottom card' simply cut each pile again, so the pack can be assembled as in step 3.*

5. *Deal out the cards one at a time. Their chosen card will be the one after your 'bottom card'.*

6. *To make a bet, deal a few cards past your victim's chosen card. At this point bet that the next card you turn over will be theirs. Having seen their card already dealt, and assuming you are referring to the cards in your hand, they are likely to accept the bet.*

7. *Turn over the patsy's card from the ones already lying on the table and order your alcohol.*

- If you 'sense' you are being cased, you probably are. Stop walking, stand with your back to a wall, put your hand over your wallet and clutch your bag tightly. You will no longer be an easy target and the thief will pass you by.

The Italian fake-baby scam

This is getting a bit old hat now, but worth a mention for the comedy value. Basically, if someone trips and tosses you their baby, let it drop. You'll be left holding a doll and by the time you realise this, the 'baby's' mum along with your bag will have vanished.

- To recap, babies are flying left, right and centre in Italy. Don't get involved.

- If you aren't in Italy, catch the kid. What are you? A moron? It's a harmless defenceless baby, for crying out loud.

The Malaysian bird-poo decoy

This is just a glorified pick-pocket variation. Pick-pockets often rely on diverting your attention away from their nefarious activities and there is no better way than distracting someone by pointing out that they are covered in bird shit.

Unbeknown to you, someone will have smeared your back with bird shit and while you and the friendly Samaritan are cleaning it off, someone else is cleaning you out.

- There are hundreds of variations on this theme. Not only is there the aforementioned bird shit decoy, I have also seen the Indian ink stain decoy, the Spanish free flower decoy (someone tries to pin a flower to you), the Indonesian Mustard Splat Decoy and the Nepalese Loose Thread Deception. Not to mention the Honduras Spit Decoy, Brazilian Ice-cream Decoy and the Stinky Dog Shit Deception of the Philippines. Do you see a pattern here?

 HAVE NO MORALS? Then roll right up and download a PDF file of card tricks at www.deanstarnes.com. Impress your niece and win drinks from your fellow backpackers or, failing that, impress the backpackers and win drinks from your niece.

- If someone, for whatever reason, alerts you to a wardrobe malfunction, grab hold of your possessions for you are about to be robbed, unless you're Janet Jackson, in which case your left tit is probably hanging out.

The Indian gift

Never look a gift horse in the mouth. In Rajastan (India) I was approached by a man selling puppets. He hounded me up and down the street. Did I want a puppet? Don't they make lovely gifts? Do you see them dance? It went on and on, there was no escape.

I was polite but firm. The puppet pedlar was not easily discouraged. Presumably hundreds of tourists daily gave him the cold shoulder and he remained unshakable. Eventually he resorted to a popular Indian ploy – that of asking about my holiday and my home country. These questions, while disingenuous, are damn hard to ignore. It just doesn't feel right to ignore someone who is politely asking you about your home and I was reluctantly dragged into a conversation.

And then something weird happened. Instead of eventually working the conversation back to his puppets as I suspected, he simply gave me one. I insisted that I couldn't possibly accept such a generous gift. He insisted I could. I countered that I had no gift I could give in return. He didn't expect one and asked me not to doubt his generosity. Eventually I accepted the gift in the spirit it was given on the condition I could buy my new friend a drink (a compromise he suggested).

When my new friend insisted on a particular bar, I knew I was obviously being scammed. I named another bar. He refused, adamant we should go to this somewhat distant bar. The more he insisted, the more apparent it became that any drink I would be served would be drugged. I remained steadfast that my offer to buy a drink was valid but only in a bar of my choice. Eventually, he agreed. He shot off down an alley saying he would be back in a few minutes. I waited half an hour, he never showed and, incidentally, he took his puppet when he left.

- Never accept free drinks from a stranger. In this day and age drugs are readily available and the practice of spiking drinks is becoming commonplace.
- No, they aren't really after your kidneys. That is an urban myth. Why would they target a foreigner when there are more accessible local victims? Ever heard of those stories in which the protagonist wakes up in a bath filled with ice and a few stitches in his back where his kidneys were removed? It's bullshit; you're more likely to lose your virginity and money – possibly both.

The free drink for your troubles scam

Obviously drugging is a popular pastime because on the same trip in the same Rajastan town, I met a man who approached me asking if I could read aloud a letter that he had received from a distant friend. Having had no formal education he could neither read nor write. Nothing makes you feel as good about yourself than

The remains of a fishing fleet in the town of Moynaq, Uzbekistan. Canals and other efforts to keep the once prosperous Aral Sea fishing industry alive were abandoned in the early '80s. Just as well; by 1985 all of the 20-odd species of indigenous fish were extinct.

HELL ON EARTH – 'DARK' TOURISM

The world isn't always pretty. Some of our actions have led to horrifying consequences, harrowing deaths and blighted landscapes. To 'view' such cursed places is to take stock of not just what we have done, but warn us of what we are capable of doing.

WHERE WORK WILL NOT MAKE YOU FREE
Auschwitz-Birkenau, Poland

Knowing that over a million European Jews, gypsies and Russian POWs were systematically murdered here does little to prepare you for the horror of Auschwitz. It is not until you see the eerie photos, read the hastily written letters and stand in a 'starvation cell' (the cells in which prisoners were given neither food nor water until they died) does the enormity of this tragedy begin to sink in.

HIGH AND DRY, Aral Sea, Kazakhstan or Uzbekistan

Ever since the Russians diverted rivers to irrigate cotton in the '60s, the Aral Sea – once the fourth-largest lake in the world – has been shrinking. Today you'll find the rusting remains of boats, stranded in a desert wasteland 150 km from the current water's edge.

GOING, GOING … GONE, West Antarctic Ice Shelf

If you want to see what remains of this ice shelf, you had better be quick; 14,000 sq. km has already melted, and that is just the tip of the global warming iceberg.

'TO KEEP YOU IS NO BENEFIT. TO DESTROY YOU IS NO LOSS.'
The Killing Fields of Choeung Ek, Cambodia

A visit to the peaceful mass graves of Choeung Ek would seem divorced from the atrocities that were committed here were it not for the Buddhist stupa made of skulls. To save on bullets, many of those murdered here by the Khmer Rouge were killed with hammers, axes, spades or sharpened bamboo sticks.

THE DEAD ZONE, Chernobyl, Ukraine

On the night of 26 April 1986, as a result of an unsuccessful experiment, Chernobyl's No. 4 reactor exploded and triggered the world's worst nuclear disaster. Today it's possible to visit the 'exclusion zone' and the ghost town of Prypya on tours. Pack your lead undies and keep to the centre of the road (radiation levels are two-and-a-half times higher at the road's edge).

when helping your fellow man; particularly when it costs you nothing to do so. As I read the letter the man was so pathetically grateful and so obviously thrilled by hearing from his friend that I couldn't help but be caught up in his enthusiasm and offered to take dictation if he wanted to reply. I think I even offered to buy the stamp and envelope.

We set off for a café that he knew, to compose the letter. Since we were standing at my hotel's front door I suggested we go upstairs where there was a balcony coffee house, but he refused, insisting that we go to his friend's café. The rest is the same as the Free Indian Gift scam. I left it at 'I am happy to write a letter on your behalf but I am unable to accompany you to your café' and walked inside. He never followed and I never saw him again.

The great Thai gem scam

Year in and year out backpackers fall for this. My sister almost fell for it and I have used it to get free taxi rides around town. Sooner or later in Thailand a dodgy túk-túk driver will tell you of a deal that's too good to be true. And he will be right – it isn't true. The exact details vary, but the upshot is you are able to buy quality gems (often rubies or emeralds) which you'll be able to sell to jewellers back home for a substantial profit. Thousands and thousands of dollars are yours, just sign on the dotted line – the one right beneath your credit card impression. This scam appeals to your greed. Backpackers are notorious for trying to stretch that last dollar and this get-rich-quick scheme proves just too tempting. After all it's not illegal to buy gems, and the trader will assure you it's relatively risk free. The only problem is that the stones are virtually worthless. They are probably gems, only of such poor quality that they may as well be rocks on the ground outside.

- If it's too good to be true then it's too good to be true. The Moroccan carpet scam works the same way as the Thai jewellery scam. The world is a small place – if you can profitably import and export items, then someone who knows far more about it will already be doing so.
- Many túk-túk drivers are paid to bring customers to jewellery scams. It's possible to negotiate free rides by agreeing to stop at a few shops; just don't fall for the scam.
- Gambling rackets, in which someone offers to deal you the winning hand if you agree to split the winnings, are also popular in Thailand. Instead, when you do bet big, not only will they not deal you the winning card as promised, you'll be unable to complain to the police afterwards. After all, what can you say – that when you did place your huge bet, they were unwilling to cheat?

When enquiring about transportation fares (as in this boat ride beside the ghats at Varanasi, India), 'As you like' means as he likes, not you. To avoid arguments, settle on a price first. That way, if you don't like it you are still free to walk away.

Pakistan's Wild West

In the countryside beyond Peshawar and Pakistani law in the Kohat Frontier Region, is the small town of Darra Adam Khel. Nothing would be unusual about this particular one-street, dusty town were it not for the fact that every shop, except for the odd tea stall or butchers, sold guns, and men lounged outside their showrooms eyeing strangers whilst boys hurried to and fro with armloads of rifle stocks and steel barrels. Women and girls were conspicuously absent. There was little traffic and the peace was shattered only by the product-testing crack of small arms' fire.

Darra Adam Khel is anything but a tourist attraction, and like other parts of the lawless North Western Frontier Province (NWFP), a permit is needed to enter. The nearest city, Peshawar, at the east end of the fabled Khyber Pass, is a wild and woolly place in its own right and it is not unusual to see men, armed to the hilt as if expecting imminent invasion, strolling the local markets. Tourists who venture beyond the city's edge must have an armed tribal escort, but despite this precaution, a number are kidnapped from the area (and later released unharmed) every year. Permits are issued by the Chief of Police and mine was declined with a smile on the grounds that '… a stray bullet is not good for tourism'. Even though my travelling companion Eric (a wise-cracking New Yorker) and I couldn't fault his logic, we boarded a local bus and headed out of town to this village of guns.

Moments after stepping off the bus we were surrounded by men all heavily laden with an impressive selection of weapons, long bushy beards and mirrored sunglasses.

Feeling like extras in a B-grade terrorism movie, we were eventually pulled aside by the local police representative

While I could not buy a gun (to the disappointment of several stall holders), I was able to borrow a Kalashnikov, buy some bullets and let rip on the outskirts of town. I managed to obliterate several bushes. If I was ever attacked by a hostile tree, I'd kill it. I kid you not – them trees better be careful.

The gun smithies of Darra Adam Khel may be low-tech but they are still horribly efficient at turning out replicas of guns from around the world. Each workshop consists of a few men equipped with simple tools who specialise in making one component of a gun, working cooperatively together until the arms order is filled.

who demanded our permit. In such circumstances it is a tradition to oil the wheels of bureaucracy with gifts. In the West, we call this bribery, but in many Eastern countries a bribe is seen to be like a tip, only given in advance. Our offer to buy the permit from him directly was refused. We offered to donate money to the local police station; he remained adamant that we return to Peshawar. We offered to pay him to escort us back to the bus stop in an indirect way through the village. Again he refused all such suggestions.

Resigned to our departure, I mentioned that a German tourist had seen the village only last week without such problems and the attitude of the constable changed immediately. He asked the name of the tourist and, once satisfied that we had not been sent by higher authorities, immediately began the finer points of the financial negotiation. In the end it came down to 10 dollars apiece after our student discount (and he even wanted to see our ISIC cards).

Keeping us to the side streets with much scurrying and, as I wildly imagined at the time, ducking for cover, we explored the smithies and closet-sized workshops. A Darra gunsmith, we were told, given a rifle that he has never seen before, could duplicate it in 10 days and then, using the new templates, make an additional copy every two or three days thereafter. Handguns, being more complicated, take a little longer. There were hundreds of tiny shops, where men, all using simple hand tools, specialised in making one part of a gun – from wooden stocks to bullet casings. While I was there, they were working to complete an order for 10,000 American M-16 rifle replicas. Naturally they wouldn't say for whom.

Some of the more unusual weapons, available to anyone with money, were guns disguised as pens or walking sticks, and for the more serious rebel, anti-aircraft rocket launchers. Dealers estimate that somewhere between 400 and 700 guns are produced in Darra daily and the arms industry employs 40,000 men in the area.

For their part, the Afridis were a friendly hospitable people. They were only too happy to pose for photographs or sell me bullets for a semi-automatic Russian style *Kalashnikov*, so I too could wander into the hills and fire off rounds at menacing trees.

We asked our police friend who were buying all these guns? He simply shrugged, slid his hands deeper into his pockets and looked the other way. Eventually we learnt that the current order of 10,000 guns was destined for Afghanistan, but whether they were to stay in Afghanistan or were destined for another market, we never found out.

To change the direction that our conversation had taken, our guide launched into a story about a group of Japanese that caused him to double over with laughter. Apparently frightened by the sound of people firing their guns into the air, an elderly Japanese woman had put up her umbrella as a shield against stray bullets.

*I visited Darra Adam Khel before September 11

THE MOUNTAIN THAT EATS PEOPLE

The remains of Cerro Rico (the rich pinnacle) still tower over what was once the wealthiest city in the New World. During the 16th century the mountain provided over two-thirds of the world's silver and funded the Spanish economy, wars and its crown's high-flying extravagance for more than two centuries. And as the world's richest mountain was mined, a city grew in the shadow of Cerro Rico, where it was rumoured that the very streets were paved with silver – Potosi.

But every silver lining has a cloud. In order to extract the precious ore, the Spanish forcibly 'employed' local Indios and African slaves to do the work for them. The price of Potosi was paid in human misery. Over four centuries, eight million workers died in the mines and for the locals the streets of Potosi flowed with their blood.

The 16th century came and went. The wealth was exhausted. The Spanish left and today Potosi is among the poorest cities in Bolivia. Bolivia itself is the poorest nation in South America.

The mine, however, still remains.

Today over 9000 miners eke a living in the catacombs of Cerro Rico. With primitive tools and dynamite, they chip and blast the rock in appalling conditions; constricted spaces, frequent accidents, low oxygen levels and asbestos growing naturally from the roof of the mine result in the life expectancy of a miner to be only 40–45.

If you buy gifts for the miners – 97 per cent proof alcohol, dynamite, coca (as in cocaine) leaves and cigarettes – you can accompany a guide into the very heart of the mines. The tour is extremely claustrophobic; at times you have to crawl and slide through tunnels too small to walk upright in, and breathing is difficult because of the altitude (the mine is at 15,000 feet) and dust.

Our guide proudly claimed that only five tourists had ever died in the mines, although he added wistfully that none were Spanish. Carts pregnant with boulders rumbled through larger tunnels and at one point the guide yelled 'Rapido! Rapido!' and we ran for our lives through the dark tunnels attempting to outrun a cart bearing down on us. Thankfully we reached a widened area and were able to press ourselves against the wall as two miners roared past us on their loaded cart back into the horrifying depths and impenetrable dark heart of the mountain.

A miner chews coca leaves, used to stave off the effects of hunger, cold and altitude.

Preparing a charge of dynamite in the mines above Potosi, Bolivia.

Chapter Seventeen

Return to sender

'Too often travel, instead of broadening the mind, merely lengthens the conversation.'

– ELIZABETH DREW

If you travel far enough, every road is a dead end. Sooner or later you either run out of money or you run out of energy; often it's both.

For some the thought of going home is filled with trepidation, for others it comes as a relief. Don't be alarmed if you find yourself more excited at the prospect of going home than you were by the thought of leaving in the first place. Even the most avid traveller will get sick of sightseeing, get fed up with the unfamiliar food and tire of the repetitive nature of having to introduce yourself to everyone you meet. Once the romance of travel has died, it can be difficult to rekindle the spark. Therefore it's handy to know your 'use by' date – the optimum length of time you enjoy travelling at any one time. For some, one week is enough, for others one year is too short.

Tell-tale signs that it is time to go home

- Your clothes no longer fit. This could be for any number of reasons. They may have simply been stretched by Third World washing techniques or you may have picked up a disease, lost a quarter of your body weight and be at death's door. Either way, it's a sign.
- You've stopped losing track of the days and now have trouble keeping track of the months.
- You spend a considerable part of each day fantasising about the contents of your parents' refrigerator and planning the 'perfect meal'.
- You know 'off by heart' the exact order of all the 5000 songs on your iPod.

TIPS ON AVOIDING HOMESICKNESS

Homesickness can be severe; feelings of longing, anxiety and depression can also be accompanied by physical ailments such as ulcers, diarrhoea, headaches, vomiting and tears.

Since many people travel home in their minds long before they step on board an aircraft, the trick is to avoid dwelling on what you have left behind.

- *Towards the end of your trip, avoid dwelling on returning to loved ones. Unchecked, those happy thoughts of reunion can soon sour to separation anxiety.*
- *Because homesickness is exacerbated by the contrast in foreign environments, seek out the familiar. This may be as simple as a burger at McDonald's or taking in a movie at the cinema.*
- *Do what ET did – phone home. Keeping in regular contact with your partner and family can help ease the space between you.*
- *Keep yourself busy. Don't sit around the hotel pining for home.*
- *Focus on all the new experiences you're gaining, not on the things you're missing.*

And if all that fails, go home – travel is meant to be fun.

BATTLE TESTED

Life after travel

If you have been away for some time, it's natural to feel excited to be back home. Unfortunately the euphoria of being surrounded by friends and family is short lived; about three days – tops. By then, everyone has heard your stories, seen your photos and read your blog. Once the realisation sinks in that you're not half as exciting as you thought you were, you'll be once again trawling the Internet for discounted flights. Within a surprisingly short time the drudgery of everyday life has resumed and the two-month trip through South East Asia fades into memory. By the time your credit-card statement arrives, you'll have remembered the reasons you were so desperate to leave in the first place.

At this point it is easy to become depressed and it's quite possible to find yourself all misty-eyed about the time you were stuck on a train for 27 hours without a roll of toilet paper. Very soon your feet begin to itch, until the day comes when you spy a picture – say one of a perfect beach – that sends you scurrying into the nearest bookshop to buy a guide book. Well, to save you all that hassle, I'm thoughtfully providing that photo here. *Bon voyage.*

Koh Phi Phi, Thailand.